HOTEL CONVENTION SALES, SERVICES, AND OPERATIONS

HOTEL CONVENTION SALES, SERVICES, AND OPERATIONS

Pat Golden-Romero

Hospitality & Convention Industry Educator and Consultant

ELSEVIER

AMSTERDAM • BOSTON • HEIDELBERG • LONDON
NEW YORK • OXFORD • PARIS • SAN DIEGO
SAN FRANCISCO • SINGAPORE • SYDNEY • TOKYO
Butterworth-Heinemann is an imprint of Elsevier

Butterworth–Heinemann is an imprint of Elsevier
30 Corporate Drive, Suite 400, Burlington, MA 01803, USA
Linacre House, Jordan Hill, Oxford OX2 8DP, UK

 Recognizing the importance of preserving what has been written, Elsevier prints its books on acid-free
paper whenever possible.

Library of Congress Cataloging-in-Publication Data
Application submitted

British Library Cataloguing-in-Publication Data
A catalogue record for this book is available from the British Library.

ISBN 13: 978-0-7506-7902-2
ISBN 10: 0-7506-7902-6

For information on all Butterworth–Heinemann publications
visit our Web site at www.books.elsevier.com

Printed in the United States of America
07 08 09 10 11   10 9 8 7 6 5 4 3 2 1

To Steve and Ryan for their patience and support.

CONTENTS

PREFACE

During the first half of my hospitality career I was always in the minority—my undergraduate degrees were in the same field in which I had chosen to work. Though I'd obtained my degrees from well respected academic institutions, there were a limited number of Hotel Management college programs in the U. S. Today, many of the both 2- and 4-year college programs, in every hospitality industry related discipline, are experiencing record growth. The tremendous industry support provided to these institutions is quite evident at career placement fairs; graduates interview with multinational hospitality corporations. I am happy to say that I'm no longer in the minority!

During the second half of my hospitality industry I began teaching in the aforementioned programs. I noticed that the vast majority of those enrolled in college programs in this discipline, entered school with some previous industry experience. Additionally, they often continued working many hours while enrolled in school, either out of necessity or because of their enjoyment of their work. Over the last 16 years countless students have provided valuable contributions to my classes from their own "work experience." This book and the accompanying instructor's guide include relevant examples and case studies from some of those students who've kept in touch and shared their hospitality industry successes.

Through out my teaching career I have tried to share this philosophy with students: "I truly believe that this is one subject in which actual work experience is necessary to be an effective teacher." This book represents the *marriage* or joining of my dual careers in this interrelated, exciting industry. I am privileged to have this opportunity to share my knowledge and experience with you.

WHO SHOULD USE THIS BOOK

The book has been created for a few different audiences. This includes students enrolled in a hospitality, meeting & convention, or tourism management program. The accompanying instructor's guide, which includes comprehensive course and testing materials, will facilitate the learning process through "real world" case studies. It will also be useful for those already engaged in industry careers *selling* or *servicing* the hospitality product. The key group markets; their wants and needs are explored, and effective marketing strategies are examined.

This book will also provide the beginning meeting or special event planners with more knowledge of the facility side of the planning process. Many group planners are part-time, have other responsibilities, and often receive little or no formal training. This book will provide those individuals with additional knowledge about the facility and services available at the destination, thereby improving their overall meeting success.

It has been my experience, that as, hospitality industry *suppliers* gain experience, many gravitate to the *planner side*. Regardless of your current focus Hotel Convention Sales, Services, and Operations will improve your understanding of both sides, with often overlapping responsibilities, facilitating alternative career exploration.

ORGANIZATION OF BOOK CONTENT

Each chapter offers a consistent structure beginning with learning objectives, main topics, industry "insider tips," discussion questions, internet and additional resources. The book also features terms and definitions from the Convention Industry Council (CIC) Glossary of Terms. Located towards the end of each chapter, these definitions have been developed through industry wide collaboration. A number of chapters have an appendix which features useful CIC event planning guides and forms, also created through industry wide cooperation. Each chapter contains samples, contributed by industry sources, of standard forms and procedures.

The first chapter of *Hotel Convention Sales, Services, and Operations* begins with an introduction to the key elements of this vast industry. Chapters 2–5 discuss each group market segment; their facility requirements, and services available at the destination. Chapter 6 is devoted exclusively to the marketing and advertising strategies employed, to develop business from each group segment. Chapters 7–10 focuses on the negotiation process, contracts; event planning and facility coordination of group services. Chapter 11 provides an overview of the key components of the exhibition trade show industry and ancillary service providers. Finally, Chapter 12 presents some of the current industry trends and discusses their potential impact.

Pat Golden-Romero
Temecula, CA
April 2007

ACKNOWLEDGEMENTS

The author would like to acknowledge the tremendous support I've received from both, industry and academic colleagues; their insight and suggestions throughout this process have been invaluable. Many of them have kindly contributed samples, quotations and consented to interviews, which are referenced in the appropriate chapters. A very special thank you to Patti J. Shock for her guidance and tremendous support over the last 20 years!

ABOUT THE AUTHOR

Pat Golden-Romero has spent her entire career in the hospitality and convention field on both the industry and academic fronts. In addition to her years of experience in hospitality convention, catering and marketing management, she has instructed and developed college curriculum in these subjects for over 16 years.

She is currently an adjunct professor teaching in the Hospitality, Tourism and Convention Management programs at: University of Nevada Las Vegas; San Diego Mesa College; and Florida Gulf Coast University. She provides hospitality training and consulting services to hospitality industry clients, world wide. Pat Golden-Romero holds a M.A. degree in Education & Curriculum Design from Alliant International University; a B.S. degree in Hotel and Restaurant Management from the University of Wisconsin-Stout; and a A.A.S. degree from Schenectady County Community College in New York.

THE CONVENTION AND MEETINGS INDUSTRY: AN OVERVIEW

LEARNING OBJECTIVES

After studying this chapter, you will be able to discuss:

- The economic impact and multiplier effect of the convention and meetings industry
- The growth of the convention and meetings industry, and current trends
- The types of facilities that house meetings and conventions
- The types of organizations that hold meetings and conventions

INTRODUCTION

About 30 years ago, in the mid-1970s, the business of planning and executing meetings in both hotels and convention halls began to undergo changes. At that time, both independent and chain hotels alike relied mostly on business from vacationers and individuals (also known as transient) to fill their rooms. The large function rooms in many hotels, designed and used as banquet and reception facilities, also could accommodate meetings. Today, the group meeting and convention market is recognized as the most significant market segment necessary to ensure the hotels' room occupancy, as well as food and beverage revenue requirements.

In the 1970s, few hotels in major U.S. cities and resort destinations had enough function space and guest rooms to book convention groups. Overall, convention groups at that time had an image that focused less on meetings and education and more on entertainment. Until recent years, the typical convention attendee was a middle-aged white male; today's convention-goer is now reflective of the workplace—women and minority groups have altered that demographic profile.

The stereotype of a three-day junket of fun for many convention groups also has been replaced by days of intensive educational programs that upon completion, awarded attendees continuous education credits (CEUs) in their vocation or field. The food and beverage functions at meetings and conventions also have become representative of the creative culinary landscape, replacing the so-called "rubber chicken banquet circuit" of years past. The audiovisual and computer technology needs of groups today require true expertise on-site to ensure that each meeting and presentation goes off without a hitch! Additionally, the meeting planners—people who represent companies and association groups—over the years have become quite knowledgeable of the process.

Therefore, all these requirements have created a need for a department that can seamlessly coordinate and execute these overlapping areas. Thus, the convention services department has become an integral part of the hotel organization chart. This chapter examines how these factors and emerging trends have contributed to the growth of the convention and meetings market. We will look at the financial impact of this global industry in both private and public sectors of the economy. In the last 20 years, state-of-the-art hotel and convention centers have been built to fulfill the need for facilities. This chapter also discusses the key facility requirements for meeting groups. Finally, we will explore the main categories of the group meetings market.

Recently the CIC (Convention Industry Council), conducted a study on the economic impact of this broad, interrelated industry, titled, *The Economic Impact of Meetings, Conventions, Exhibitions, and Incentive Travel.* Figure 1.1 is a summary of the key points from the *2004 Economic Impact Study*, from the CIC Web site. The accompanying pie chart shows the total direct spending by industry segment, with conventions and exhibitions generating the most spending: 55.5 percent ($122.31 billion). Additionally, the study reports that "the largest share of the convention and exhibition dollar (35%) is spent in hotels and other facilities." These facts further demonstrate just how interdependent these hotel and convention industries are on each other.

This summary illustrates the usefulness of this report and application to many segments of the meeting and convention industry. Further information on the facts and findings of this study can be located in the appendix at the end of this chapter.

The billions spent in total by all these convention and meetings market segments have a far-reaching financial impact. For example, the U.S. Department of Labor classifies jobs in the hotel, restaurant, and tourism industry as part of the service sector of our economy. Additionally, a large number of jobs are created both directly and indirectly by the convention and meetings industry.

SERVICE SECTOR ECONOMIC IMPACT

Jobs are created and revenue occurs in other industries indirectly through foreign and domestic delegate spending by conventioneers. This is known as

FIGURE 1.1

2004 ECONOMIC IMPACT STUDY

The Economic Impact

of Meetings, Conventions, Exhibitions, and Incentive Travel
A Summary

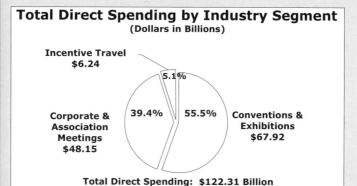

Total Direct Spending by Industry Segment
(Dollars in Billions)

Incentive Travel
$6.24

5.1%

Corporate &
Association
Meetings
$48.15

39.4%   55.5%

Conventions &
Exhibitions
$67.92

Total Direct Spending: $122.31 Billion

The meetings, conventions, exhibitions, and incentive travel industry...

Is a 365-day a year business that operates in communities large and small.

Generates more than 36% of the hotel industry's estimated $109.3 billion in operating revenue.

Directly accounts for nearly 17% of the air transportation industry's operating income.

Generates spending and tax collection that trickle down to every sector of the local economy, from taxis and restaurants to retail stores and other services.

Supports 1.7 million jobs in the United States – One in every 86 individuals is employed in some aspect of the industry.

CONVENTION INDUSTRY COUNCIL
8201 GREENSBORO DRIVE
SUITE 300
MCLEAN, VA 22101
1-703-610-9030
FAX: 1-703-610-9005
www.conventionindustry.org

Taken as a whole, meetings, conventions, exhibitions, and incentive travel generated $122.31 billion in total direct spending in 2004, making it the 29th largest contributor to the gross national product.

These are just some of the key findings from a new study conducted by VERIS Consulting, LLC for the Convention Industry Council (CIC).

Facts & Figures
The industry's total direct spending is $122.31 billion. 1,710,000 full-time equivalent (FTE) jobs are supported by the direct spending of the industry.

Association-sponsored events accounted for two-thirds, or $81.94 billion, of the direct spending industry total. Corporate-sponsored events accounted for the remaining third, or $40.37 billion.

The largest share of the convention and exhibition dollar (35%) is spent in hotels and other facilities. The rest is widely distributed throughout local economies. After air transportation (24%), the biggest categories of attendee, exhibitor, and sponsor spending were: restaurant and outside catering food & beverage outlets (14%) and business services (12%).

A Useful Tool
The Convention Industry Council's 2004 Economic Impact Study is a useful tool for industry professionals, as well as communities at large, when planning, budgeting, and advocating for issues related to meetings, conventions, exhibitions, and incentive travel. The Study also:

➤ Provides compelling statistics to assist in attracting public funding from both local governments and private investors;

➤ Illustrates benefits of industry in terms of jobs created, business sales and tax revenues; and,

➤ Provides a baseline report that can be used to estimate long-term impact.

> **Purchase your copy of the Convention Industry Council's *2004 Economic Impact Study* today at www.conventionindustry.org**

Courtesy: CIC (Convention Industry Council) (2005).

the *multiplier effect*. As we said in the introduction, by the 1970s and 1980s, hotels and resorts began to expand their facilities to accommodate groups and compete for this emerging market. To remain profitable, most hotels no longer could rely on the leisure vacation and individual business traveler markets to fill their guest rooms year round. At the same time, many people, some with newly earned college degrees in a new program, Hotel and Restaurant Management, began careers in hotel group sales departments. Hotels with 400 or more guest rooms and meeting facilities will have a Group Sales department with a director and sales managers assigned to each of the market segments.

Based on the hotels' marketing plan, occupancy, and revenue goals, each salesperson must qualify and book a certain amount (or quota) of groups in their respective market.

For example, a group like a national associations' annual convention may need 200 to 300 rooms for three nights, with meeting space and multiple food and beverage functions. However, association groups traditionally require very low group rates because the majority of the delegates are paying their own way and will not be reimbursed. Additionally, planners for associations expect low room rates and complimentary meeting and exhibit space due to the large quantity of guest rooms they can provide.

This is where the "dance" of negotiating between the seller (facility) and the buyer (group planner) begins. Today, the hotel sales director must train their managers to evaluate every group for the total revenue potential: guest room nights, plus food and beverage and other services. Research is also regularly conducted to determine the groups' history (did they really use all the guest rooms the hotels held for them in previous years?). However, many association groups like to meet in different regions of the country each year, and this will impact attendance as well.

As you can see, for each group market segment there are many factors for the hotel or facility to consider before it even quotes a group room rate. Regardless, hotels derive much more revenue from any group business and therefore actively advertise and compete for this market. In Chapters 2, 3, and 4, we will also discuss identification of the needs of each type of group customer. Since the 1980s the people who plan the meetings and conventions for associations, corporations, and organizations have become more knowledgeable about the profit centers for hotels. Planners who are responsible for numerous meetings through the year often manage a staff and belong to their own trade association. These organizations offer educational programs at their own conventions so that new and seasoned meeting planners can gain more planning expertise.

However, the growth of the meeting industry is impacted by many factors, most notably, the economy. During the recession of the early 1990s, few corporation meetings were held off-site. Consequently, many hotels went bankrupt by the mid-1990s. The demand for training meetings grew in the late 1990s as a result of daily advancements in computer technology. Every few years the cycle alters so that sometimes it's a buyer's market (planners), and other years it's a seller's market (facility).

TYPES OF FACILITIES THAT HOLD MEETINGS AND CONVENTIONS

Multinational hotel chains have invested millions in renovating and upgrading their entire hotel properties, to provide facilities and services required by large meeting and convention groups. These well-known and recognized full-service hotels—such as Marriott, Sheraton, Hyatt, Westin, and Holiday Inn—compete with each other as well as other properties within their own chain or brand.

In addition to the traditional hotel, let's look at other facilities or "venues" used for meetings. Remember, each market or group planning a meeting has different needs and objectives. For example, corporate meeting groups require people (usually employees) to attend, and the corporation (employer) typically pays for everything—including hotel, meals, and travel—related to the meeting. Conversely, attendance at an association convention is optional, and attendees pay out of their own pockets. This results in fluctuating attendance and a greater need for low-cost hotel rooms.

On the other hand, incentive groups need very little meeting space, but they do require a full-service resort with luxurious hotel rooms and amenities. Fortunately, there are more than enough different types of facilities to accommodate these needs. First, we'll explore conference facilities.

Conference Centers

Conference centers are a relatively new concept that offer state of the art dedicated meeting facilities. Designed with the latest in meeting technology and soundproofing, these self-contained environments often feature built-in theaters and ergonomic chairs that are still comfortable after six hours of meetings. Today, the concept has evolved so that the design features and services provided at a conference center are quite varied. However, their marketing strategies remain focused on providing meeting facilities that are superior to hotels, since they don't double as banquet rooms. Most conference centers differ from hotels in the following ways:

- Their Meeting package pricing includes rooms, meals, and refreshment breaks
- Their Inclusive package concept ensures no unexpected charges for meeting planners
- They are suitable for small groups of 50 to 200 people who want to be treated like a big group, with an attentive staff and good service

As this concept has grown in popularity with meeting groups, some conference centers have been either acquired or built by some of the leading hotel chains. Therefore, this concept has evolved so that there are now conference facilities built to accommodate each niche. Other features may include:

- Conference center facility only; no hotel or overnight facilities (limited-service chain hotels often are built near these facilities to house conference attendees)
- Conference center with or without guest rooms, located away from city and distractions; a self-contained environment with meals on-site (meal package)
- Full-service hotels with adjacent conference center buildings

Two well-known companies successful in building and operating facilities are Benchmark Hospitality and Harrison conference centers (the latter has been purchased by Marriott Corporation). The one thing all conference centers have in common is that they're all designed for smaller groups, usually under 300 people.

All-Suite Hotels

All-suite hotels first appeared in the late 1970s with Embassy Suites quickly dominating this category. Their unique configuration features a two-room suite with a bedroom separate from a kitchenette and living room area. Each Embassy Suites hotel offers meeting and function facilities suitable for groups of up to 300 people. Most all-suite properties include:

- Spacious two-room suites for all attendees
- Complimentary buffet breakfast and evening reception daily (available for all guests, not private)

CONVENTION CENTERS

Historically, these facilities were designed for convention meeting groups of up to several thousand people, with a trade show area for 200 to 300 exhibits. Convention center function space can be quite versatile with air walls that can create more meeting rooms for smaller groups, known as *break-out rooms*. The centers also double as entertainment locations for concerts. For many cities this center may also be the *only* facility that can accommodate banquets for 1000 people or more. As a meeting venue convention centers are unique in the following ways:

- They don't have guest rooms, but are connected to (or within walking distance of) a large hotel.
- They are usually feasible for only large conventions.
- Convention space is booked through the convention center sales department or local convention bureau sales staff.
- Convention center space can be booked up to 10 years (or more) in advance for very large conventions; guest room blocks will be reserved at numerous nearby hotels (known as a citywide convention).

UNIVERSITY AND COLLEGE CAMPUSES

Campuses are a newer, affordable alternative, especially for groups who meet during the summer, although meeting space has become more limited as colleges increase their marketing efforts. This has forced repeat customers to secure space further in advance.

As a meeting venue campuses offer the following unique features:

- They have large amounts of meeting space (classrooms), rooms (student housing), and function space (student dining space) available during the summer
- They can offer lower group rates than hotels during a high-demand (summer) period

Each of these meeting facilities venues will be discussed in greater detail, along with site selection criteria and industry procedures, in later chapters.

TYPES OF MEETING PLANNERS

Today, meeting planners in general have received much more professional training than in the past. As mentioned previously, there are now numerous associations for all types of meeting planners to join. These groups offer training sessions (known as continuing education) to their members, which often are held during the convention.

Association Planners

The vast majority of association meeting planners are full-time, planning three to five meetings annually. Their job title is Planner, with the association's annual convention as their primary responsibility. This convention is the main source of income for that association, and attendance at these three- to four-day events is usually over 400 people. Types of associations include trade, professional/scientific, educational, veterans/military, and technical.

Smaller associations in any of these categories may not have a full-time planner. Similar to corporations, the association would also outsource this function. Organizations known as association management companies often are hired to manage the meeting and convention requirements of multiple associations. Planning needs may also include association board meetings, usually held quarterly. In general, the association meeting segment combined represents the largest group business revenue source for hotels and convention centers.

Corporate Planners

A large percentage of corporate meeting planners perform those duties only once or twice a year, so their full-time position could be in marketing, sales, management, training, or operations. When corporations cut back on the number and types of meetings held, some eliminate this position altogether and instead hire planners only when needed. Unfortunately, this often happens during a slow economy. Consequently, the task of planning one corporate meeting could be contracted to any of the following types of organizations:

- Event planning company
- Travel and meeting management
- Destination management
- Independent meeting planner
- Site selection
- Incentive meeting management

Also, it is interesting to note that many planning professionals who start a firm with one of the preceding titles have background in hotel group sales and services departments. Planners who have worked on the supplier or seller side can be effective negotiators for their clients (group holding the meeting.)

However, there are many companies that have enough meetings to warrant having a meeting planning department. This department may also handle all travel arrangements for individual business travelers for that company as well. In this case, travel agents who rely on the hotel group sales departments to coordinate the meeting logistics may actually be the only planners for that corporation.

The largest segment of full-time corporation meeting planners is found in the insurance industry. All types of insurance companies hold a variety of meetings that their agents are required to attend. Additionally, this segment plans incentive travel programs that are rewarded to the insurance agents for their sales volume. Only the most luxurious full-service resorts and destinations are used for these programs. Planners in this segment can work either directly for an insurance company or for an incentive travel company. Remember, though, that unlike associations, corporations do not promote meetings outside their own employees or stockholders.

Nonprofit Organizations

There are many types of groups that are known collectively by the acronym SMERF, which stands for social, military, educational, religious, and fraternal. Meeting planners under this umbrella often hold the job title executive director. The issue common to all SMERF groups is cost. Like associations, many meeting attendees are paying on their own. Many of their annual meetings or conventions can have over 500 to 800 attendees.

Government and Union Planners

The final types of planners we will look at are government agencies and labor unions; these are similar to SMERFs in regards to meeting cost issues and the planner's job title. What often separates them are the following key concerns: most government employees are reimbursed only for meeting-related travel and meals expenses within the *per diem*. This is a fixed amount of money allowed that is set for each city by the federal government.

In general, hotels or other meeting venues must be able to meet these requirements to be successful with securing the business. However, that is just the start. Later in the book we'll learn more about the proper servicing to ensure that the group is satisfied and will hopefully return again and again.

MEETING INDUSTRY REPORTS

Throughout this book you will see many important quotes, statistics, reports, and general contributions from a variety of convention industry trade publications. Most of these publications survey their subscribers—multiple types of meeting planners—on industry trends. The survey results in the *2005 Meetings Market Report* from *Meetings Media* are an example of this practice.

This survey is a propriety *Meetings Media* online study that was distributed to 8,512 *Meetings Media* subscribers. (As an incentive to complete the survey, respondents were offered a chance to win one of four $50 American Express gift cards. The survey generated 430 completed responses.) *Meetings Media* reports this is their second annual report.

The charts in Table 1.1 report the demographics of the survey respondents: independent, association, and corporate planners. The results also report the level of support their respective organizations provide for each segment.

Table 1.2 is from the same survey, and identifies trends in types of facility and meeting attendance.

ADDITIONAL 2005 MEETINGS MARKET REPORT HIGHLIGHTS

The following is an excerpt from the summary of that report. It is provided in this introductory chapter to assist you with industry trends and in defining specific terminology used throughout this book.

POST-9/11 RECOVERY

With continuing fallout from the events of 9/11, corporate cutbacks and accounting scandals, plummeting stock prices, SARS, and the escalating war in the Middle East, it was a challenge to just muster up the courage to drag oneself out of bed in the morning last year, much less hop a jet to travel across the continent for a meeting.

Planner Demographics

While nearly four of five planners surveyed are female (a statistic that generally reflects the industry), 44 percent of independent planners are male

Continued

(56 are female). Independents are also the most tenured, with 67 percent indicating that they have been in the meetings industry for 11 years or more. Training on the whole is up, with the career growth of planners who said they receive support in the form of memberships to major trade organizations such as MPI or PCMA rose 5 percent over results from the 2002 survey. Association planners registered a 28 percent growth rate in trade association membership over 2002 results, but this high figure was dampened by a drop of 14 percent and 3 percent, respectively, of corporate and independent planner memberships.

Association and independent planners benefited from qualified third-party training, which was up 19 percent and 12 percent, respectively, from the previous survey. Corporate planners had the least amount of training, with 30 percent saying they had no continuing education support.

Financial Trends

In general, survey results show that while planners may not have had a banner year in 2003, it did trend upward—or at least stayed the same—from the year before. "We had the exact number of meetings budgeted in 2003," says Elizabeth Campbell, director of corporate events and travel for Livermore, California-based Discovery Toys. "However, most budgets were decreased as the events were being planned and executed. The challenge in a nutshell is decreasing budgets, more importantly, the decreasing of established budgets after contract commitments have been made—and yet expectations and program elements remain the same if not higher."

Planner optimism is perhaps fueled by an expected spike in attendance as the economy improves, with companies having more money available to send employees to meetings, and associations enjoying membership with fatter wallets. Most planners expect their attendance in 2004 to increase. Approximately 30 percent of all planners reported that their organization's sales or memberships increased during the 12 months before the survey was taken, with 36 percent of association respondents indicating a rise in membership and 28 percent of corporate planners saying their companies enjoyed an increase in sales. A staggering 34 percent believe the number of meetings they hold will increase during the next 12 months, with 35 percent of corporate planners and 29 percent of association planners expecting more meetings. Independents forecast a 43 percent rise.

Anatomy of a Meeting

A total of 41 percent of all planners said more complicated contract negotiations were the most evident way their meetings had changed in the last year, followed by an increased workload due to reduced staffing (37 percent) and more concern for security (36 percent).

Complicated contract negotiations were singled out by 41 percent of respondents for two years running. Planners, as always, had a few tricks up their sleeves when it came time to sit down at the bargaining table. Attendees booking outside of the room block, which all too often triggers attrition clause enforcement, was listed as a major concern by 27 percent of respondents. Attrition was a major concern for 36 percent of association planners. Finally, 37 percent of all planners and 46 percent of association planners said that booking outside of the block was at least of minor importance.

Courtesy: Meetings Market Report, *Meetings Media* (2005).

TRENDS AND PRACTICES

In conclusion, let's look at a few current trends in the meeting industry.

Technology

Advances in computer technology have changed the way hotel sales departments communicate with potential customers.

- Hotels have an RFP (request for a proposal) form on their own Web sites that planners can use to submit their meeting dates and function space requirements.
- Hotel sales managers now carry laptops on business trips, enabling them to check group availability online in real-time with the client.
- Event and meeting planning computer software programs are now available and used by many (types of) planners.
- Hotels now use software programs called Yield and Revenue Management, which determine the ideal rates (to quote) for a particular piece of business to meet the hotel's revenue and budget requirements. This is a component of the negotiation and contract process.
- To remain competitive, hotels have installed high-speed T1 lines in all guest rooms, enabling faster Internet access for meeting attendees.
- Full-service staffed business centers are available (often 24/7) for attendees to use during their stay or meeting.
- Videoconferencing capability also has been made available and affordable for groups to use, increasing the audience size and participation.
- Individual attendee reservations and almost all registration functions can be made online or on-site at the convention desk.
- Audiovisual production companies tape meeting sessions, which are purchased by members unable to attend the event, providing an additional source of revenue for the organization.

TABLE 1.1
2005 MEETINGS MARKET REPORT

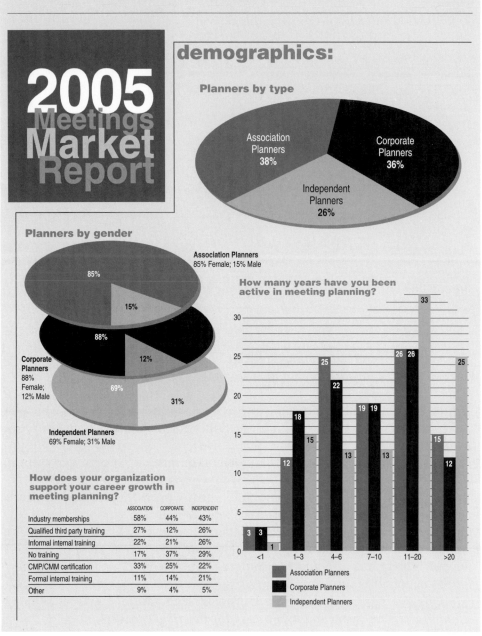

demographics:

Planners by type

- Association Planners 38%
- Corporate Planners 36%
- Independent Planners 26%

Planners by gender

- Association Planners: 85% Female; 15% Male
- Corporate Planners: 88% Female; 12% Male
- Independent Planners: 69% Female; 31% Male

How many years have you been active in meeting planning?

	<1	1–3	4–6	7–10	11–20	>20
Association Planners	3	12	15	13	26	15
Corporate Planners	3	18	22	19	26	12
Independent Planners	1	25	25	19	33	25

(Note: values read from bar chart; 13 also shown for 7–10)

How does your organization support your career growth in meeting planning?

	ASSOCIATION	CORPORATE	INDEPENDENT
Industry memberships	58%	44%	43%
Qualified third party training	27%	12%	26%
Informal internal training	22%	21%	26%
No training	17%	37%	29%
CMP/CMM certification	33%	25%	22%
Formal internal training	11%	14%	21%
Other	9%	4%	5%

Source: 2005 Meetings Market Report.

TABLE 1.2

FACILITY AND MEETING TRENDS

trends:

What types of facilities do you use for most of your meetings?

	ASSOCIATION	CORPORATE	INDEPENDENT
Several chains	74%	61%	71%
Independent hotels	46%	45%	60%
Conference centers	35%	49%	39%
Convention centers	46%	35%	34%
Boutique hotels	24%	18%	36%
Special venues	19%	23%	27%
No particular type	14%	14%	10%
One particular chain	1%	1%	2%

What is the approximate attendance at the meetings and events you plan?

	ASSOCIATION	CORPORATE	INDEPENDENT
1–50	63%	55%	51%
51–100	47%	49%	48%
101–200	50%	40%	44%
201–300	38%	30%	45%
301–500	32%	25%	24%
501–750	24%	12%	23%
751–1,000	17%	13%	14%
Over 1,000	40%	13%	19%

Source: 2005 Meetings Market Report.

Second-Tier Cities

Planners have been made aware (by convention and visitors bureaus) of the benefits of selecting sites in smaller cities or destinations. Known as second-tier, these cities are serviced by smaller airports (with major airline carriers) that are also more accessible and often more cost effective. Additionally, many large cities now have a second airport; within 40 to 60 miles of the main one, which offers the same benefits.

We will further explore these and other trends in the last chapter of this book. The appendix also includes some supporting articles in their entirety.

REVIEW QUESTIONS

1. Describe the amenities and services typically found at an *all-suite hotel* in both the guest accommodations as well as the meeting facilities.
2. Describe the amenities and services typically found at a *conference center* in both the guest accommodations and the meeting facilities.
3. List and define at least three technological developments that have shaped the meeting and convention industry since the 1970s.
4. List and describe the key survey results presented in the *2005 Meetings Market Report*. Discuss how these demographic trends have shaped the industry.

REFERENCES

Convention Industry Council (CIC). (2004, 2005). *CIC Press Release 2004 Economic Impact Study*.

Meetings Media. (2005). *Meetings Market Report*.

GLOSSARY

Note: Most chapters in this book contain a Convention Industry Council (CIC) Glossary of Terms. These terms represent the development of the first comprehensive standardized glossary terminology for the convention and meetings industry, developed by APEX (Accepted Practices Exchange), an initiative of the Convention Industry Council that is bringing together all stakeholders in the development and implementation of industry-wide accepted practices to create and enhance efficiencies throughout the meetings, conventions, and exhibitions industry. Reprint permission has been provided by the CIC.

Conference Center: A facility that provides a dedicated environment for events, especially small events. May be certified by the IACC (International Association of Conference Centers).

Second-tier City: A city where space limitations of the convention center, the hotels, or the air lift (airport) make the city more appropriate for smaller meetings and events.

APPENDIXES

The following documents are provided as a resource. Reprinted with permission.

Appendix A: CIC Press Release

The following is a press release regarding the CIC 2004 Economic Impact Study. The complete study is available for purchase at www.conventionindustry.org.

FOR IMMEDIATE RELEASE – September 13, 2005

CONTACT: Mary E. Power, CAE
President & CEO
Convention Industry Council
(703) 610-9030

MEETINGS INDUSTRY IS 29TH LARGEST CONTRIBUTOR
TO THE GROSS NATIONAL PRODUCT
The Convention Industry Council's 2004 Economic Impact Study shows the strength of the industry

McLean, Virginia – September 13, 2005 – The Convention Industry Council (CIC) released today its 2004 Economic Impact Study, which provides the most current findings of the economic impact of the meetings, conventions, exhibitions, and incentive travel industry in the United States. The study provides a macroeconomic analysis of the industry's direct spending and employment growth.

"CIC is pleased to present this study on the economic impact of the meetings, conventions, exhibitions, and incentive travel industry," said Mary E. Power, CAE, president and CEO of the Convention Industry Council. "Conducted by VERIS Consulting, LLC of Reston, Virginia, this report estimates the economic impact of this industry to the national economy. With this study, CIC hopes to increase public awareness of the industry as a vital economic engine."

Summary of Findings
The meetings, conventions, exhibitions, and incentive travel industry is a 365-day-a-year business that operates in communities, large and small, across the country. Taken as a whole, it generated $122.31 billion in total direct spending in 2004, making it the 29th largest contributor to the gross national product. That is more than the "pharmaceutical and medicine manufacturing" industry and only slightly less than the "nursing and residential care facilities" industry.

The industry's spending and tax revenue ripple through every sector of the local economy, from restaurants and transportation to retail stores and other services, while supporting 1.7 million jobs in the United States. It generates more than 36% of the hotel industry's estimated $109.3 billion in operating revenue, and its attendees account for nearly 17% of the air transportation industry's operating income.

Facts & Figures
The industry's total direct spending is $122.31 billion. Direct Employment Impact, the number of full-time equivalent (FTE) jobs supported by the direct spending of the industry, is 1,710,000 jobs. Direct Tax Impact rose to $21.40 billion.

Association-sponsored events accounted for two thirds, or $81.94 billion, of the direct spending industry total. Corporate-sponsored events (including incentive travel) accounted for the remaining one third, or $40.37 billion.

The largest share of the convention and exhibition dollar (35 percent) is spent in hotels and other facilities. The rest is widely distributed throughout local economies. After air transportation (24 percent), the biggest categories of attendee, exhibitor, and sponsor spending were: restaurant and outside catering food & beverage outlets (14 percent) and business services (12 percent).

Key Findings
2003
Total Direct Spending- $119.09 billion
Total Direct Employment- 1.70 million
Total Direct Taxes- $20.84 billion

The credible, well-researched facts and figures presented in the Convention Industry Council's 2004 Economic Impact Study will be useful to industry professionals as well as communities at large when planning, budgeting, and advocating for issues related to meetings, conventions, exhibitions, and incentive travel. The Study also:

*Provides compelling statistics to assist in attracting public funding from both local governments and private investors;
*Illustrates benefits of the industry in terms of jobs created, business sales, and tax revenues; and,
*Provides a baseline report that can be used to estimate long-term impact.

Due to the broad nature of the industry, data from a number of reputable sources, each specializing in a particular aspect of the industry, was researched, aggregated, and analyzed. CIC and VERIS Consulting wish to thank the following organizations for contributing their research and data to this project:
* Air Transport Association of America (ATA)
* American Hotel & Lodging Association (AH&LA)
* Center for Exhibition Industry Research (CEIR)
* The Incentive Federation
* International Association of Convention and Visitor Bureaus (IACVB)
* Meetings & Conventions Magazine
* SITE Foundation
* Travel Industry Association of America (TIA)
* U.S. Bureau of Labor Statistics
* U.S. Bureau of Economic Analysis

The Convention Industry Council's 30 member organizations represent more than 100,000 individuals as well as 15,000 firms and properties involved in the meetings, conventions, and exhibitions industry. Formed in 1949 to provide a forum for member organizations seeking to enhance the industry, CIC facilitates the exchange of information and develops programs to promote professionalism within the industry and educates the public on its profound economic impact. In addition to the Economic Impact Study, CIC is responsible for the Certified Meeting Professional (CMP) Program, APEX (Accepted Practices Exchange), and the Hall of Leaders.

###

Click here to view a summary of CIC's 2004 Economic Impact Study.

Source: CIC, 2005.

Appendix B: APEX Industry Glossary

The glossary shown here is available to anyone seeking definitions of commonly used industry terms.

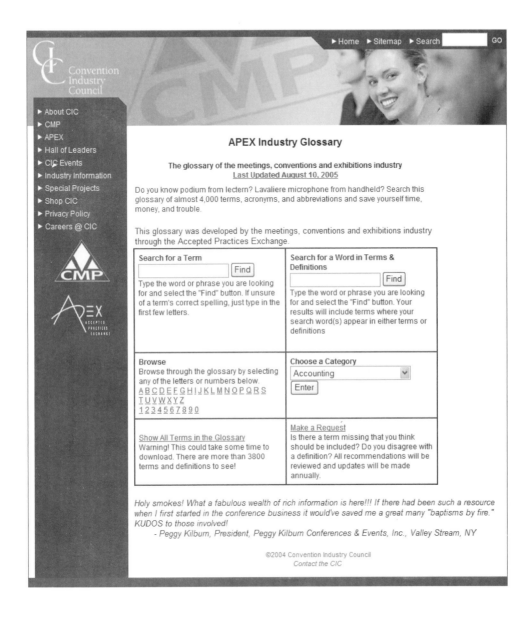

THE ASSOCIATIONS, CONVENTION, AND MEETINGS MARKET

LEARNING OBJECTIVES

After studying this chapter, you will be able to discuss:

- Categories of associations and definitions
- Associations that hold meetings
- What facility services and amenities are important to association planners
- Types of meetings
- The resources available to hotels for identifying association planners

INTRODUCTION

There are numerous types of associations, and they serve many purposes. One element common to all associations is their need to gather their members for business, professional, and social activities. This aspect is particularly important to the hospitality industry, which provides the facilities and services for these gatherings. This chapter provides an in-depth look at associations, their types, and the purposes they serve. It analyzes the types of meetings these groups conduct and how they go about selecting particular sites for their conventions and meetings.

DEFINITIONS OF ASSOCIATIONS

Associations are composed of people who share a common interest. The CIC (Convention Industry Council) defines an association as an organized group of individuals and/or companies who band together to accomplish a common purpose, usually to provide for the needs of its members. An association is usually nonprofit.

A *Trade association* is defined as group of persons or businesses in a particular trade or industry. Generally these organizations are exempt from federal income tax under Section 501(c)(6) of the Internal Revenue Code.

This chapter explores associations groups, their purposes, their responsibilities to their members, and the needs for meetings and conventions.

First let's discuss the main categories of associations: *vocational* and *avocational*. *Webster's Dictionary* defines these as follows:

Vocational: A trade, profession, or occupation.
Avocational: Something one does in addition to his or her vocation or regular work, and usually for pleasure; a hobby.

All of the types of associations we'll examine in this chapter fall within these two categories. Today many adults belong to and may be active members of both a vocational and an avocational association. They may belong to an vocational association for their profession or business benefits. Additionally, they may engage in a leisure activity or hobby for which they belong to an avocational association. People often choose to attend local or national chapter conventions for either type of association.

ASSOCIATION PURPOSE AND BENEFITS

These members who, as stated in the definition, "band together to accomplish a common purpose" become the main purpose of the association. The association is made up of its members and the benefits provided to them. The most standard membership benefits usually include the following:

- Annual national convention and tradeshow
- Professional continuing education and certification programs
- Opportunity for interaction and networking
- Research and statistical data
- Group hotel, travel, and professional discounts
- Influence on legislative and lobbyist efforts

Impact of Associations' Meetings and Conventions

The Destination Marketing Association International (DMAI) (formerly known as International Association of Convention and Visitor Bureaus IACVB) reports that they have as members over 500 associations that hold at least one annual meeting or convention per year. Add to this the state and regional chapters of associations that also hold their own meetings. Though smaller in attendance, these still provide room nights, as well as food and beverage revenue for urban hotels across the country. Financial benefits to the local economy at the destination go way beyond the obvious hospitality industry related services. Just log on to the Web site of any city or area convention and visitors bureau for the latest statistics, which are reported to board members and the general public. (A partial list of CVB Web sites is provided in the appendix.)

The CIC Economic Impact Study, previously discussed in Chapter 1, also shows the tremendous financial impact of the association, and of the meetings and convention industry, on the economy. Most large associations belong to the American Society of Association Executives (ASAE) and the Center for Association Leadership, the trade association for association executives. (Please note that this organization recently changed its name to include *the Center for Association Leadership*.)

Additionally, their Web site provides further insight into the ways associations are advancing the economy:

- Associations' annual budgets now exceed $21 billion, which translates into billions of dollars more in indirect benefits to the U.S. economy.
- Although largely tax exempt, associations still pay more than $1.1 billion annually in local, state, and federal taxes.
- Associations employ 260,000 people full time and another 35,000 part time.
- The ripple effect of association activities on other sectors of the economy is demonstrated by the impact of association meetings and conventions on the travel and hospitality industry. According to ASAE research, association-sponsored meetings and conventions now account for more than 26 million overnight stays in hotels each year.
- Associations dominate the $102 billion U.S. meetings business. Ninety-two percent of associations hold meetings, accounting for 67 percent of the total meetings industry, according to a study by the CIC.

The association maintains statistics and conducts research on a wide variety of topics pertaining to its members, who represent almost every known industry, profession, and avocation. Figure 2.1 shows the homepage from the ASAE & The Center for Association Leadership Web site.

Now we'll look at the various types of associations, along with the meetings and events held, so we can better understand the facility needs of each. But first, what do most of these associations attendees (known as delegates) have in common?

- Unlike corporate meetings, attendance isn't required.
- The majority of association delegates who attend conventions pay their own way.
- Delegates need lower room rates as well as lower travel and registration fees (for the preceeding reason).
- Delegates intrinsically need to derive a benefit from attending (educational sessions, which offer certifications, can provide this).

Figure 2.2 is also from the ASAE and the Center for Association Leadership Web site. This example shows their monthly publication and services, which

Figure 2.1

ASAE & the Center for Association Leadership Homepage

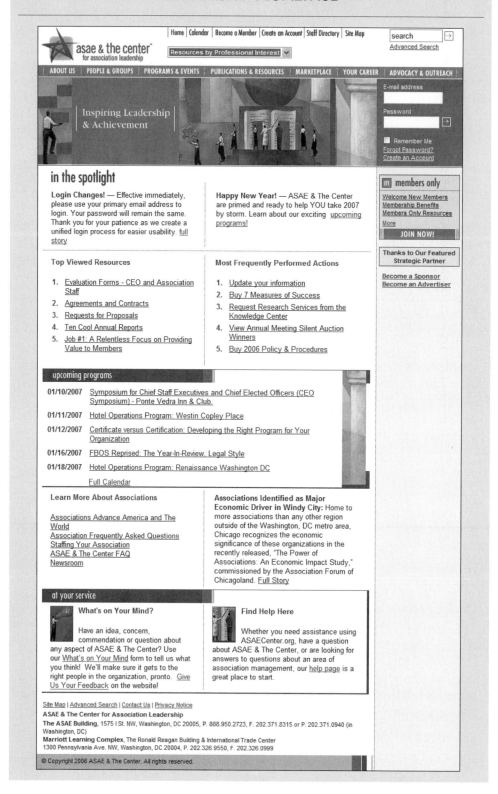

FIGURE 2.2

ASAE MONTHLY PUBLICATIONS

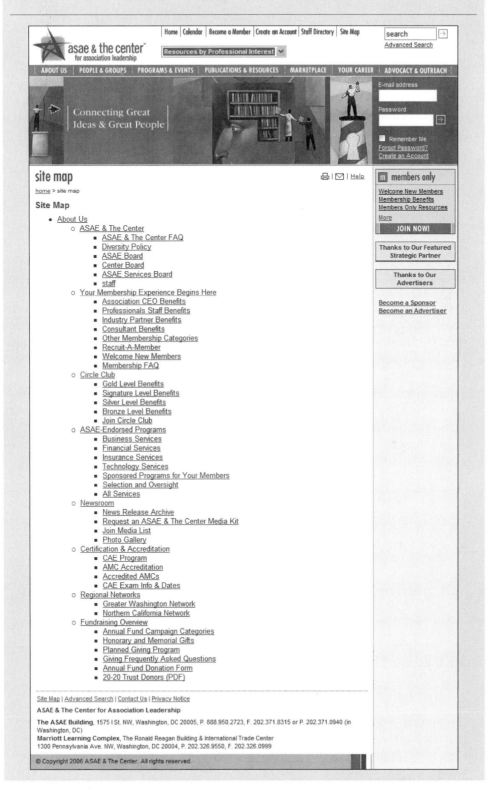

further illustrates the collective power and value of each association and their respective members.

Defining the Value of Associations

Valuable characteristics of associations are as follows:

- America's trade, professional, and philanthropic associations are allocating one of every four dollars they spend to member education and training and public information activities, about three times the amount they spend on direct lobbying of government.
- Americans active in associations devote more than 173 million volunteer hours each year, time valued at more than $2 billion, to charitable and community service projects.
- Ninety-five percent of associations offer education programs for members, making that service the single most common association function. This is followed by convention planning and other convention activities (89%), using Web sites and e-mail to share information with members (81%), and public information activities (79%).
- In terms of annual spending, membership education and training is also the single largest budget item for associations, accounting for $3.6 billion per year, or about 18 percent of the average association's budget. Additionally, association members spend in excess of $10 billion annually to participate in these education programs.
- Other noteworthy association activities include industry research, which 7 out of 10 associations offer at a total cost of $615 million a year; and setting industry product and service standards for their industries, which three of five provide at a total cost of about $884 million annually. The survey found that members spend more than $1.1 billion to comply with these association-set standards, which safeguard consumers and provide other valuable benefits.

Size of Conventions

Of the reported 500 associations that hold an annual convention, the number of attendees requiring hotel guest rooms can vary greatly. Current industry statistics break down as follows.

Annual Convention

Average Number of Attendees:

Under 100 attendees = 12 percent
100–149 attendees = 23 percent
150–199 attendees = 53 percent
2000 or more attendees = 12 percent

TYPES OF ASSOCIATIONS

The following are descriptions of the largest types of associations that hold meetings and conventions.

Trade and Professional Associations

Most vocational associations fall into this category. Members typically work within the field or industry and may have very specialized disciplines for which they have their own association. One example of a professional association is the Association of Realtors, which has members representing many different real estate companies. The members each have an interest in the profession but may be owners, realtors, brokers, or more than one of these. Additionally, other categories of members include companies that provide services to real estate companies, like printed advertising materials or specialty items (i.e., refrigerator magnets, calendars). Furthermore, they will likely become an exhibitor at the annual convention.

Educational Associations

Educational associations are organizations of professional educators, both teachers and administrators. This category also has many developed subgroups for the many academic subject disciplines and levels, be it college, primary, public, or private school. One area almost all educational associations have in common is the school calendar. Since they can meet only during the summer break, their conventions are normally one to two days longer than other associations.

WHEN CONVENTIONS ARE HELD

According to an ASAE survey, the most popular months in which annual meetings or conventions are held are April, May, June, September, and October. For the majority of associations, the most popular arrival day of the week is Monday. Avocational associations often hold their meetings over weekends and are therefore not included in this data.

The most common duration of a meeting or occupancy pattern (main arrival day through main checkout day) is Monday through Thursday.

TYPES OF FACILITIES SELECTED

The site selection process is described in more detail later in the book. However, it is important to consider what criteria is important to association planners. Planners are routinely surveyed and asked to rank those critical factors that can vary greatly year to year.

There are many factors that go into the site selection process for the many different types of meetings and conventions held by associations. Table 2.1

TABLE 2.1
RANKING OF FACILITIES

Scale: 1 not as important, 2–3 somewhat important, 4–5 very important

	Column A Meetings	Column B Convention
Meeting room facilities	1	2
Guestroom facilities	1–2	1–2
Overall appeal	1	1
Air transportation	2	2
Membership appeal (city image)	2	2–3
Affordability	1–2	2
Dining/Entertainment	2	2–3
Climate	2–3	2–3
Recreational facilities	2–3	3
Exhibit facilities	1–2	4–5
Accessibility by highway	2–3	2–3

Source: Abbey, J. (2003).

shows how the types of facilties and destinations used by assocations for meetings are ranked for meetings and conventions.

THE DECISION-MAKING PROCESS

Years ago, all aspects of association management and meeting planning were done on a voluntary basis. Back during those days the author made many, many hotel presentations to general memberships, whose vote would make the final decision on the destination and site selection process. Today, as associations have grown in size and diversity of responsibility to those members, the planning function has evolved as well. Small associations often hire a multi-management firm for administrative functions, and the volunteer board plans the meetings. A full-time staff member; whose job title is usually Association Executive, is limited to the larger associations. Additionally, the sole Association Executive will also handle the administrative functions. Understanding the unique structure of an association can assist the hotel sales manager in determining how to effectively market their services and facility. The Association Executive will usually have convention planning experience, whereas the volunteer board member most likely will not. Table 2.2 shows the attendance and length of association meetings.

TYPES OF EVENTS AND THEIR REQUIREMENTS

Each type of meeting has specifications that help determine the type of facility that will be utilized:

Board and Committee Meetings   Often held in full-service resort properties (with golf facilities) on a quarterly basis.

TABLE 2.2
TYPES OF ASSOCIATION MEETINGS HELD

Type Meeting	Attendance Range	Duration (days)
Board meetings	20–40	1–2
Educational seminars	110–130	2–3
Professional/Technical	130–140	2–3
State/Regional meeting convention	130–150	2–3
Other types of meetings	150–170	2–3

Source: Abbey and Astroff, 2003.

Seminars/Workshops	Training and continuing education, classroom setup needed for meeting space. Repetitive pattern (for many this is the fastest growing segment of associations meetings).
Professional/Technical	Program on new developments relevant to the association members. Larger educational classroom setup needed.
State and Regional Conventions	National associations may sponsor regional or state chapter meetings; both have a smaller number of attendees.
Annual Conventions	Held in conjunction with a trade show or exhibition. Multiple hotels may be required for sleeping and meeting facilities. Meeting size varies from large (general session) to small (committee meetings). Multiple food functions.

MEETING ROTATION CYCLE AND OTHER AREAS GOVERNED BY ASSOCIATION BYLAW REQUIREMENTS

Treated as a separate issue are the requirements some associations have that can definitely impact or ultimately determine the destination and location on where a meeting or convention will be held. It is important, therefore, that the seller (facility) be completely aware of these requirements before time and money is invested in the sales solicitation process.

Numerous associations have one or more of these requirements:

- Can hold meetings only within the same state in which they are located
- Can hold meetings only where there are union members working in the facility
- Must rotate or alternate meeting sites around the geographic regions of the United States (or internationally as scope and membership location dictates)
- Can rotate meetings only within the regions of the state

Keep in mind that the cycle for some large associations may also include more than one convention a year or annual regional and state chapter conventions. Exceptions to their "pattern" can occur if regions or chapters are not financially prepared to host the national convention. Smaller associations may have a convention only every other year. Another important factor is the location of the membership base. For example, if the majority of members reside in proximity to one destination, and members voice concern over travel costs, this may supersede any rotation schedule

Lead Time

In addition to the preceeding areas, the hotel sales representative must be cognizant of the lead time associations require. Common sense dictates that the larger the group, the longer the lead time. For annual conventions this still holds true, with the very largest associations requiring five or more years, although the average-sized association needs only two to four years. As you'll learn in Chapter 7, there is a frequent turnover in the hotel sales business. The same is true of the Association business, but for different reasons. Many association planners are volunteers who are elected board officials. Even though the site selection decision was made during their term, they may no longer be on the board at the time the convention occurs. The lead time for other types of association meetings is much shorter; eight months to one and a half years, the latter for quarterly board meetings.

TRADE SHOWS

A trade show or exhibition (1) provides a major source of revenue from exhibitors and (2) showcases services of interest to members while attending a convention.

Creating and maintaining a successful and profitable trade show is a major undertaking for any association executive. Chapter 11 provides a planning overview that is applicable to associations and other types of planners. In reference to lead time, it is important that groups are monitored closely by the facility to ensure they don't exceed the space on hold. Associations, often eager to increase exhibitors (and revenue), must communicate closely with the convention services manager.

Convention and Visitors Bureaus

Convention and visitors bureaus (CVBs) can be beneficial to association planners and groups, as shown in Figure 2.3.

In Chapter 7 we will explore the impact of attrition on the meeting industry. With this issue foremost on the minds of most association planners, CVBs have recently begun to provide much-needed assistance. Author Ruth Hill, in the article, "Association Meetings—CVBs Add Value for Attendance Building"

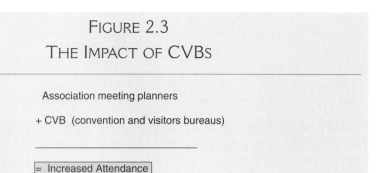

FIGURE 2.3
THE IMPACT OF CVBS

Association meeting planners

+ CVB (convention and visitors bureaus)

= Increased Attendance

(*Meetings West*, August 2004), had the following to say about how CVBs increased services to convention groups, from marketing to convention services. Here are just a few examples of how they have responded to what association planners have asked for:

*The Atlanta CVB and other bureaus across the country are becoming more aggressive in helping groups build attendance, particularly for those valuable citywides, in order to compete in the marketplace.

*The Austin CVB purchased a new e-marketing system that will be particularly helpful to association planners, and it is free to those who book Austin. This software helps association planners build attendance by doing e-mail blasts about registration and housing.

*The San Diego CVB offers planners a "tool kit" to help e-market a convention. The bureau sets up a link from their Web site, geared to association members (attendees) with information about the city such as restaurant and entertainment venues. It helps save a lot of Web designing time and generates some excitement, which boosts attendance.

*The Chicago CVB offers sophisticated software to associations with large exhibitions or trade shows held in conjunction with their annual convention. It is designed to generate leads to increase the number of exhibitors and attendees through telemarketing or direct mail without lead duplications.

The article includes many other examples of ways CVBs are valuable, especially to association planners.

RESOURCES

As you can see, CVBs at every destination work diligently to cultivate and secure association group business in this competitive industry. Therefore, most hotels with at least 400 guest rooms and comparable meeting space join the local convention and visitors bureau as well as their "lead" referral program. For the hotel and convention center industry, the process of identifying qualified leads and decision makers has become very sophisticated. In Chapter 5, additional examples of beneficial joint CVB marketing tools are provided. This subject is also covered quite well by numerous textbooks, college courses, hospitality sales executives, and consultants.

SUMMARY

You can see why the association market segment is singularly responsible for the majority of a hotel's group marketing plan. These multifaceted potential *opportunities* for hotels and convention facilities warrant careful study and prequalification of the group's meeting and guest room needs and history. Otherwise, the planner (and seller) will only be frustrated if time is wasted on a courtship that will never come to fruition because the facility didn't do their homework. To book a piece of this multibillion dollar market, you may have to start with a small board meeting to show how well the facility actually can provide the services promised by the sales department.

REVIEW QUESTIONS

1. Define the terms *vocational* and *avocational*. Give an example of each.
2. List and describe at least three types of meetings held by associations.
3. What facility amenities and services do these planners look for when planning a meeting or convention?
4. Describe and list the two main revenue producers for an association.
5. Describe at least three marketing strategies and sales techniques that are successful for facilities in developing the association business.

REFERENCES

Abbey, J., Astroff, M. (2003) *Convention Sales & Services*, 6e. Cranbury, NJ: Waterbury Press.
ASAE & the Center for Association Leadership (2005)
Destination Marketing Association International (2005)
Hayes, T. (August 2002) The association segment provides reliability to beleaguered suppliers, *Meetings West*.
Hill, R. A.(August 2004) Association meetings taking care of business, *Meetings West*.

ADDITIONAL RESOURCES AND WEB SITES

www.asaenet.org	ASAE & the Center for Association Leadership
www.asae.org/publications	Association Management publication (published by ASAE & the Center for Association Leadership)
www.pcma.org	Professional Convention Management Association
www.conventionindustry.org	Convention Industry Council

GLOSSARY

Articles and Bylaws: Rules adopted by an organization for managing its internal affairs.

Association: An organized group of individuals and/or companies who band together to accomplish a common purpose, usually to provide for the needs of its members. Usually nonprofit. **See also** *Trade Association*.

Association Agreement: 1) A union contract covering companies and unions that bargain on an area-wide basis. 2) A union contract negotiated by a group of employers through an employer's association with the union representing their employees.

Association Booth/Stand: An exhibit booth/stand at which an association provides information about its purpose and services to members and prospective members.

Association Staff: An individual who works for an association.

Attendee Brochure: Direct mail piece sent to current and prospective attendees that promotes the benefits of attending a specific event.

Attendee Scope: Where attendees come from. It is directly related to the spending characteristics of attendees who fall into each of these categories: *International*: Draws a national and international event audience; 15% or more of event delegates reside outside of event host country. *National*: Draws a national event audience; more than 40% of delegates reside outside of a 400 mile (640 km) radius of event city. *Regional*: 60% of delegates reside within a 400 mile (640 km) radius of event city; delegates may reside in a multistate area and/or a regionally homogenous international area. *State/Province*: More than 80% of delegates reside in event state/province (or event-sponsoring state/province when held in state/province other than home state/province; more than 20% of delegates reside outside a 50 mile (80 km) radius of event site. State/provincial audiences are less inclined to use air travel and local auto rental than regional audiences. *Local*: 80% of delegates reside within a 50 mile (80 km) of radius of event site; local audiences typically do not require overnight accommodations.

Trade Association: Group of persons or businesses in a particular trade or industry. Generally these organizations are exempt from federal income tax under Section 501(c)(6) of the Internal Revenue Code.

Trade Center: Special purpose office building oriented toward a specific group of users. Typically, wholesalers in a specific industry (e.g., furniture, apparel) have showrooms to exhibit products to buyers.

General Session: A meeting open to all those in attendance at a event.

Plenary Session: General assembly for all participants.

APPENDIXES

The following two articles pertain to association meetings convention industry trade publications. Collectively, they provide further insight and varying perspectives into the association meetings market. Reprinted with permission.

Appendix A: Association Meetings: Taking Care of Business

Not so long ago, association meeting planners organized logistics, hired speakers, printed and mailed out brochures, and then waited for phone and mail responses. Due to planners' labors, many members routinely attended the organization's annual meeting, where they dropped in on a couple of education sessions, applauded a keynote speaker, and enjoyed camaraderie with industry friends at a reception or on the golf course. Expectations remained the same year after year.

But today, expectations among association members have changed, as has the role of the planners who serve them.

The old formula doesn't work anymore and planners are aware that they must deliver an "experience" to ramp up attendance and participation. Unlike their corporate counterparts who often execute events for a captive audience of company employees, association planners must create events to tempt members who usually pay their own meeting expenses. What those members want now is a lot more than a couple of workshops and an awards banquet.

"There is so much free information available today—on the Internet and elsewhere—it's got to be the experience," confirms John H. Graham, IV, president and CEO of American Society of Association Executives (ASAE). "Twenty-five years ago, the purpose was to be educated. Education is still the answer, but you must offer an experience around it. It's now about how the member is treated before he or she goes to the meeting, how registration is done, and what amenities are included in the package. Association meetings, like so many other things in our society today, are experience driven."

Graham adds that mainstream meetings are dying in the association realm. Like old-style restaurants that only offer meat and potatoes on a plate without a garnish, association meetings lacking extras are disappearing. The job of the organization's meeting planner is to serve up an experience that members can't duplicate anywhere else.

With the rise in member expectations has come the more prominent role of meetings—and their planners, both internal and independent—in the realm of strategic association management.

Face Time at Meetings

Meetings are the face of an association, says Amy LeDoux, CAE, CMP, vice president of meetings and expositions for ASAE's Center for Association Leadership. But organizations are putting more of a premium on them than ever before, she says.

"Organizations realize meetings are their prime interface with their members and a lot more organizations are understanding the importance of meetings as a strategy for their people," LeDoux explains. "So the value of the meeting professional has increased. This is because they are gaining ground as strategists."

Offering education is something any organization can do, LeDoux adds. But the larger task is helping associations create communities.

"It's our job as planners to help people make those important connections at meetings," she says.

Thus, while value and ROI are important to both corporations and associations, they mean something very different to each. While corporations place emphasis on additional sales transactions and revenues to measure ROI, associations measure value by surveying member feedback regarding the overall experience the association provides them.

The more strategic role association planners now have in their organization's management dictates the need for additional training, LeDoux says, and ASAE members have a new roster of opportunities to glean such professional development.

"At our annual meeting this August in Nashville we will have programming called 'Meetings and Expositions Days,' a kind of conference within a conference, targeted to senior level meeting planners," she says.

The M&E Days will focus on strategy and leadership, sales, marketing, and branding, and it will be open to planners as well as other industry people, such as senior hotel sales executives.

Also, coming this fall is the first installment of ASAE's new Business of Meetings Certificate Program (see sidebar, this page), which entails coursework designed to help planners think beyond logistics.

Stakeholder Strategies

Learning to be more strategic requires planners to have higher regard for all stakeholders, including themselves, says Sally Goldesberry, CMP, CMM, senior manager of meetings and exhibits for the Society of Petroleum Engineers (SPE) in Richardson, Texas.

"Planners who are strategic are secure in their jobs today because associations are looking at their organizations as a business even though they may be nonprofit," Goldesberry says. "The effective association planner will make sure they are doing best practices, evaluating their meetings, and finding ways to get input from stakeholders to help them be more strategic."

In Goldesberry's realm, exhibitors rank with members in stakeholder importance. SPE has new initiatives to partner with trade show exhibitors to support their marketing efforts and participation, and discussions with exhibitors now revolve more around their ROI than what size booth they want, Goldesberry adds.

Those discussions have led SPE to develop new marketing tools to assist their trade show partners.

"We are developing various marketing tools that our exhibitors can use in our shows, such as e-technologies to support them in more of a mass marketing effort to bring more people into the show," Goldesberry explains. "Exhibitors evaluate their own customers, but we provide the e-invite at a small, or no, cost to them.

"Also, for small to midsize exhibitors, we are providing a theater—an exhibitor showcase—for scheduled presentations, so they can better compete with larger exhibitors who have their own theaters on the show floor," she continues. "We are offering extended hours during the reception on the night before the official opening day. And, of course, we put food on the show floor to encourage attendees to visit and stay longer."

Listening to exhibitors talk about what works for them is also important, according to Goldesberry.

"Associations may be driven by programming, but it's important to acknowledge that exhibitors spend a lot of money to be in our shows, and they are certainly important stakeholders," she says.

Goldesberry adds that SPE members are also targets for the association's strategic e-marketing efforts.

"Years ago, the idea was to print your brochure and just wait for a response," she says. "There wasn't much follow-up back then, but with e-marketing we can do a lot more to get people to attend conferences. This includes working with industry publications to get articles published that enhance our marketing strategies in both print and on the Web."

Strategic meeting planning today can extend beyond headline conferences, according to Jana Brown, senior manager of conference events for the 22,000-member Golf Course Superintendents Association, based in Lawrence, Kansas. The international organization has one major annual event, and 104 chapters across the U.S. mount regional events throughout the year. Brown says her role in the association now places her in an advisory position, as she assists members at the chapter level with contract negotiations and other management tasks.

"Chapters are asking us for more help in doing venue selections and contract negotiations," she says. "Before, they did it themselves but they are now looking for ways to improve efforts."

Brown's expanding role may soon involve giving support across the borders, as her organization plans on developing initiatives to form multiple international chapters.

Outsource Partners

Member expectations for unique meeting and conference experiences has been one catalyst for the merging of associations with similar profiles in recent years. Mergers stimulate streamlining of member services and reduce the duplication of programs. They may also spawn larger meetings for the new organization and a bigger roster of session tracks.

Independent planner Charles S. Massey, CMP, and president/CEO of Synaxis Meetings & Events, in West Hollywood, California, says growth by merger is one trend that prompts some strategic partnering among those who plan.

"Associations may outsource certain tasks to small association management companies, who in turn 'co-source' with others," Massey says. "In our case, we've had one major association client whose management company has outsourced the logistics to us for over 10 years. As we've gotten busier in the past two to three years, we've had to think strategically and even 'co-source' with some competitors. We have realized the team approach is a good creative solution, so long as you can build a team with people you trust."

Source: Hill, R. Meetings MidAmerica, July/August 2005.

Appendix B: The Association Segment Provides Reliability to Beleaguered Suppliers

Association meetings, formerly given little appreciation by suppliers and destinations, are now being courted like the belle of the ball.

As the economy boomed in the late 1990s, hotels and destinations focused increasingly on lucrative corporate groups, with many properties lowering the available number of rooms for meetings altogether so there would be more room for high-revenue independent corporate and leisure travelers.

That was before the combination of a sputtering economy and Sept. 11 caused much of the corporate and leisure business to dry up.

In the poor economy, corporate groups have been canceling or scaling back significantly, but with the average association drawing about 26 percent of its revenue from its annual conference—second only to the 41 percent that comes from dues—the meetings must go on, says Chris Vest, a spokesman for the Washington, D.C.-based American Society of Association Executives.

"Most of our contacts and colleagues in the hospitality community have been very forthcoming about the fact that corporate business has slacked off to a significant degree post-September 11, and that association meetings and conventions have really been the sort of backbone of their group business," Vest explains. "I think association meetings have always been an important part of their business, but it seems as if it's gotten even more vital in the past eight months."

Loyal Customers Letty Canizalez, national sales manager for the San Diego area's Loews Coronado Bay Resort, says that as corporate groups are downsizing and cutting product launches, associations remain dependable.

"If you book something in association, it's hardly ever canceled," she says. "And they are loyal. If the really love your hotel or [chain] they keep coming back."

She says that with many attendees of association meetings paying their own expenses, as opposed to going on a company tab, the price is key. With the soft hospitality market causing lower prices, she says groups that usually meet in three-star hotels are how able to consider her property or other resort properties.

In San Francisco, where the technology boom pushed room rates to all-time highs, some properties were reserving fewer rooms for groups and were pricing many associations out of the market, says Jeff Doane, director of sales and marketing for The Fairmont Hotel San Francisco.

"There was a real synergy between the association market and this hotel for a number of years," he explains." And then the economy got hot and we went through our renovation and I think we tried to reposition ourselves and avoid that market a little bit, which was definitely the wrong decision because [the association market] is such a perfect match for this hotel. So we are very interested in re-establishing the ties we had with the association market."

He says his hotel's high ratio of meeting space to rooms, 55,000 square feet to 600 rooms, makes the San Francisco Fairmont a good bet for associations, plus he says associations tend to look for properties that capture the essence of a destination, which he says The Fairmont does.

Doane says San Francisco hotels were lulled into a false sense of security by the strong leisure and independent corporate travel that was pushing up ADR and filling rooms.

"I think in general that you learn certain hard lessons when you go through economic times like we have over the past year and a half, and you realize how important [long-standing] relationships are to the hotel business," he says. "Hopefully, it's a lesson we've learned well enough."

Mark Theis, vice president of the San Francisco Convention and Visitors Bureau's convention division, says the City by the Bay is traditionally a three-legged stool of a destination relying on equal parts group, independent corporate, and leisure travelers. But now he says the group business, which is comprised of 65 percent to 70 percent of association meetings, is carrying the bulk of the weight.

"Candidly, two years ago all the hotels were dropping [the number of rooms they would set aside for group] blocks to get the higher-yielding corporate business and high-yielding corporate traveler," Theis notes.

He says there fortunately is enough of a base of stable association business to help somewhat offset losses in other sectors. The CVB has added more sales and marketing resources to attract the group business in recent months, and also to spread the word that the city has more availability and lower prices than in recent years.

"Clearly, this has been an eye-opening slap in the face that everyone needs to be reminded of who are our customers that are with us in good times and bad times, and we as a community don't lose sight of our regular, loyal customers," Theis says. "It also wakes us up to ensure we don't get sloppy when [other segments of business recover]. The last months have re-educated the masses to ensure that we are not overlooking these people, and it's forced us to sell smarter and friendlier than perhaps two years ago."

Richard Grant, spokesman for the Denver Metro CVB, says CVBs have been less guilty of slighting associations because they have always made large associations their emphasis. "A convention bureau does what a hotel can't do on its own. It's hard for them to go after a citywide [alone]," he explains.

Quantity Counts But it is not the citywide meeting alone that the CBVs try to court. Grant says an association can have as many as 50 additional meetings each year in addition to the annual convention. "Another beauty of going after the association market is you may fail to get their big meeting, but you may pick up some smaller meetings; it puts you on their radar," he says.

Grant says that because associations spend more than $56 million of the $83 million spent annually on meetings, conventions, and seminars (according to ASAE figures), it is a segment that shouldn't be overlooked.

Kent Lindeman, owner of Corte Madera, Calif.-based association management firm Holland-Parlette Associates, says he is now considering destinations and properties for his associations that he hasn't sent out RFPs to in years.

He says San Francisco is the prime example of what's happened in recent years. He hasn't had one of his four national association meet in San Francisco in five years because of escalating prices, but is now including the city in RFPs again.

He says second-tier cities have benefited the most because associations that once would not have considered meeting in a second-tier city were forced by economics to go there and were pleased with the results.

"A lot of groups we have, have gone to a second-tier city and they liked it," Lindeman says. "They felt it was a comfortable fit and they didn't get lost in the destination." He says another trend is that hotels are lowering attrition penalties from the once 90 percent to 100 percent threshold to as low as 70 percent or 80 percent.

Lindeman adds that low prices are now pushing many associations to book as far as six years out so they can lock in good rates. Personally, he prefers to book no more than three years out because properties can change so much in six years.

But he doesn't blame those who are booking further in advance when hotel sales staffs are wooing the business so strongly. Denver's Grant says associations have traditionally placed accessibility, facilities and cost at the top of the list when considering a destination. But in recent years three other factors have joined those concerns: safety of the city, location of the center and services provided, and the image and drawing power of the city.

Denver is working to polish its image. "It's tougher to sell the glitz and romantic images of the city, so we've spent a lot of time branding the city so that everything you see about it is consistent: that it's a young, highly-educated, energetic city," he explains.

San Francisco's Theis says that his city's appeal as a tourist destination helps it to draw association meetings because the groups know that attendance will be high when held there.

Source: Hayes, T., Meetings West, August 2002.

THE CORPORATE MEETINGS MARKET

LEARNING OBJECTIVES

After studying this chapter, you will be able to discuss:

- What corporate meeting planners require of the facility
- The role of the independent or third-party planner
- The requirements of the corporate and association markets
- Types of company or corporate meetings held

INTRODUCTION

The term *corporate* is somewhat misleading. It is actually comprised of both companies and corporations. In this chapter we will learn about the different types of businesses that make up this market, which is equally as important (as associations) to hotels and other group facilities. Meeting planners for this segment hold a variety of job titles. We will explore these as well as the diversity of meetings for which they are held responsible.

Only recently have records been kept, which provide a more accurate comprehension of the size and scope of the financial impact of the meetings industry. In recent years, the United States Department of Commerce periodically has released information records on the number of meetings held. The data is provided by corporations on a voluntary basis and is not meant to be comprehensive or represent any standard of measurement. In 2001, 147,613 corporations reported the following:

- In total, they held approximately 1,684,061 meetings annually
- Total expenditures for meeting spending were estimated to be $45.8 billion

TABLE 3.1
MEETING TYPES

Type Meeting	Attendance Range	Duration (days)
Sales Meetings		
National	150	3–4
Regional	60	2–3
Professional/Technical	Varies	2
New Product/Dealer meetings	130–150	2–3
Management meetings	Varies	2
Training meetings	30–50	3

Source: Abbey (2003), *Meeting News*.

Table 3.1 lists the types of meetings held by corporations and companies.

EVENT REQUIREMENTS FOR EACH TYPE

Each type of meeting has certain requirements, as described here.

National and Regional Sales Meetings. These have seen the most growth in the corporate meetings market. They offer good potential for repeat business. These represent the largest and fastest growing segments of the corporate meetings market. The broader scope of national meetings results in large space requirements than regional. Both offer good potential for repeat business.

Professional/Technical Meetings. These often utilize seminar and workshop formats, with lecture and demonstration conducted by consultants, educators, and vendors. In general, a large amount of meeting space is required.

New Product Introduction/Dealer Meetings. These may involve sales staff for new product introductions and campaign rollouts. Top company management and press may attend. They are usually lavish food and beverage events.

Management Meetings. These are usually small in size, but first class hotel facilities are required. They may require multiple geographic locations for simultaneous live video-conferencing.

Training Meetings. All levels of employees need training. These require meeting space with little distraction. Meeting space that is designed for long-term comfort is a plus. They are set up like conference centers, with good lighting and ventilation. Good servicing can be a plus to ensure repeat business.

Meeting Seasons

In their annual State of the Industry report, *Successful Meetings* found that the popularity of months to hold corporate meetings breaks down as follows:

January–March	25.9%
April–June	24.9%
July–September	25.3%
October–December	23.9%

Days of the week to hold corporate meetings:

Weekdays (Monday–Friday)	59.8 %
Weekends (Friday–Sunday)	16.8%
Weekdays and Weekends	23.5 %

Source: 2005 Successful Meetings State of Industry Report, *Successful Meetings*

SITE SELECTION

Just like associations, corporate planners are also routinely surveyed and asked to rank those critical factors that impact site selection decisions. The type of site selected varies greatly, depending on the main purpose of the meeting. As just mentioned, resort-level amenities are required usually for top management and board-level events. Conversely, an airport hotel location can provide a very cost-effective, distraction-free environment for training meetings.

Equally important is the size of the hotel: corporate groups of 100 rooms (or fewer) try to avoid large convention hotels because they don't like that "little fish in a big pond" feeling. Meeting planners are routinely surveyed by trade publications. Table 3.2 shows how they ranked those critical factors that impact site decisions.

TABLE 3.2

FACTORS CONSIDERED IMPORTANT TO CORPORATE MEETING PLANNERS IN THE SELECTION OF A FACILITY/HOTEL

Factors Considered "Very Important"	Corporate Planners
Number, size, and quality of meeting rooms	84%
Cost of hotel or meeting facility	82
Negotiable food, beverage and room rates	79
Quality of food service	76
Number, size and quality of sleeping rooms	74 ·
Availability of meeting support services and equipment, such as audiovisual equipment	59
Efficiency of billing procedures	58
Assignment of one staff person to handle all aspects of meeting	54
Previous experience in dealing with facility and its staff	53
Efficiency of check-in and check-out procedures	49
High-speed Internet access	42
Meeting rooms with multiple high-speed phone lines and computer outlets	40
Number, size and quality of suites	30
Proximity to airport	28

Source: *The 2004 Meetings Market Report conducted by* Meetings & Conventions magazine.

Unlike the association market, planners for companies and large corporations are difficult to identify by their job titles. In some cases, one person may plan only one event, and then have someone else plan the next.

Job Titles

These are some of the positions that involve some meeting planning responsibility:

- Company president (small businesses only)
- Marketing and sales managers
- In-house corporate travel department manager (expected to evolve as impacted by travel industry trends)
- Corporate office-level executives
- Administrative executive assistants
- Independent meeting planners
- Full-time meeting planners

Only large corporations have this position. In the next chapter we will discuss other corporate market segments, such as the insurance and medical fields, which require full-time planners.

Also unlike association planners, their corporate counterparts rarely join trade associations specifically created for meeting planners. Often, only corporate planners who are full time planners themselves. managing a department of planners, choose to belong to associations like:

- P.C.M.A.: Professional Convention Management Association
- M.P.I.: Meeting Planners International
- Alliance of Meeting Management Companies (AMMC)
- The Society of Corporate Meeting Professionals

Note: A detailed description of the scope of each is provided at the end of this chapter.

Lead Times

In general, when compared to associations, all corporate meetings have a much shorter lead time. Sales meetings usually have the longest lead time—8 to 12 months.

Remember that corporate meetings follow no cycle, but are held only when there is a need. During economic recession or a limited growth period, most companies will cut back or even cancel meetings. Conversely, the beginning of an economic recovery may "green light" a meeting that was previously canceled, resulting in a very short lead time. Even in times of limited growth, certain types of meetings, such as sales meetings, are still held, but again, with

TABLE 3.3
LEAD TIMES

	Last Year	Current
Management meetings	6 months	3 months
Training meetings	6 months	12 months
Sales meetings	3 months	6 months
Incentive travel	12 months	6 months

Source: *Successful Meetings* (2005).

a very short lead time. Under these circumstances, the corporate planner must be more budget conscious, even with the short lead time. The facility often must rethink its yield management strategy in what is often called a "buyer's economy." Only when it becomes a "seller's economy" can the principle of lead time be effectively applied.

In the annual State of the Industry Report (*Successful Meetings*), many surveyed corporate planners stated "one of their most challenging areas is shortened or unrealistic lead time for planning." A section of the report titled, "Shrinking Lead Time," compared the previous and current year, in which the lead time had been cut virtually in half (see Table 3.3).

Attendance and Payment

As previously mentioned, unlike associations, where attendance is voluntary and attendees pay their own way, corporations require their employees to attend. Consequently, all sleeping, meeting room, and group meal functions are paid for by the corporation. Individual charges such as room service, health club, or gift shop—known as incidentals—often are paid for by the employee. These charges will go on a separate incidental hotel bill. We will examine account billing more fully in a later chapter.

Site Selection Companies

The corporation or company may contract with an independent planner. Sometimes these planners don't receive a fee for their services and instead must negotiate with the facility for a commissionable group room rate. Today, there are many types of contracted arrangements made between intermediaries that may include everything from site selection to on-site meeting management.

FROM THE AUTHOR

Most independent planners I have worked with over the years, including myself, have extensive hospitality industry experience, as both a buyer and

FIGURE 3.1

BOHANNON & ASSOCIATES, INC. BUSINESS CARD

Serving Meeting Planners and the Hospitality Industry Since 1983

BOHANNON

& Associates, Inc.

Laura C. Bohannon, CMP, *Problem Solver Specialist*
MPI Sacramento/Sierra Nevada Chapter President 2005-06

978 Fieldgate Way • Gardnerville, NV 89460
775-265-8815 • 775-720-0333 cell • 775-265-8816 fax
Laura@bohannon.biz

seller. Many have formed their own companies after their position as a full-time corporate planner was eliminated—an industry trend that occurs whenever there is a weak economy. Whatever their background, independent planners often are hired to plan meeting and site logistics from concept to execution.

Figure 3.1 is a sample business card from Bohannon & Associates, Inc., an independent site selection planning company that offers multiple services.

The following interview was conducted with an established independent planner whose company has evolved into a full service meeting and event management operation.

Interview

Describe the main services that your company provides to meeting groups and planners.

Our agency takes the clients needs and works quickly to find the right venue for their program. We negotiate the rates for their program and we review the contract prior to the client signing it. We also step in and act as the clients' agent when there are any disputes that the client feels they cannot handle alone. Having worked in the hotel business for 12 years and as a planner for the past 11 years I feel that I can easily remedy most challenges because I know where both sides can afford to bend and where they cannot afford to lose.

Please briefly summarize your hospitality industry background, prior to forming your present company.

I started in the industry in 1983 as a Sales Manager for the Sheraton Hotel in Beaumont, Texas. I left to become a Director of Sales of a small suite hotel after the first year and stayed in that position, in Austin, Texas for the next three years. Marriott's Regional Office in Dallas recruited me to help open more than 10 Courtyard by Marriott hotels as a Regional Sales Manager for the following two years. After vacationing in beautiful Monterey, California I decided to move there and stayed in one place for nearly seven years as an Associate Director of Sales at The Monterey Plaza. Once my first daughter was born it was time for me to slow down a bit and work at my own pace. I had a strong rapport with my long-term clients who entrusted me with their business once I became an independent site selection, third-party planner. After three years in business I started managing full-service conventions and now, nearly 11 years later, my company handles all aspects of meeting planning services from managing very large trade shows to designing and implementing large public events.

CERTIFICATION

Independent planners have long struggled for acceptance and respect for their hard work. Most belong to one or more of the industry trade organizations listed in the resource section of this chapter. Additionally, a well-respected certification, CMP (certified meeting professional), is available for experienced independent (and all types of) planners who, upon successful completion of the exam, will receive this designation. The certification program is administered by the CIC, an organization cited throughout this text. According to the CIC Web site, "the CMP program continues to grow world-wide with more than 11,000 Certified Meeting Professionals in 29 countries."

CERTIFIED MEETING PROFESSIONAL (CMP) PROGRAM
SETTING THE STANDARD OF EXCELLENCE

Through the CMP Program, individuals who are currently employed in meeting management have the opportunity to pursue continuing education, increased industry involvement and industry-wide recognition by achieving the CMP designation. The requirements for certification are based on professional experience and an academic examination. The foremost certification program of today's meetings, conventions and exhibitions industry, the CMP designation recognizes those who have achieved the industry's highest standard of professionalism. Established in 1985, the CMP credential was developed to increase the proficiency of meeting professionals in any component or sector of the industry by:

Continued

SOURCES OF BUSINESS FOR THE CORPORATE MEETING MARKET

Many of the sources in this market, as with the association sector, come through networking. All hotel corporations have regional or national sales and marketing support through advertisements and sales offices. These offices generate leads for individual hotels in a region and can save the planner time by determining availability at all hotels in the desired destinations. Unlike a Convention and Visitors Bureau, who will not show favoritism, hotel sales managers will offer only the hotel properties that they represent.

Corporate managers and executives who *occasionally* plan meetings typically don't like to be contacted by hotels, until they have a need. So the less obtrusive, the better. It's best to communicate with the regional hotel sales office when prospecting for new business. Word-of-mouth referrals can work miracles for this market. Relationships are built from successful meeting servicing. This is a great way to get leads on other company divisions who hold meetings, if not in your city, then in others where there may be affiliate properties.

Figure 3.2 is an ad from the Web site homepage for Helms Briscoe. They are an independent site selection firm, offering (free) services to all types of

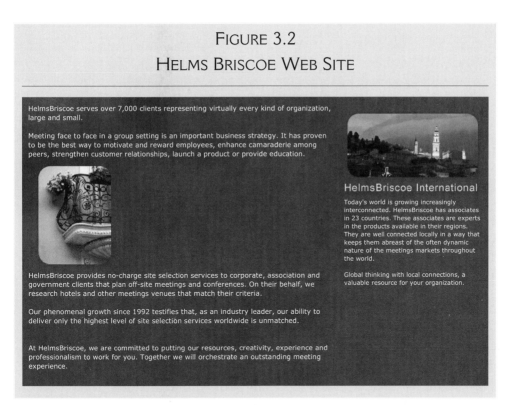
Source: WWW.helmsbriscoe.com

planners. Meeting planners may also be solicited by hotel representation firms. These organizations generate group leads for hotels, sometimes on a monthly retainer agreement or commission basis.

RETURN ON INVESTMENT, JUSTIFYING YOUR EXISTENCE

Corporate planners who do plan multiple meetings per year are often torn between their full time job responsibilities and having to justify to their bosses the required time commitment. If the corporation considers the related activities a support or peripheral function, then it may be relegated to an "administrative activity." Hotels have developed advertisements that should appeal to the planner who has no time to do the research. The other target audience here is the planner who is continually frustrated by the number of hotel sales and servicing staff he or she must deal with, just to plan one meeting. This is a common complaint, although not exclusive to the corporate market segment.

One-Stop Shopping

In later chapters we will discuss the steps for planning the entire event. We note this challenging issue here because hotels now have a hotel contact just for corporate planners. Similar to the concept of *one-stop shopping*, one request on the hotel's Web site will accomplish booking and planning a meeting for 50 to 75 people. True, it could be an association group, but beyond board meetings, all other types of meetings are larger than this.

Following are some examples of how hotels—whether chains or independent—are trying to distinguishing themselves by servicing the small group segment. The following are excerpts from *Meetings Guide to the West* (May 2000).

Hyatt's Meetings Connection (MC) managers act as liaisons between hotel operating departments and planners. MC managers are trained to be planner advocates who ask the right questions about guest room needs, meeting requirements and specifications, catering, transportation details, AV needs, and VIP services. One of their chief responsibilities is to act as consultant, to fill in the gaps in the experience of a planner who may not plan meetings on a full-time basis.

Fred Shea, vice president of sales for Hyatt Corporation, says small meetings amount to about 70 percent of his company's meetings business, so it is Hyatt's objective to give personalized attention. "Smaller meetings are very important to us, and our MC people take a group all the way through, from booking to servicing when they arrive on-site," he explains. "In some cases, they hand off to a services manager, but personalized attention is how we do it, either way."

At the 510-room Grove Park Inn & Spa in Asheville, N.C., meetings represent about 60 percent of business, so Pola Laughlin, associate director of sales, says groups with 20 or less sleeping rooms on peak nights get the attention of Meetings Express staff people.

"Our small specialist people do contracts, BEOs, dinner reservations—everything they need. It's a one-stop service," she says. "There's never any breakdown, because we also have convention managers who work with larger groups. Meetings Express staff people never work with them."

The following is one meeting planner's experience with holding meetings at Mandalay Bay. Robert Mansfield, manager of performance improvement for Kia Motors, holds meetings two to four times per year at Mandalay Bay for the automaker's dealerships, ranging from 15 to 50 peak room nights for each. He says that having one person assigned to his group from the time he calls to check for availability until the end of the event emulates the personalized service of smaller properties. He prefers to meet at larger properties because of the diversity of recreational opportunities available. After a bad experience at another Las Vegas property, he began to rethink that proposition, but after moving the meetings to Mandalay Bay, he is content.

According to Danielle Babilino, vice president of hotel sales at Mandalay Bay Resort and Casino (Las Vegas, 3,300 rooms), small meetings fill a variety of needs for her property, including last minute fill-in business. Since many small meetings involve corporate decision makers, the possibility exists of attracting larger business later through a positive experience, making smaller meetings a priority for Babilino and her staff. Mandalay provides the decision maker in any size group with a pin identifying them as such so that staff can quickly identify them.

"The VIP Pin program is for decision makers—these are the people that if they say jump, we say how high," she says. "Even though they are a smaller meeting, there are still people in that meeting that are decision makers and need to be treated like decision makers." Babilino says the intimacy a smaller property may provide is offset by the resources of a large hotel, pointing out that Mandalay has 16 restaurants, the House of Blues, the Mandalay Events center, the Shark Reef aquarium, and more all on-site.

"The tendency to get lost in the shuffle is a lot greater [in a large hotel]; you tend to lose the attention of the property," Mansfield says about his previous experience.

Hilton Hotels Corporation recognizes that "the planner for a smaller meeting may be less experienced, or this may be something they do on an ad hoc basis, so they may not know the ropes of a hotel," says Linda Simpson, western regional vice president of sales and marketing. She says that giving the client one person to work with who can handle all the meetings' needs from food and beverage to audiovisual is key for small meetings. "One source gives them time back, and we understand and appreciate the number one thing everyone needs back is time," she says.

Hilton treats smaller meetings differently from the onset of the process, with Dallas-based Hilton Direct handling calls regarding availability at any of the company's hotels. The ability for a customer to make one phone call to inquire about multiple hotels in multiple destinations is "spot-on in relation to efficiency for the customer," Simpson says. The ad in Figure 3.3 focuses on the many resources Hilton Direct provides.

IN CLOSING

In this chapter we have reviewed the diverse corporate and company meeting market segment. As you have learned, this market can provide a substantial amount of rooms and Food & Beverage revenue for hotels.

For smaller hotel facilities, which can't accommodate large conventions, it is the primary market they solicit and *must* book to remain profitable. In the next chapter we will explore another segment of the corporate market: Incentives. This segment has unique characteristics that set it apart from the corporate market.

REVIEW QUESTIONS

1. List the major facility services required by a corporate meetings planner.
2. Define the terms independent or third-party planner. Give examples of the services they provide.
3. Compare and contrast the different site requirements of corporate and association groups.

FIGURE 3.3
HILTON AD

Source: Ad courtesy of Hilton Hotels.

4. How does the issue of *room rate* differ between corporate and association meeting planners?
5. List the common types of meetings held by companies and corporations.
6. What does the term *one-stop shopping* refer to? Provide some examples.

REFERENCES

Abbey, J., (2005) *Convention Sales and Services*, 7e, Cranbury, NJ: Waterbury Press.
Convention Industry Council, CIC Web site. (2006).
Bohannon, L. (2005) Interview. Bohannon & Associates.
Hill, R., Hayes, T. (May 2004) 2004 Meetings Guide to the West.
Kovalski, D. (August 2005) Micro management, *Corporate Meetings and Incentives*. Article reprint on Web site.
State of the Industry Report. (2004, 2005) *Successful Meetings*.

ADDITIONAL RESOURCES

Independent Site Selection and Planning Firms

www.davidgreenassociates.com
www.conferon.org

Related Industry Trade Groups

The following organizations are among the 32 related industry trade groups that belong to the CLC (www.conventionindustry.org).

The Society of Corporate Meeting Professionals (SCMP)*

217 Ridgemont Avenue
San Antonio, TX 78209
T: (210) 822-6522
F: (210) 822-9838
www.scmp.org

*This group currently is without a Board of Directors.

Member Profile

The Society of Corporate Meeting Professionals (SCMP) membership consists of corporate meeting professionals and convention/service professionals. SCMP exists to further industry education and promote professionalism in the corporate meeting arena.

Professional Convention Management Association (PCMA)

2301 S. Lake Shore Drive Suite 1001
Chicago, IL 60616

T: (312) 423-7262
F: (312) 423-7222
www.pcma.org

Member Profile
The mission of the Professional Convention Management Association (PCMA) shall be to serve the association community by enhancing the effectiveness of meetings, conventions, and exhibitions through member and industry education and to promote the value of the meetings industry to the general public.

Alliance of Meeting Management Companies (AMMC)

7465 Prarie Lake Drive
Indianapolis, IN 46256
T: (317) 842-9852
F: (317) 576-9851
www.ammc.org

Member Profile
AMMC strives to become the premier organization for meeting management consultants; to serve the business management needs of meeting management consultants; to establish an identity for the meeting management consultant industry both in the meetings industry (planners and suppliers) and in the general business community; to create a network that supports the members; to encourage and promote high standards and ethics in the meetings industry; and to safeguard and promote the interests of its members.

Meeting Professionals International (MPI)

3030 LBJ Freeway
Suite 1700
Dallas, TX 75234
T: (972) 702-3000
F: (972) 702-3036
www.mpiweb.org

Member Profile
Established in 1972, Dallas-based Meeting Professionals International (MPI; www.mpiweb.org) is the largest association for the meeting profession, with 18,000 members in 64 chapters and affiliates. As the global authority and resource for the multibillion-dollar meeting and event industry, MPI empowers meeting professionals to increase their strategic value through education, clearly defined career pathways, and business growth opportunities. Its new plan, Pathways to Excellence, is designed to elevate the role of meetings in business via creating professional development levels to evolve member careers to positions of strategic understanding and influence; influencing executives about the value of meetings; and intensifying supplier business opportunities.

APPENDIX

Micro-Management, by Dave Kovaleski

The following complete article on micro-managing corporate meetings is provided as a resource. Reprinted with permission.

Micro-MANAGEMENT

DON'T TALK TO LYNN RIDZON ABOUT ROI. She's too busy saving her company millions of dollars to think about it.

Ridzon's meeting department at the Bristol-Myers Squibb Co. in Princeton, N.J., has embraced a process called CSM—consumption and specification management—that assesses internal meeting and travel consumption patterns in detail to identify needs and eliminate unnecessary expenditures.

It's a micro-approach to scrutinizing meeting expenditures and making changes such as placing meetings at less-expensive venues, combining multiple meetings, and implementing per-person meeting caps.

"In addition to cost savings as a result of contract negotiations, you need to step back and look at why you're doing things, how you're doing them, where you're doing them, and who is attending," says Ridzon, director of global meeting management.

She has certainly proven her value to Bristol-Myers. In the first year of implementation, her department saved more than $6 million on meetings alone—this on top of the negotiated savings that the company realizes annually through its consolidated meeting management processes. This year, BMS has targeted about $10 million in incremental savings.

While Ridzon's success with CSM is clearly earning her respect from senior management, her cost-avoidance approach could not be further from the new ROI method that Meeting Professionals International is touting as a way for planners to get a seat at the table. ROI methodology is a macro-approach that has planning executives measuring the business impact of their meetings—sales generated, skills learned, etc.—in dollars and cents. "My problem with ROI," she says, "is that I don't develop the content for our meetings. If your core job responsibilities are the logistics of meetings, then I think CSM is an excellent way to prove your value and iterate your expertise."

How It Started

Two years ago, the global strategic sourcing department at BMS approached Ridzon with the concept of CSM—which it was ultimately planning to roll out companywide. "We were looking at other ways to drive procurement benefits in the organization," says Bill Stirling, vice president, global sales/marketing and IT sourcing. "We had already implemented category management and strategic sourcing. CSM is an internally driven process in which we analyze and challenge the quantity and specifications of what is being procured."

When the program was introduced in late 2003, meetings were part of the first wave of projects. "Meetings and travel were our flagship departments for this initiative because we have a lot of spending and visibility in those areas," he explains.

It helped that BMS's meeting department had already been centralized for more than 10 years and had a proprietary system of tracking meeting spend called MARRS (Meeting Analysis Registration and Reporting System), which was developed and designed by the meeting management team in conjunction with their internal IT group.

"Data is key," says Stirling. "It's fortunate that Lynn's team has a very robust data repository."

The first step was to give Ridzon and her staff of 15 more authority. The company mandated meeting registration policy in 1998, but it needed to be enforced by senior management. "Lynn needed more clout in terms of compliance," says Stirling. "The more meetings we can direct into Lynn's group to manage, the better off we are."

Ridzon's staff is divided into three areas: internal meetings, external meetings, and the resource center, which sends out the requests for proposals, does site searches, negotiates contracts, produces budgets, and tracks expenses. In the past, her staff would have worked within the parameters of the meeting request to negotiate the best deals on meeting space, hotel rooms, and airfare. Now, they are supported by the CSM policy to take a closer look and ask questions to figure out ways to avoid costs.

The process of probing for more information—and having the authority to do so—is at the heart of CSM. "It's about needling down to what are the objectives of the meeting and what do we need to do to meet them," explains Ridzon.

For example, when a meeting request comes in, one of the first questions Ridzon asks is: "Is this a national or regional meeting?" By looking at the audience and the part of the country they're from, she can determine the most cost-effective meeting site. If a group from the Northeast requests a meeting in Florida, she might suggest a regional venue to save money on airfare. If a request comes in for a training meeting at a resort in a top-tier destination, she might funnel it to an airport hotel or a smaller city. "Do you really need a resort if you're going to have a training meeting that runs from 7 in the morning until 10 at night?" she asks.

Another cost-saving measure has been to insist that people use meeting facilities at company sites, including an area the company uses for sales training meetings. "We found that the utilization rate of these rooms was only about 30 percent," says Stirling. Now, groups use the space for smaller meetings that used to be booked off-site.

"There is a lot more scrutiny," adds Stirling. "Not only are venues challenged, so is attendance." Lynn's team, along with the hosts, determine who, and how many, really need to attend.

Ridzon's department also reports up through the corporate travel department, which has several money-saving CSM policies that affect meetings, such as mandating 14-day advance air bookings and eliminating first-class travel.

Per-Night Spending Caps

Also as part of the CSM initiative, Ridzon instituted per-person, per-night caps, with different spending limits for various types of meetings. "We have eight different meeting types, and every meeting goes into one of those buckets," she explains. From training meetings on the low end to incentive trips on the high end, each type of meeting has a maximum allowable per-person, per-night rate. While not set in stone, these guidelines put a stake in the ground. For a company that runs about 300 meetings annually, the savings are huge.

Another tool Ridzon has at her disposal is the authority to combine meetings. "We review disparate meeting requests and recommend that certain meetings be joined together because they are maybe on either end, the same audience," she explains. "So you're saving thousands of dollars, minimally, by combining two or three or even four meetings."

This has been done several times in the past year, most recently with a training meeting, a national sales meeting, and a marketing meeting. They were all national meetings, scheduled around the same time, with crossover attendees. Her staff picked a site in the middle of the country (Dallas) and booked a venue for a week, with meetings scheduled back-to-back. By limiting travel expenses, room nights, and venue costs, they saved thousands without any disruption to the meetings.

Looking Inward

The concept of consumption management is not new within procurement circles, but as a formalized travel and meetings policy, it's cutting edge, says Anna Flynn, vice president, Institute for Supply Management, a leading procurement industry association in Tempe, Ariz. "I've only seen a few companies where people have actually put a program together." Earlier this year, Flynn took an in-depth look at the BMS CSM initiative in a case study published by CAPS Research (www.capsresearch.org), an arm of ISM.

The typical approach to controlling cost is to do so externally—that is, manage expenses through relationships with suppliers and negotiating. CSM takes a different tack: looking internally. "If you say you want to manage costs, maybe you need to look back inside your organization and figure out where you're driving costs in the first place," says Flynn.

Bringing the CSM initiative to meetings and events is indicative of what is happening throughout corporate America, she says. Procurement departments are taking a closer look at meetings and events, which have been overlooked in the past. "The idea is to create more structure and discipline, from a sourcing standpoint."

At BMS, meeting planners manage the CSM program while maintaining a close working relationship with procurement. "There was a lot more interaction when we were rolling it out, but now it runs pretty smoothly," says Stirling. Now, they talk on a weekly basis, and Ridzon attends monthly review meetings with Stirling and his staff. She also participates with the procurement CSM team in developing quarterly reports that are sent to the chief financial officer and executive management of the business unit.

A big challenge for CSM when it comes to meetings is imposing such a program without upsetting internal clients and attendees. If the accommodations or the venue or the transportation is inconvenient or unsatisfactory and affects the program or attendees' morale, these kinds of cost-avoidance measures can backfire. "The real danger is not fully capturing all the intangible costs," says Flynn. "You [don't want to] start cutting back on certain things that may seem like a luxury but may be essential to creating the right learning environment."

In cases in which individuals have objected to meeting recommendations—which has happened, but on a limited basis—there is an appeals process. Any changes need to be supported by a justifiable business reason and be OK'd by senior management.

Part of the Culture

Embedding the CSM concept into company culture is critical, says Stirling. His solution has been to communicate the benefits of CSM by providing training seminars and involving employees by asking them for their money-saving ideas through an internal, online "idea bank."

When procurement came to Ridzon with the CSM initiative, she embraced the change, but not without impressing upon them the nuances of meetings and events. "Meetings are a different type of category. You are not just purchasing a commodity, you are really purchasing a service," she says.

She also educated them about the supplier relationship management part of the job. "We were able to communicate that sourcing meetings is something that's different from transient travel and does require expertise in the area," she says. Ridzon taught procurement to look at each meeting individually, which requires consistent processes and procedures for placing meetings. As she puts it: "Each meeting has its own personality and needs, so you have to understand what the objectives [of each one] are."

So far, overall, the feedback from procurement, the company's senior management, and various department heads has been positive.

"I think everybody's on the same page here," she says. "How can someone say, 'You're wrong, I really want to spend $50,000 more'?" From a business perspective, what we're doing makes all the sense in the world."

CSM at Bristol-Myers Squibb

WHAT IS IT? Consumption and specification management, a procurement-driven initiative that analyzes meeting expenditures and authorizes planners to make changes such as placing meetings at less-expensive venues, combining multiple meetings, and implementing per-person meeting caps

WHEN DID IT START? 2003

SAVINGS IN THE FIRST YEAR: $6 million

SAVINGS TARGETED FOR 2005: $10 million

The Problem with ROI

Lynn Ridzon is not interested in taking responsibility for meeting ROI based on meeting content. "I wouldn't even know where to begin, and, believe me, I have a lot of experience in meetings management," she quips.

She questions what is being put out there by the industry on ROI. "The models they're suggesting people use to measure ROI are so convoluted that nobody who manages a substantial number of meetings would ever have the time or resources to be able to implement the process," says Ridzon, director of global meeting management, Bristol-Myers Squibb, Princeton, N.J. She's referring to the ROI Methodology, developed by Jack Phillips, founder of the ROI Institute, Birmingham, Ala., which Meeting Professionals International has thrown its support behind as a tool to measure the intrinsic value of meetings. However, MPI brass, as well as Phillips, have stated that the methodology is not for everyone.

At BMS, planners can provide input on content or suggest venues or set-ups for certain types of seminars. "But we're not in a position where we are setting the objectives of meetings. We are supporting the communication of that message through a meeting program."

Planner responsibilities differ from company to company, so some planners might find their situation more suited to measuring ROI, says Ridzon. Nonetheless, she thinks the CSM makes more sense for most planners than ROI and is a more efficient and effective way for them to prove their value.

"It's something you can control. And it's right in your own back yard—you know this stuff. If logistics management is your primary responsibility, you are there to support the ability of the meeting host to get their meeting objectives and message across in the best possible way."

Industry leaders champion the idea of elevating the profile of the meeting planner within corporate America. But Ridzon thinks CSM—not ROI—is the way to go. "When your company is looking at a huge spend for meetings and it's being managed appropriately and you're showing great cost savings, then you definitely will get a seat at the table," she says.

THE INCENTIVE, SMERF, AND OTHER MARKETS

LEARNING OBJECTIVES

After studying this chapter, you will be able to discuss:

- The SMERF markets: social, military, educational, religious, fraternal
- The incentive market and the unique requirements of this segment
- The tour and travel market, and how it has drastically changed in recent years
- The senior, theater, and sports market segments

INTRODUCTION

The following markets can provide a significant amount of both individual and group room nights for some types of hotels. Some of these markets also have meetings and trade shows, which can provide more than incremental revenue. These markets, however, are not presented in order of their revenue potential. Historically, each hotel individually evaluates the potential of each market segment and then develops its marketing plans accordingly.

TOUR AND TRAVEL MARKET

The tour and travel market is like a large umbrella that covers many other markets. In recent years, this market has undergone unprecedented change in booking practices and procedures. Until the late 1990s, retail travel agents were responsible for the majority of both group and individual bookings for both transportation and accommodations. Since then two huge events have collectively brought about this change.

The first was the Internet, which quickly revolutionized how people planned and booked their own vacations and business trips. According to American Express, "45 percent of all travelers now use the Internet as their primary planning resource, up from 35 percent in 2003." According to Forrester Research, "More and more people research Web sites for destinations, hotels, and airlines on their own PCs and laptops without having used a travel agent." Reports from the famous Cal Neva Resort in Lake Tahoe, Nevada confirm this trend: "Individual website reservations made directly by the customer have increased 30 to 40 percent, in the last six months, while travel agent bookings have decreased substantially, even though we still pay 10 percent commission."

Consumers were expected to spend $37 billion online in 2003 for air travel, hotel, and car reservations, and online hotel and lodging bookings should experience 142 percent growth over the next five years, says Forrester Research. And room nights booked online in the third quarter were up 51.6 percent over last year, according to TravelCLICK's eMonitor.

Second, but not independently, the airline industry has slowly cut the commissions to travel agents. Since mass air travel first began, commissions of around 10 percent had been standard to agents for their services and issuing of airline tickets. Subsequently, commissions became the standard by which other major travel services, especially hotels, reward travel agencies for their business.

Late in the 1990s the major airlines, in a drastic cost-cutting move and an attempt to ward off bankruptcy, began the commission reductions. By the beginning of the new century, most airlines had implemented plans to phase out commissions. Contrary to industry analysts' predictions, however, as of late 2004, most large hotel corporations have not followed suit and are still paying commissions, albeit reduced from the original standard of 10 percent.

At the same time, there has been an increase in the amount of leisure time for some travelers, whereas others often need to combine business and (family) vacations into one trip. As previously mentioned, many well-traveled individuals no longer rely on (or see the benefit of) a travel agent, thereby rendering the retail travel agent obsolete.

Consequently, almost all agencies now must charge a fee for their services when booking airfare and/or a hotel, as the commissions had previously provided their lion's share of income. As customers have become more comfortable using the Internet, they have simultaneously been targeted for the major "Internet-only price" discounts advertising campaigns by the major travel industry corporations. Though there are many contributing factors, the end result has been that many retail and wholesale travel/tour companies have gone out of business since 2000. The recent increase in travel-related business failures has not gone unnoticed by the consumer, resulting in an increase in travel insurance and bookings made directly by the user.

The travel/tour agencies that have survived the downturn in business are those that began developing alternative market segments up to one decade prior. The successful travel planning company today has active salespeople soliciting all types of groups that travel, usually for leisure purposes. Travel arrangements for individual corporate business travelers today are routinely made through their own offices.

Impacts on the Hotel/Convention Industry

Since the late 1980s a number of travel agencies have become the in-house travel department for large corporations with many employees who travel frequently. Historically, these types of agreements have successfully trimmed the travel budgets through volume discounts. This leads us to the impacts on the hotel/convention industry. Many in-house travel agents are asked to gather bids for room rates from hotels for company meetings, which usually involves some event planning. From the perspective of the hotel sales department, this type of business (corporate group) can yield higher returns (higher room rate and function revenue) than the individual tour and travel market. Both small (ten or fewer) and large tour groups have reaped package discounts through this system, which is integral to this market. Transportation is a very important factor because it can include the means to arrive at a destination (airlines, motor coaches, railroads, or limousines); or it can be the final destination itself (such as cruise ships). Moreover, transportation conveyances can be used at the destination for group movement and entertainment (e.g., deep-sea fishing boats or special excursion trains).

Familiarization or "Fam" Trips

One long-established travel industry promotional technique is still available, although it has become harder for members of the tour and travel industry to qualify for this strategy. Familiarization or "Fam" trips are designed to give travel intermediaries a favorable impression of the property or facility that they can then relate to their customers. Usually, most of the expenses for such visits are picked up by the sponsoring property. For the facility seriously pursuing the group tour market, the investment could produce major dividends. This strategy and other market applications will be discussed further in Chapter 5.

INCENTIVE TRAVEL MARKET

Technically, the incentive market is part of the corporate market discussed in Chapter 3. However, this segment alone provides substantial revenue to many full-service luxury resort properties. Therefore, we will treat it as a special category.

Incentive travel is an award that is offered as a prize or motivation to employees or distributors who achieve the goal established by a company. Historically, incentive programs have been successfully used for those in sales or selling positions. Since it is a reward, only the most exclusive and exotic destinations, resorts, and cruises are chosen. Meetings are usually limited to four to six hours total for incentive programs. The itinerary is developed with the IRS guidelines in mind for incentive rewards. For further information on current government reporting requirements, contact SITE: Society of Incentive Travel Executives (see Additional Resources at the end of the chapter). The larger companies that plan these motivational programs belong to SITE.

The industries that generate the most incentive programs are insurance companies, automobile dealers, and home appliance distributors (from hot tubs to refrigerators). As incentive demand has increased, so has the need for professionals to organize these programs. Known as incentive travel houses, these companies negotiate directly with the hotels, airlines, and related travel services. There are a multitude of services that incentive houses can provide if the client needs complete coordination. The important thing is to know what will motivate different people and create the right program for each, all at the same destination!

Incentive Industry Tradeshows

The Society of Incentive and Travel Executives partners with the Motivation Tradeshow (ITME) to annually bring together the major buyers and sellers of incentive products and services. Only destination and hotel facilities desirable to this market would consider making the investment for a booth at this show, which usually has a waiting list. Remember, too, that there are many other nontravel industry products that compete for the incentive industry dollar. The leaders in these product lines also are represented at this show.

So what destinations and activities get people motivated these days? What are the latest trends with programs? The following is paraphrased from an article on incentives by Carolyn Blackburn, in *Meetings West*, September 2004 issue.

Group incentive travel now includes activities from wine-pairing culinary classes to off-road Hummer tours. Groups range from the mid to late 20s to the early 60s. Activities include white-water rafting, water skiing, horseback riding, golf, spa treatments, fine dining, and bungee jumping.

Some of the factors that influence this decision are:

- Incentive budget economy (how strong is the economy in the country in which the sponsoring group is headquartered?)
- Buying power (strength or the U.S. dollar/exchange rate in the countries being considered at the destination)
- Political climate/post-9/11 terrorist alert level (customer "fear factor")
- Value: amenities compared to other destinations
- Uniqueness of experience (have these participants experienced this type of trip before?)

According to industry experts like Rhonda Brewer, vice president of Pricing and Proposals at Maritz Travel Company, pure incentives (all fun and reward no meetings required) are rare these days. They generally have been replaced by incentive programs "that incorporate a meeting component." "Pure incentives are fewer and fewer between for tax purposes," she says. "Groups network a little, bond and build." A budding trend is to motivate top sellers by offering more than one travel option to be taken within a certain time frame after a months-long sales period. After all, some people prefer mountains instead of the ocean, and some enjoy bringing along their families, whereas others would rather there wasn't a child in sight, not even their own.

Incentive Booking Trends. "There's a lot of last-minute booking now: "What used to be a year to 18 months is now four months and sometimes less." *Internationally*: Europe, Mexico, or the Caribbean; Asia: Hong Kong and Thailand. *Domestically*: Hawaii, Florida, Phoenix/Scottsdale, Southern California."

9/11. Then came 9/11. On that day, Maritz had 57 programs in operation. "We had participants all over the world that we were trying to get home," he recalls. "We had one small program in a rural area of Italy; it was very difficult to get them connected back to Rome, and then get them connected back to the United States."

In fact, despite moving incentives closer to home in the wake of 9/11, planners say they are still able to offer high levels of satisfaction. The United States has produced many great resorts with spas. Some are just so top notch that people don't have a problem taking their people to domestic locations now, too. Resorts with spa and golf are now destinations in themselves. They have all the function space right there. Domestically, four- and five-star quality resorts are being utilized by incentive groups. High-end clients want special functions like a private rodeo for their top producers.

How much longer will it last? Are there signs of a return to "normal"? Planners across the board are seeing an increase of interest in Europe and beyond. Says Hester, "After a couple of years, people have started to feel safe again and to say, "Hey! We used to go on some great trips, what happened?" That's what is happening now. They want to go to more exotic places like Africa. That's one place that has come on very strong. There's a lot of interest in South Africa and in Kenya." Hester has recently come from a site inspection in St. Petersburg, Russia. "Everything about it is amazing and wonderful. It's got all the infrastructure to keep Western tastes happy, but it's still got a very exotic foreign flair."

Although Comb admits, "With the euro being what it is, it takes a higher budget to go to Europe," she is still bullish on international travel. "For those who are looking for more of a value, we're looking at Portugal, Spain, and Ireland," she says. "But the traditionals are coming back—Paris, London. Asia is slowly coming back, but it's not big at this time. But I'm finally seeing China opening up again, which is kind of exciting." And though Hayes, now senior account manager at Chicago-based Proactive Inc., admits that incentive travel has slowed down, her clients are still going international—to Spain. Looking ahead, Comb is cautiously optimistic: "Happenings in the world will sway people on which destinations they choose, but I think travel is back. It's exciting for our industry; people are excited to travel again."

Figures 4.1 and 4.2 are examples of incentive market ads used by resorts to attract this lucrative group market.

FIGURE 4.1
GRAND HYATT BALI INCENTIVE AD

NEW BALLROOM MAKES GRAND PREMIER AT GRAND HYATT BALI

Grand Hyatt Bali now offers an even more exciting facility for meetings and incentives following the launch of the new ballroom in July 2006, complementing the hotel's existing space.

More than 650 luxurious guestrooms and suites, as well as extensive recreational and meeting facilities that can accommodate 1,000 people all in one resort make Grand Hyatt Bali the ideal destination for all types of meetings and incentives.

FEEL THE HYATT TOUCH®

For reservations call your travel planner or Grand Hyatt Bali at + 62 361 77 1234

P. O. Box 53 Nusa Dua, Bali, Indonesia TELEPHONE +62 361 77 1234   FACSIMILE +62 361 77 2038 bali.grand.hyatt.com

Courtesy: Hyatt Hotels.

FIGURE 4.2
MARRIOTT INCENTIVE AD

Courtesy: Marriott Hotels.

SMERF

A market segment quite different from the Incentive business is the SMERF market, which refers to a number of different groups that have common attributes and requirements. The acronym SMERF, believed to have been coined long ago by hoteliers, stands for social, military, education, religious, and fraternal. Though many feel this term is passé, the hotel sales professionals who speak to my classes still recognize the market and use the term.

SMERFs share the following characteristics:

- Nonprofit
- Very price-sensitive; need low rates
- Meet during the slow (off) season and often bring family members
- The meeting planners are usually volunteer and change each year

- Range from 50 to 500+ sleeping rooms per night (often stay two singles per room)
- Vary greatly in their meeting room requirements

The bottom line is that these groups are often those that will fill slow dates, whatever the type of property and location. Often SMERF attendees representing an avocational association hold future potential business from their profession as well.

Under the SMERF umbrella, there are almost too many substitutions for the groups that hold each letter title. For example, some have used the R to refer to reunion groups, and since there are no real hard and fast rules, this alternative is acceptable. Additionally, some use the S for social, where reunions might be categorized. The reunion market segment has really grown with the help of the Internet. School alumni from high schools to colleges have found each other online, and enlisted groups large enough to hire a professional web-based planner to organize their reunions. Figure 4.3 is an example of a Web site for a reunion planning company.

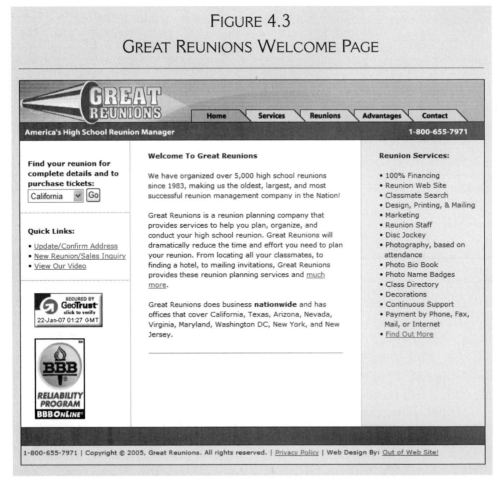

FIGURE 4.3
GREAT REUNIONS WELCOME PAGE

Source: www.greatreunions.com

The rest of the SMERF segments—education, religion, and fraternal—all provide significant sleeping room blocks, food and beverage, and usually need substantial meeting space as well. Though these segments may seem to be very much alike, they each have specific needs. Figure 4.4 shows the home page of a publisher of monthly magazines geared toward these market segments (www.meetingsnet.com). The MeetingsNet homepage describes the organization as follows:

> MeetingsNet is the meeting industry's portal for information and resources related to planning meetings and events. Published by Primedia Business Magazines & Media, a unit of PRIMEDIA, the Meetings Group of magazines provides comprehensive coverage of meeting planning issues, trends, and events in five focused areas: association, corporate, insurance/financial, religious, and medical. For more specific information related to the niche meetings categories that our magazines cover, please visit our individual magazine sites. The Meetings Group also publishes a weekly e-newsletter, *MeetingsNet Xtra*. The newsletter provides timely information and analysis of the news and events that shape the five meetings industry niches covered by the print magazines.

Each of the SMERF market segments has its own international association, but they have enough issues in common to make it beneficial to share resources and articles, which is why some articles are published in more than one segment. For more in-depth information on the trade associations for each segment, please go to their Web site.

INSURANCE MEETINGS

Like incentives, the insurance meeting market is part of the corporate market. However, they also fall into a special niche market, in part due to the large amount of money spent by the insurance industry. Interestingly, the insurance industry (typically large corporations) is the largest user of incentive travel awards. They are shown by meeting planners surveys consistently to be the number one spender annually. The number of insurance companies changes frequently, as mergers and acquisitions occur often. This activity alone creates a need for numerous meetings. Each insurance company can hold up to 20 meetings a year including national and regional conventions, training seminars, and conferences. This segment also has many professional meeting planners with titles like vice president, marketing director, and meeting planner.

Since insurance companies are corporations, most planners in this category are members of one or more meeting management associations. One is the Insurance Planners Conference Association (ICPA). The largest insurance plan-

FIGURE 4.4
MeetingsNet Web Page

Source: www.meetingsnet.com

ners usually belong to the Professional Convention Management Association (PCMA; www.pcma.org). This segment includes planners representing the larger groups that belong to the trade association, the Religious Conference Management Association (RCMA), which represents over 200 different denominations. As the PCMA homepage in Figure 4.5 shows, this organization has much diversification in its membership. PCMA began as a health care member organization but has expanded to include the scientific, engineering, and insurance industries.

Resources

Either PCMA or ICPA are a valuable source for identifying planners. PCMA, particularly, has a large supplier of hotels and facilities in their membership. The annual convention trade show brings together many suppliers and buyers. (If you look at the PCMA history page, which details the chronology, you'll see that in the mid-1980s, the educational foundation began to launch its meeting and convention management curriculum. I was very involved in that process as the instructor for those courses at a community college in San Diego. Since then, according to their Web site, the textbooks and curriculum have been adopted by over 22 colleges offering certificates and degrees in meeting and convention programs globally.)

RELIGIOUS GROUPS

The largest religious conventions bring 10,000 to 30,000 attendees to cities, typically booking every hotel and motel room available. Known as a citywide convention by the local Convention and Visitors Bureau (CVB) (more on this service in a later chapter), religious conventions can last a week or longer. Many planners representing the larger groups belong to the trade association that represents over 200 different denominations, the RCMA. Refer to their Web site for additional information on this association. In general, religious groups meet during the weekend, typically slower periods for downtown city hotels.

Resources

At most destinations that do not have a strong tourism market, this is the ideal SMERF for the local CVB to solicit. Therefore, the initial contact will usually be through their leads program. Membership in the RCMA can be another useful resource; they also hold conventions for suppliers. Figure 4.6 shows the RCMA Web site homepage (www.rcmaweb.org).

GOVERNMENT GROUPS

This vast market segment is composed of literally thousands of government agencies throughout the United States. In general, the government segment is controlled by the *per diems* established by the U.S. General Services Adminis-

FIGURE 4.5

PROFESSIONAL CONVENTION MANAGEMENT ASSOCIATION (PCMA) HOMEPAGE

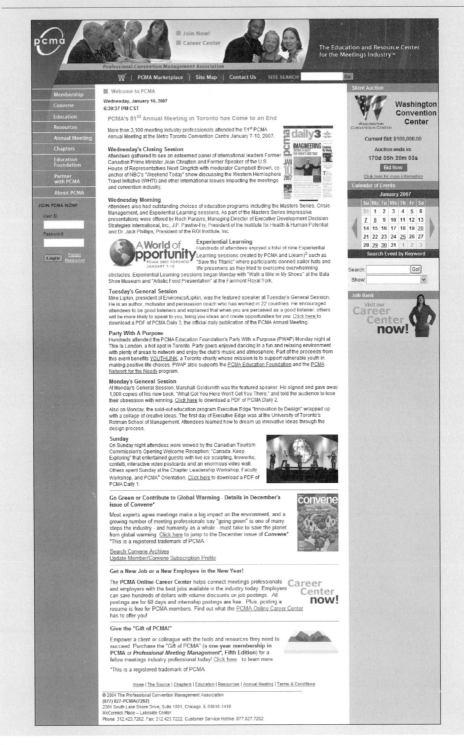

Source: www.pcma.org

Figure 4.5

Professional Convention Management Association (PCMA) Homepage—*Continued*

Sunday, August 21, 2005, 10:25 AM CST

Welcome to PCMA

The mission of the Professional Convention Management Association shall be to deliver breakthrough education and promote the value of professional convention management.

Online Registration for the 2006 Annual Meeting is now open to PCMA Members! Click here for more information about the Annual Meeting and to register.

PCMA recently introduced a framework for the delivery of meetings education. Click here for more about the Principles of Professional Performance (PoPP).

New LegalAdvantage Program
Protect your organization from potential financial and legal liability by attending A Closer Look at Vendor Contracts and Intellectual Property

Latest News

PCMA Members to Be Honored by NYSAE
8/18/2005
The New York Society of Association Executives (NYSAE) will honor five women in the meetings industry - all PCMA members - as "Meetings Industry Icons" during NYSAE's Parade of Stars on Feb. 6, 2006.

Scott Beck Named Salt Lake CVB President and CEO
8/18/2005
Scott Beck, general manager of the Salt Lake City Marriott City Center, has been chosen to lead the Salt Lake Convention and Visitors Bureau as president and CEO.

International Association Meetings Decline
8/18/2005
There have been fewer international meetings held over the past five years, according to the Union of International Associations (UIA), a non-profit research institute and information clearinghouse based in Brussels.

Room Block Management Guide Published
8/18/2005
Conferon Global Services (CGS) has published The Guide to Room Block Management, providing best practices for blocking rooms, managing housing and registration, and developing incentives for attendees and exhibitors to book in the block.

SUBSCRIE

Quick Links t
What's Hot

Join PCMA

Online Memb
Directory

Online Memb
Renewal

RFPs for PCM

PCMA/MPI Mu
Education Prc

Community S
@PCMA

NEW! PCMA S
Verification P

Travel Partne

Terms and Conditions

Home | The Source | Chapters | Education | Resources | Annual Meeting

FIGURE 4.6
RELIGIOUS CONFERENCE MANAGEMENT ASSOCIATION (RCMA) HOMEPAGE

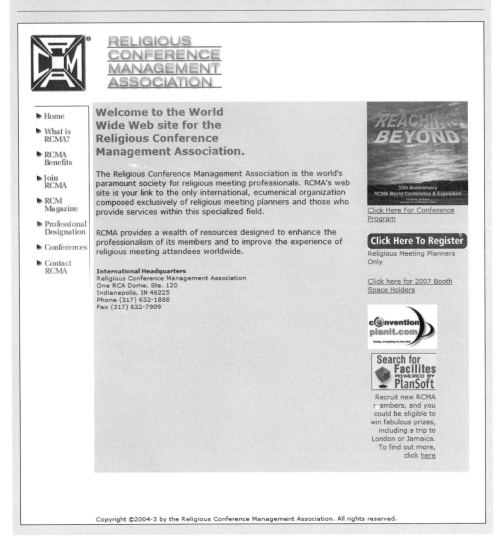

Source: www.rcmaweb.org

tration (GSA), which determines the amount of money that will be allowed for travel-related expenses. *Most* planners (and there are multiple categories), belong to the Society of Government Meeting Planners (SGMP). This association is also part of the publishing resource MeetingsNet Web site; refer to this site for additional information on this association. The government market segment has very well-established guidelines for bids requests for proposals, which are discussed in later chapters. This segment typically books short term, four to eight months out. Additionally, other government meetings that can go over the *per diem* amounts can be identified through networking government contacts and research via the SGMP membership.

Resources

Hotels and their respective food and beverage outlets must first be aware of the *per diems* (dollar amounts) that are listed for each U.S. city in the government publications. Therefore, hotels interested in this market establish government room rates in their marketing plan and decide on the desired amount of rooms and revenue and during which periods they would like to fill with this business. Figure 4.7 is from the SGMP Web site (www.sgmp.org).

EDUCATIONAL MEETINGS

Educational groups almost exclusively meet during the summer and will use dormitories and college classrooms when necessary. As with other SMERFs, room rate is paramount, as most attendees (educators) pay all or part of their own expenses.

Resources

Almost all meeting planners are full-time educators who are volunteering their time. Only some belong to planners associations. Those individuals can be located through the Meetingsnet.com Web site publishing group, which has a link to their trade association. Local college and universities often can provide educational association directories.

FRATERNAL PUBLIC SERVICE ORGANIZATIONS

This market is composed of two types of groups, both of which are strong advocates of community service. First there are the fraternal service organizations. The most well-known community civic groups have familiar names: Rotary, Kiwanis, Lions Club, and the Loyal Order of Moose. Other well-known groups in the fraternal category include International Shriners and veterans-related groups, such as American Legion and VFW (Veterans of Foreign Wars). Planners in this category are almost all volunteers. These organizations all have chapters in each city, which hold local monthly meetings. They are undoubtedly well known for the wide variety of community events they run.

The second type consists of college sororities and fraternities. They have large events only during the summer and may need only overflow guest rooms and meeting space. They often use college dormitories and classrooms. Planners for the largest events often are paid, and book two to three years in advance.

FIGURE 4.7

SOCIETY OF GOVERNMENT MEETING PLANNERS (SGMP) HOMEPAGE

Source: Society of Government Meeting Planners www.sgmp.org

Resources

For the fraternal market, hotel executives can start by becoming active in these organizations locally, as well as donating their time, hotel function space, and support. Leads can be attained initially through networking and inquiries for regional or national upcoming events. For sororities and fraternities, the alumni office on college campuses usually can provide contact information.

MEDICAL AND HEALTH CARE MEETINGS

Composed of the broad health care professions, including pharmaceutical companies, this is a fast-growing segment.

The majority of medical meetings are usually fewer than 200 people. Types of meetings include introduction of new products by drug manufacturers (pharmaceutical) and conferences on new surgical procedures and treatments.

CEU *Continuing Education Requirements for Medical Specializations*

These meetings are attended by all levels of health care professionals and held during peak periods of fall and spring. Almost all meeting planners are professional and belong to the Professional Convention Management Association (PCMA). Additionally, the Meetingsnet.com Web site publishing group has a link to the trade association that focuses on medical market planners.

Resources

Hotels that wish to develop this market should join either or both of the preceding associations.

LABOR UNIONS

There are estimated to be at least 150 different labor (trade) unions, which collectively represent hundreds of thousands of members. This is a vast market that holds numerous regional and national conventions. Two critical factors determine site selection: low room rate, and whether the hotels' employees are members of any union. For example, the restaurant or food and beverage employees are often members of one union, whereas other departments may be represented by a completely different union. Meetings held usually include national/regional conventions, national/regional conferences, and executive committees. (The hotel may not be considered for the bigger events until these occur). Planners are often professionals who hold the title of Union Secretary.

A related article on the impact of unions from the MeetingsNet Web site can be found at the end of this chapter. It addresses the growing impact of union contracts on the hotel and convention industry. The article succinctly describes the recent fallout when labor contract negotiations failed in two major convention cities. When workers (union members) walked off their jobs, management was challenged to provide excellent service for in-house convention groups. Additionally, the article offers strategies for meeting planners to protect their meeting.

Resources

The local union office can provide contact information for the Union Secretary office or the meeting planner; one can be found in every large city. Union conventions can draw upwards of 10,000 or more members, though local and regional meetings are typically much smaller.

ADDITIONAL MARKETS TO CONSIDER

Finally, there are a few additional markets that warrant consideration for possible group or individual frequent or even small group meeting business. Each hotel should follow its respective marketing plans, which, if done correctly, will have predetermined the market mix based on the positioning of that property. Since this is not a marketing textbook, I have included only one chapter on hospitality strategies. Therefore, the following markets should be considered only as possibilities to investigate for further development:

Theater or arts market. Is the hotel in or near the theater district? Contact theater operators, production companies, and actors guild; or stage crew, artists (display local artists work).

Sports and teams market. Wide variety of group events for all types of hotels. Teams from Little Leagues, other youth-oriented activities to professionals, all need hotel accommodations when they travel. Contacts include the coach, athletic director, or team manager. In addition to sleeping rooms, special meal arrangements are often required.

Senior citizen market. Wide variety of group business including Grey Panthers, American Association of Retired Persons (AARP). This is the fastest growing age group and will only continue to grow as more baby boomers (people born between 1946 and 1964) reach retirement age.

SUMMARY

These market segments will continue to provide substantial revenue for the hospitality industry both directly and indirectly. Different from both the association and corporate group business, the SMERFs have limited budget and date flexibility. Seasoned hotel sales professionals know that this is the ideal market segment to fill those slow periods. However, in a buyer-driven economy, there is still much competition. The competition for the high-end, full-service incentive market is palpable but limited to only the most high-end resort facilities. In general, there is such a wide variety of rooms and meetings business opportunities here that most hotels can be successful with developing one or more of these market segments.

Author's note: Appendix B, at the end of this chapter, is a comprehensive directory of third-party planning companies and organizations. The directory includes detailed descriptions of their event planning services as shown on their respective Web sites.

REVIEW QUESTIONS

1. Discuss the term *tour and travel* and describe at least two events or trends that have dramatically impacted this market segment.
2. Define the term *SMERF* and list the major markets that comprise this segment.
3. List at least three features SMERF have in common and describe a corresponding benefit a hotel can provide for each.
4. List at least three requirements unique to the incentive market. What type of hotel can effectively secure business from this market segment?
5. Discuss the requirement of the insurance and religious group markets.

REFERENCES

Abbey, J. (2005) *Convention Sales & Services*, 7e. Cranbury, NJ: Waterbury Press.
Blackburn, C. (September 2004) Incentive trends, *Meetings West*. Meetings Media.
Levine, N. (2003) Cal-Neva Resort, Lake Tahoe Nevada.

ADDITIONAL RESOURCES AND WEB SITES

Incentive and Motivational Planning Companies

www.maritztravel.com	Maritz
www.efmcdonald.com	Carlson Travel Group

GLOSSARY

DMC: Destination Management Company. Professional company engaged in organizing events of all types, and their related activities.

Familiarization Trip: Fam Trip. Offered to potential buyers of a venue, a program designed to acquaint participants with specific destinations or services and to stimulate the booking of an event. Often offered in groups, but sometimes on an individual basis.

Ground Operator: Company or person in a city handling local transportation and other local travel needs.

Incentive: Reward offered to stimulate greater effort.

Incentive Event: A reward event intended to showcase persons who meet or exceed sales or production goals.

Incentive Travel: A travel reward given by companies to employees to stimulate productivity.

Incentive Travel Company: Company that designs and handles some or all elements of incentive travel programs.

Operator: A loose term that may mean Destination Management Company.

Per Diem: Per day. Some event attendees, such as government employees, have a limited amount of money they can spend per day on food and other expenses. Daily allowance for items like food, lodging, etc.

Professional Congress Organizer (PCO): European term for DMC; local supplier who can arrange, manage, and/or plan any function or service for an event.

Refundable Deposit: A deposit made by the destination management company to a venue that may be returned to the DMC under certain conditions agreed to by the venue.

Religious Meetings: An event for attendees to discuss nonsecular subjects.

SITE: Society for Incentive Travel Executives.

SMERF: Meetings acronym for a category of meeting market segments including Social, Military, Educational, Religious, and Fraternal groups.

APPENDIXES

Appendix A: The Impact of Labor Unions

The following complete article on hotel labor unions is provided as a resource.

In case you didn't know it, there's an elephant in the hotel. It even has a name—labor—and in 2006 it could turn into an 800-pound gorilla. Next year, hotel contracts expire in several major cities. In Chicago, New York, Boston, Toronto, Honolulu, Sacramento, and Monterey, Calif., contracts are up at most of the major hotels, while contracts are also up for some hotels in Cincinnati and Detroit, one in Seattle, and one in San Francisco. And after the recently settled dispute in Los Angeles, where a two-year contract was agreed upon, add that city to the list. All told, employee contracts at more than 400 hotels will be up for renewal next year—more hotel contracts at more hotels than the industry has ever seen.

Many fear that current labor disruptions in San Francisco and, until recently, Los Angeles, are the tip of the iceberg compared to what could happen in '06. David Scypinski, senior vice president, industry relations, Starwood Hotels and Resorts, compared the economic effects to the downturn after 9-11. "It could create a chain of events that hurts the industry and hurts the economy," he says. It's no accident that the stars have aligned this way, says John Wilhelm, president, Unite Here, the union that represents hotel and restaurant employees. "We thought, if we line up as many contract expirations as possible in one year, they're going to have to pay attention. That may be naive on our part; perhaps they will continue to have the same kind of head-in-the-sand approach with workers as they are apparently exhibiting with customers," he says, citing that many hotels are imposing stiff penalties for reduced attendance or cancellation.

While negotiations have not yet started for next year's contracts, Wilhelm says he is concerned about 2006 based on what has transpired in San Francisco and Los Angeles this year. In San Francisco, hotel labor and management at 14 hotels have been at odds since last September after a worker strike and subsequent lockout. Employees went back to work in November when the two sides agreed to a 60-day cooling period, which ended in January. Employees are back at work, but no contracts have been signed, and the picketing and boycotting continue. This spring, in the most visible protest yet, 37 union members were arrested for civil disobedience while picketing in front of the San Francisco Hilton.

In San Francisco, "there's no reason for optimism that I've heard about," says Wilhelm. Among the hotels involved are the Hilton San Francisco, Four Seasons, Fairmont, Sheraton Palace, Omni Hotel, Grand Hyatt Union

Square, and Westin St. Francis. Several large groups have moved their meetings from the boycotted hotels. In Los Angeles, contracts at eight hotels within the multi-employer group including the Westin Century Plaza, Sheraton Universal, Hyatt Regency Los Angeles, Hyatt Regency West Hollywood, Millennium Biltmore, Regent Beverly Wilshire, Westin Bonaventure, and Wilshire Grand Hotel were unsigned for more than nine months until a settlement was reached in June. During that time, some 114 meetings had been relocated from the boycotted hotels, according to the union. In June, a two-year contract was reached, which means the two sides will be back to the table again in 2006. As to whether the negotiations in San Francisco could drag out for another year and a half, Wilhelm says, "I guess that's possible, but that would be foolish in the extreme. The boycotts will continue and the business uncertainties will continue, but I can't control what the employers do, so I don't want to say it's not possible." Scypinski is hopeful that the dispute in San Francisco will be resolved soon, but he is not holding his breath. "If they were serious about negotiations, they would be at the table right now," he says. "We've given them a fair package. The problem is, they just want to go ahead and play it out until next year, when they have this huge amount of potential leverage, and suddenly, they come to us with the hammer."

In San Francisco, the two sides have met around 45 times over the past 10 months. "We want to get back to the table as soon as possible," says Steve Trent, general manager, Grand Hyatt Hotel, San Francisco, and spokesman for the multi-employer group, which represents the 14 hotels. The major stumbling blocks in the negotiations include the length of contract, health care, pensions, and workers' rights. With regard to health care, the union wants to maintain the coverage that it has had in the past. The hotel group says its proposal would not change eligibility for regular employees, only some part-time workers. Joe McInerney, president of the American Hotel and Lodging Association, is optimistic that the two sides can reach an agreement in San Francisco and avert further strikes in 2006. "If they want to cripple the industry, so be it. But there are reasonable people on the union side, and they are trying to work for their members."

What does this mean? In San Francisco, Mark Theis, vice president, convention division at the CVB, stresses that it's not as bad as it seems. "There might be some random demonstrations that last an hour or two every other week, but nothing like there was before Christmas." As far as widespread cancellations and moved meetings, Theis says that most groups have held their meetings in the city as scheduled. What hurts is the unsettled nature of the dispute. "It just creates a layer of ambiguity and grayness on San Francisco as a desirable meeting destination," Theis says. To counter that, the CVB is calling clients six to eight months out to keep them abreast of what is happening.

Despite the uncertainties surrounding the hotel labor situation, there are precautions you can take. First, there is the matter of hotel contracts. Strikes, threats of strikes, even picketing are covered in force majeure clauses, but there has to be a reason to exercise the clause to cancel the meeting. Keep in mind, however, that if performance is not an impossibility, the clause may be challenged by the hotel if it states that the defense to performance is limited to "impossibility" and does not provide for the defense of commercial "impracticability." With regard to hotel cancellation clauses, planners should review contracts carefully with counsel to ensure maximum protection in the event of cancellation. Also, contracts should require hoteliers to provide "a reasonable estimate of the actual damages the hotel will suffer" if the group cancels. Strikes and threats of strikes are covered in cancellation insurance. However, coverage is not available if the buyer knows the strike is coming.

In the RFP process, planners should ask pointed questions about labor unions at hotels. Be proactive in communicating with the hotel and the union to get specific information on how the meeting might be affected. Work with the hotel to find out how it can accommodate the group if there is a disruption. CVBs are knowledgeable about the labor environment in a given city, so they may be able to provide valuable advice and resources. If circumstances dictate that you can't hold a meeting at a particular hotel, ask the hotel about moving the meeting to another property within the chain. Meeting professionals also can exert pressure by making their concerns known to CVBs, local government officials, hotel owners and management companies, unions, and industry associations. Labor is a hot topic among industry organizations, so stay tuned for informational forums and white papers. If unwanted solicitations come from union representatives, CIC recommends that planners take notes and get the contact information from the caller and forward the information to management or counsel. Finally, don't avoid cities that have new contracts due in 2006. Planners have to continue to make decisions that are good for their organizations, understanding that they may have to make last-minute adjustments.

Source: www.meetingsnet.com

Appendix B: Directory of Third-Party Planning Companies

WE ARE PLEASED TO INTRODUCE the first directory of third-party planning companies to readers of *Corporate Meetings & Incentives*. These paid listings include association management companies, destination management companies, incentive travel companies, independent meeting planning companies, and special event planning companies. Companies are listed alphabetically with a description of their services within each listing. Be sure to visit the outsourcing directory online as well at meetingsnet.com.

ASSOCIATION MANAGEMENT COMPANIES

J. Edgar Eubanks & Associates
One Windsor Cove, Suite 305
Columbia, SC 29223
MaryAnn Crews, President
(803) 252-5646, (800) 445-8629
Fax: (803) 765-0860
mcrews@jee.com; www.jee.com

Category
Association Management Company

Company Description
Established in 1971, first association management company in South Carolina. Currently manage 10 associations: one local, two state, and seven national. Served clients average of 15 years. 11 employees, president with 20 years of association experience, three VPs with 22 years' experience, five executive directors. Meeting planning, financials, and publications are areas of specialization. Provide full service for most associations.

Professional Industry Associations
SC Chamber of Commerce, National Federation of Independent Businesses, SC Society of Association Executives, American Society of Association Executives, International Association of Association Management Companies

McVeigh Associates, Ltd.
275 Dixon Avenue
Amityville, NY 11701
Douglas Hunt, Director, Business Development
(631) 789-8833, (800) 726-5655
Fax: (631) 789-9726
dough@mcveigh.com; www.mcveigh.com

Category

Association Management Company

Company Description

McVeigh Associates is a full-service meeting and incentive management company with global capabilities and program expertise that includes, but is not limited to, incentives, sales meetings, advisory boards, product launches, association meetings, investigator/opinion leader programs, and special events. Traditional services are blended with and completed by emerging technology to provide all clients with the industry's most cost-effective and creative project management.

Professional Industry Associations

Meeting Professionals International, GEP Advisory Board, Marriott Advisory Board, International Association of Travel Agents

Certifications: Certified Meeting Professional

DESTINATION MANAGEMENT COMPANIES

Accenting Chicago Events & Tours, Inc.

225 North Michigan Avenue, 11th Floor
Chicago, IL 60601
Glenda Jindrich, President
(312) 819-5363
Fax: (312) 819-5366
info@accentingchicago.com
www.accentingchicago.com

Category

Destination Management Company

Company Description

Accenting Chicago Events & Tours, Inc., in business for 11 years, is a full-service destination management company, whose energetic staff is dedicated to producing innovative, customized programs in the Chicago area. Accenting Chicago's services include opening galas and product introductions; special events at museums, private clubs, yachts and boats, zoos, restaurants, and nightclubs. Accenting Chicago also provides incentive and interactive programs, all forms of ground transportation, meet & greets, and bilingual services.

Professional Industry Associations

Chicago Convention & Tourism Bureau, Chicago Tour Professionals Association, Greater North Michigan Avenue Association, Association of Destination Management Executives, Meeting Professionals International, International Special Events Society, Travel Contacts

Association of Destination Management Executives

3401 Quebec Street, Suite 4050
Denver, CO 80207
Sylvia Rottman, Executive Vice President
(303) 394-3905
Fax: (303) 394-3450
info@ADME.org; www.adme.org

Category
Destination Management Company

Company Description
The Association of Destination Management Executives (ADME) is composed of the premier destination management company executives/owners globally. The organization is dedicated to the education of its members in the ever-changing DMC industry segment, thus providing only the best for meetings, corporate, and incentive management professionals needing these services.

Professional Industry Associations
ADME members are also members of the American Society of Association Executives, Meeting Professionals International, Professional Convention Management Association, ICPA, An Association of Insurance and Financial Services Conference Planners, International Special Events Society, and International Association for Exhibition Management

Certifications
Many ADME members have multiple certifications, including the DMCP, ADME's Destination Management Certified Professional designation. Among our membership, the following certifications are held: Certified Meeting Professional, DMCP, Certified Special Events Professional, Certification in Meeting Management, Certified Incentive Travel Executive

Destination Concepts inc

4241 Jutland Drive, Suite 200
San Diego, CA 92117
Brynne Frost, Principal
(858) 274-7979, (800) 272-3775
Fax: (858) 274-1440
brynne@destinationconcepts.com
www.destinationconcepts.com

Category: Destination Management Company

Company Description
Combining unparalleled creativity, consummate industry experience, and continuous owner involvement in each and every program, Destination Concepts inc is your comprehensive Southern California destination management partner. DCi offers

innovative solutions for custom events beyond the conventional, presenting the very best experiences throughout Southern California with exceptional value. Pushing creative boundaries to exceed expectations, DCi specializes in progressive event design and production, strikingly original décor, and customized general session and award ceremonies. We offer dynamically interactive entertainment designed to transform mere evenings into awe-inspiring events. For superior service and flawless events, DCi is your one link to infinite possibilities!

Professional Industry Associations
Women's Business Enterprises National Council, National Association of Women Business Owners, Association of Destination Management Executives, Meeting Professionals International, Society of Incentive & Travel Executives, Healthcare Convention & Exhibitors Association, Hospitality Sales & Marketing Association International, Insurance/Financial Service Conference Planners Association, International Special Events Society, San Diego Convention & Visitors Bureau, Palm Springs Desert Resorts Convention & Visitors Authority, Anaheim/Orange County Visitor & Convention Bureau, Newport Beach Conference & Visitors Bureau, San Diego North CVB, Contact DMC Group, Gaslamp Quarter Association, San Diego Chamber of Commerce, San Diego Aircraft Carrier Museum

Certifications
Certified Meeting Professional

ME Productions
2000 SW 30th Avenue Pembroke Park, FL 33009
Laura Shaner Martin, Sales Director
(954) 458-4000, (800) 544-0033
Fax: (954) 458-4003
lsmartin@meproductions.com
www.meproductions.com

Category: Destination Management Company

Company Description: ME Productions is an award-winning, full-service destination management and event production company specializing in national and international corporate events, business theater, staging, audiovisual, music, and entertainment. The company offers complete turnkey solutions and is the largest event production company in the Southeast U.S.

Professional Industry Associations
Hotel Sales and Marketing Association International, National Association of Catering Executives, Society of Incentive and Travel Executives, Meeting Professionals International, International Special Events Society

Certifications
Certified Meeting Professionals

INCENTIVE TRAVEL COMPANIES

Jornee
915 Middle River Drive, Suite 509
Fort Lauderdale, FL 33304
Jeffrey Hockersmith, President
2004-09-01(954) 563-6272
Fax: (954) 563-0439
jeffrey@jornee.com; www.jornee.com

Category
Incentive Travel Company

Company Description
As a Global Leader in meeting management, incentive travel and special events, Jornee provides world-class business solutions to meet, and exceed, your corporate objectives. Well-known for our unparalleled customer service, outstanding creativity, and unmatched business experience, we have maintained one of the industry's highest client-retention rates. From inception to completion, we deliver experiences with measurable results!

Professional Industry Associations
Meeting Professionals International, Society of Incentive Travel Executives

streamlinevents, inc.
124 Washington Avenue, Suite E
Point Richmond, CA 94801
Annette Chinn, Principal
(510) 232-0990
Fax: (510) 291-8884
info@streamlinevents.com
www.streamlinevents.com

Category
Incentive Travel Company

Company Description
streamlinevents, inc. offers event marketing strategy, full-service meetings management, and event production. We are committed to tailoring creative and strategic events that result in participant motivation, excitement, and reward through high-impact events and programs. stremlinevents, inc. provides a complete and full range of services through a series of strategic partnerships. You never pay for too large a team or company as we right-size the team based on your needs and requirements. Our efficiency results in a greater return on investment for our clients. Based in the San Francisco Bay Area, we serve clients globally.

Professional Industry Associations
Meeting Professionals International, Professional Convention Management Association

INDEPENDENT MEETING PLANNING COMPANIES

Accurate Image Marketing, Inc.
212 S. Henry Street, Suite 200
Alexandria, VA 22314
Walter E. Galanty Jr., President
(703) 549-9500, (888) 899-4653
Fax: (703) 549-9074
WGalanty@aimmeetings.com
www.aimmeetings.com

Category: Independent Meeting Planning Company

Company Description
AIM is a complete outsourcing meeting planning/sports marketing company. With six employees, AIM manages meetings, trade shows, incentive programs, and special events and golf tournaments for associations, corporations, nonprofits, and celebrities. Our clients include Xerox, Countrywide, National Head Start Association, Aerospace Medical Association, Independent Insurance Agents and Brokers, and others.

Professional Industry Associations
Management company for National Association of Golf Tournament Directors, International Association for Exhibition Management, Greater Washington Society of Association Executives, Association of Meeting Professionals

Certifications: Company President is a Certified Tournament Director.

BA Associates Inc.
PO Box 1807
Blue Bell, PA 19422
Maureen Moroney, CMP, President
(215) 628-2265, (800) 628-0099
Fax: (215) 628-4017
maureenmoroney@cs.com
www.ba-assoc.com

Category: Independent Meeting Planning Company

Company Description
BA Associates Inc. is a meeting planning and incentive management company with 16 years of experience creating and organizing meetings, sales incentives, product launches, trade shows, and trade missions that have taken place across the United

States, Europe, and the Caribbean. The number of attendees at these programs has ranged from 20 to 2,000. Our worldwide contacts and strong contract negotiation skills enable us to bring these programs in on time and on budget.

Professional Industry Associations
Meeting Planners International, HealthCare Business Women's Association, Philadelphia Leadership Society, Board of Directors Phila. Chapter of Cystic Fibrosis, Board of Directors Women's Regional Business Council, Philadelphia World Trade Center

Certifications: Certified Meeting Professional

CM Planners
3700 Forums Drive, Suite 201
Flower Mound, TX 75028
Donna Hoye, Marketing Director
(972) 539-8298
Fax: (972) 539-2850
donna.hoye@cmplanners.com
www.cmplanners.com
Category: Independent Meeting Planning Company

Company Description
CM Planners is a comprehensive meeting planning and event management agency. We provide a complete menu of planning and event management services to corporations and associations. We have the skills, experience, buying power, and technology to design and produce effective adult-education programs (training facilitation, conferences, programs, and seminars), unique customer recognition events (incentives), negotiate the intricacies of a global sales meeting, introduce a product line, and acquaint attendees with cutting-edge technology through a user conference and/or an educational conference. Contact us today to meet the needs of your company. Call toll free (877) 626-7526.

Professional Industry Associations
Meeting Professionals International, International Association for Exhibition Management, Professional Convention Management Association, and Connected International Meeting Professionals Association

Certifications: Certified Meeting Professionals

Conference Services Caribbean Ltd.
PO Box 250
Mandeville, Jamaica Rosalie O'Meally, CMP,
Managing Director
(876) 961-0055
Fax: (876) 625-8934
Contact@ConferencesCaribbean.com
www.ConferencesCaribbean.com
Category: Independent Meeting Planning Company

Company Description

Conference Services Caribbean (CSC) provides comprehensive services for meetings and conferences. We specialize in corporate, regional, and international meetings and conferences in Jamaica and throughout the Caribbean at competitive costs.

Professional Industry Associations

Meeting Professionals International, Connected International Meeting Professionals Association

Certifications: Certified Meeting Professional

Conferon, Inc.

2500 Enterprise Parkway East Twinsburg, OH 44087
Jeff Fugate, Vice President National Sales
(330) 486-0327
Fax: (330) 425-FAXX
jeff.fugate@conferon.com
www.conferon.com
Category: Independent Meeting Planning Company

Company Description

Conferon, the nation's largest independent planning firm, manages more than 1,600 meetings for more than 575 corporate and association clients and books more than 1.8 million room-nights generating more than $300 million in group hotel room revenues annually. Established in 1970, Conferon services include Web-enabled meeting consolidation, site research/selection, contract analysis and negotiations, comprehensive on-site support, online event services including registration and housing with real-time reporting, lead retrieval, full-service graphic design and marketing, incentive/promotion services, and trade show sales and management for events from 50 to 200,000. Headquartered in Cleveland, Conferon has regional offices in Atlanta, Boston, Chicago, Denver, St. Louis, and Washington, D.C.

Professional Industry Associations

American Society of Association Executives

Corporate Meeting Solutions, LLC

11721 S. Easley Drive Lee's Summit, MO 64086 Wanda DeArmon, President
(816) 697-8840
Fax: (816) 566-2433
wanda@corporatemeetingsolutions.com
www.corporatemeetingsolutions.com
Category: Independent Meeting Planning Company

Company Description

Corporate Meeting Solutions, LLC is a full-service meeting planning company. CMS' services include site selection/contracting, budget development, attendee invitations/confirmations, registration, airline and guest room reservations, menu and event planning, on-site meeting management, payment of all meeting expenses, including participant honorarium and travel expenses, and budget reconciliation. In its four years of operation, CMS has planned almost 200 meetings. The owner has more than 14 years of meeting planning experience, primarily in the pharmaceutical and medical education fields. CMS is a small business and prides itself on providing a unique level of personal service and attention to detail that will please any customer.

Professional Industry Associations

Meeting Professionals International

Certifications: No certifications. Owner has 14 years of meeting planning experience.

Covey and Associates

Sharon Covey, CMP, President
(530) 589-2876
Fax: (530) 589-3649
coveyassoc@aol.com
www.coveyandassociates.com
Category: Independent Meeting Planning Company

Company Description

Covey and Associates is a conference management, event production, and incentive travel company. We are celebrating our 24th anniversary providing corporations and associations with creative, cost-effective solutions for all meeting and event needs. We are a one-stop services provider, which allows clients ease of doing business, and sound economics. Many of our clients are multinational corporations, with which we have enjoyed a very high percentage of repeat business. Our personalized service, expertise, and long-term supplier relationships provide clients with product excellence and enhanced ROI and have been key to our success in the meeting industry.

Professional Industry Associations

Meeting Professionals International, Cruise Lines International Association

Certifications: Certified Meeting Professional

Detailed Meetings, Inc.

3964 Dautless Drive Rancho Palos Verdes, CA 90275
Gail A. Emery, CMP, President
(310) 541-9330
Fax: (310) 943-2433
pcgemery@msn.com

Category: Independent Meeting Planning Company

Company Description

Detailed Meetings, Inc. (DMI) is a third-party meeting and event management company developed to work in partnership with your existing staff, other third-party companies, or to handle full production of a meeting. President Gail A. Emery, CMP, has almost 20 years' experience in the corporate, association, and not-for-profit industries. DMI was founded in 2003 to provide an experienced resource able to work globally within a multitude of environments and cultures.

Professional Industry Associations

Meeting Professionals International

Certifications: Certified Meeting Professional

Face To Face Events, Inc.

2699 Iversen Court Santa Clara, CA 95051
Dawn Slykhouse, President
(408) 241-8906
Fax: (408) 241-8918
dawns@facetoface-events.com
www.facetoface-events.com

Category: Independent Meeting Planning Company

Company Description

Face To Face Events is an events management company in Silicon Valley, California, that is built on a strong foundation of professionalism and trust. Our experience is in managing events in the computer industry for major associations, alliances, and corporations. With over 20 years of event planning experience, our dedicated, capable, reliable staff can assist with any of your event management needs, from the development of initial logistical requirements through the actual production and management of your event. Our goal is to create a well-planned, successful face-to-face event.

HelmsBriscoe

8535 E. Hartford Drive, Suite 206
Scottsdale, AZ 85255
Kari Moberg, Director Associate Advancement
(480) 718-2422
Fax: (480) 718-1126
kmoberg@helmsbriscoe.com
www.helmsbriscoe.com

Category: Independent Meeting Planning Company

Company Description

As the world's largest and best-known meeting site selection company, HelmsBriscoe takes the labor-intensive, time-consuming task of locating, evaluating, and contacting appropriate sites for your organization's meetings off your desk, freeing up your schedule for other priorities. We are compensated for our services by receiving a placement fee from the hotel or venue chosen by you. Because of this, there's no need to budget for HelmsBriscoe site selection services. At HelmsBriscoe, we are committed to putting our resources, creativity, experience, and professionalism to work for you.

Professional Industry Associations

American Society of Association Executives, Professional Convention Management Association, Meeting Professionals International

Certifications: Certified Meeting Professional, Certification in Meeting Management, Certified Association Executive, CMR

Hobbs & Ford, Inc.

Sarasota, FL 34238
Harriet McCreary, President/CEO
(941) 922-9767
Fax: (240) 209-0735
harrietm@hobbsandford.com
www.hobbsandford.com

Category: Independent Meeting Planning Company

Company Description

Established in 1998 this certified, woman-owned business strives to become your Event Partner of choice. Locations serving Philadelphia, Pa.; Tampa Fla.; and Washington, D.C. areas. We specialize in training of personnel and volunteers on technology, cultural/political/event-specific etiquette, people movement, and event assignments. On-site event/meeting management. Global shipping logistics for event and convention exhibits, collateral, and support materials. Air, ground, and ocean container transport with 24/7 customer service.

Professional Industry Associations

Meeting Professionals International New Jersey, Philadelphia, Potomac, and Tampa Bay Chapters; International Special Events Society; American Society for Training and Development

Make It Happen, LLC

137 Alhambra Street San Francisco, CA 94123
Linda Mansouria, CMP, CMM, President
(415) 928-5257
Fax: (415) 567-8667
lindam@makeithappenllc.com
www.makeithappenllc.com

Category: Independent Meeting Planning Company

Company Description

Make It Happen, LLC is a full-service global meeting management firm specializing in medical, pharmaceutical, biotech, and technology events for corporate, association, and nonprofit markets. We exceed expectations in service and provide strategies to meet our clients' goals and objectives. We are based in San Francisco, Calif., and have been in business more than 8 Years. The Meetings Academy, a comprehensive education and training center for the meetings industry, is a subsidiary of Make It Happen, LLC. The curriculum is designed to assist beginning, advanced, and independent meeting and event professionals and courses will be offered globally. Make It Happen, LLC, is a certified women-owned business and member of the Northern California Chapter of Meeting Professionals International.

Professional Industry Associations

Meeting Professionals International

Certifications: Certified Meeting Professional, Certified Meeting Manager

Meeting Sites Resource

2082 Business Center Drive, #172
Irvine, CA 92612
Tim Brown, Partner
(949) 250-7483
Fax: (949) 250-4105
tbrown@meetingsitesresource.com
www.meetingsitesresource.net

Category: Independent Meeting Planning Company

Company Description

Meeting Sites Resource is a leading specialist in meeting site research and hotel negotiations. For 12 years, we have partnered with customers throughout the United States to add value to their meetings and events. There is no cost or fee for our site research/contract services. Our performance advantage is our experienced people, buying clout, 48-point hotel contract negotiation process, advanced technology, customer project teams, and service guarantee. MSR is headquartered in Irvine, Calif., with satellite offices in San Diego, Long Beach, New York, Kansas City, and Dallas. Call us at (949) 250-7483 x312

Professional Industry Associations

Meeting Professionals International (three of our team on the faculty), Professional Convention Management Association

Certifications: Certified Meeting Professional

MFM Group, Inc.
Corporate Headquarters:
4856 SW 72 Avenue Miami, FL 33155-5526
Dan Lamey, Executive Vice President
(305) 667-4705, (800) 814-6548
Fax: (800) 546-9984
wdalamey@mfmgroup.com
www.mfmgroup.com

Category: Independent Meeting Planning Company

Company Description
MFM Group was founded in 1994 and has a multilingual staff of professionals based in Miami, Orlando, Las Vegas, New York, Charlotte, and Washington, D.C. MFM Group provides complete turnkey event, conference, and meeting production. We can manage a single event, or—if you decide to outsource—manage your entire event and conference production function. MFM undertakes both event-based and multiyear contractual arrangements. Our services include event, conference, and meeting production; venue site selection and contracting; creative program design; on-site management, including registration; event marketing and communications; and audiovisual contracting and management.

Professional Industry Associations
Meeting Professionals International, American Society of Association Executives, Florida Society of Association Executives, Greater Miami Convention and Visitors Bureau, Orlando/Orange County Convention and Visitors Bureau, Washington, DC Convention and Tourism Corporation

Certifications: Certified Association Executive, Certified Meeting Professional

Moons Event Management, Inc.
80 Cherokee Road Pontiac, MI 48341-1503
Molly A. Moons, President
(248) 454-0431, (800) 403-9805
Fax: (248) 454-0432
molly@moonsevent.com
www.moonsevent.com

Category
Independent Meeting Planning Company

Company Description
For 23-plus years we have provided strategic planning, creative design, program development, detailed planning and coordination, and on-site implementation for

corporate management meetings, special events, and employee incentive programs. Working on a national and international scale, we will handle your entire program from start to finish, or we can work in conjunction with your staff, to ensure your complete satisfaction and success.

Professional Industry Associations
Meeting Professionals International

SLACK Incorporated/Healthcare Education Resources
6900 Grove Road
Thorofare, NJ 08086
Robin Simon, Director of Healthcare Education Resources
(856) 848-1000, (800) 257-8290
Fax: (856) 848-6091
rsimon@slackinc.com
www.slackinc.com

Category: Independent Meeting Planning Company

Company Description
SLACK Incorporated is an ACCME accredited provider, managing more than 75 meetings worldwide each year. And as a publisher of more than 30 healthcare periodicals, we have relationships with world-renowned leaders who help develop tailor-made programs to best achieve your meeting's objectives. From start to finish, our team of dedicated project managers will work with you to organize an event to meet your needs.

Stephen Clark & Associates
3150 N. Sheridan Road Suite 21C
Chicago, IL 60657
Stephen Clark, President
(773) 281-2630
Fax: (733) 529-9884
stephenclark74@msn.com

Category: Independent Meeting Planning Company

Company Description
Hands-on meeting and incentive planning company to manage programs start to finish, as well as assist corporate meetings department with project or support help. Specialize in site search, contract negotiations, program/speaker development, and incentive programs. Also has background in corporate travel management.

Professional Industry Associations
Meeting Professionals International; and ICPA, An Association of Insurance and Financial Services Meeting Planners

Certifications: Certified Meeting Professional, as well as past Meeting Professionals International Planner of the Year

SPECIAL EVENT PLANNING COMPANIES

All Access
2605 Mesa Drive Nashville, TN 37217
Michael Owen, Partner
(615) 367-4505
Fax: (615) 367-0857
m.owen@allaccess.cc
www.allaccess.cc

Category
Special Event Planning Company

Company Description
All Access creates dazzling special events and delivers world-class entertainment for business or pleasure. Plus we come fully armed with an arsenal of savvy marketing support techniques and professional production services to support your event. We create events that deliver your message with sizzle, from invitations to thank-you notes. From Pop Stars to Pig Races, there is no limit to our imagination or talent network when it comes to providing you the absolute best in entertainment options. From the extraordinary to the outrageous, if the act is available, we can get it for you!

Professional Industry Associations
Meeting Professionals International, Tennessee Society of Association Executives, International Entertainment Buyers Association, Nashville Association of Talent Directors

Boca By Design
1500 N.W. 1st Court Boca Raton, FL 33432
Cindy Christman
(561) 447-5444
Fax: (561) 447-5445
cchristman@bocaresort.com
www.bocabydesign.com

Category: Special Event Planning Company

Company Description
At Boca By Design, we know that our success is measured by your success. Our visionary approach to corporate event planning ensures a signature style and quality that is unparalleled. From concept to execution, our team orchestrates special occasions, endowing each event with imaginative detail and flawless service.

Professional Industry Associations
International Special Event Society, Meeting Professionals International, National Association of Catering Executives, and Boca Raton Chamber of Commerce

Connexts Marketing and Corporate Communications
16-03 Radburn Road Fair Lawn, NJ 07410
David F. Williams, Production Manager
(201) 797-2727
Fax: (201) 791-2729
dfw@connexts.com
www.connexts.com

Category: Special Event Planning Company

Company Description
At Connexts, we create energy by connecting minds. Our well-balanced staff of seasoned professionals and edgy Gen Xers give our clients the best possible mix of ideas and performance. At Connexts, we have produced meetings and events for more than 20 years, using the latest technology, skilled technicians, talented speakers and performers, and our legendary attention to details. Connexts offers message development, speech writing, site selection, venue interface, staging, production, and direction. Our goal is always to deliver high-impact results and messages remembered long after the show is over. Call for a consultation and transform the way your company communicates.

Professional Industry Associations
Public Relations Society of America, New Jersey Business and Industry Association, National Association of Women Business Owners, and Women's Business Enterprise National Council

The Custom Event
164 W. Austin Avenue Libertyville, IL 60048
Bonnie Hansen Rybicki, President
(847) 362-3561
Fax: (847) 362-3830
bonnie@thecustomevent.com
www.thecustomevent.com

Category: Special Event Planning Company

Company Description
The Custom Event offers affordable and effective outsourcing for event planning needs. In the Chicago area or wherever business leads, our group of seasoned, award-winning producers provides the resources and expertise to deliver impactful live productions such as product and brand launches, sales meetings, theme platforms, client events, celebrations, trade shows, teambuilding, etc.

Professional Industry Associations
Meeting Professionals International, Chicago Convention & Tourism Bureau

Certifications: Certified Meeting Professional

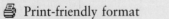 Print-friendly format   E-mail this information

Source: Corporate Meetings & Incentives publication. From their Web site.

THE ROLE OF CONVENTION BUREAUS AND OTHER DESTINATION MARKETING ORGANIZATIONS

LEARNING OBJECTIVES

After studying this chapter, you will be able to discuss:

- The role of the convention and visitors bureau in planning a meeting or convention
- The role of destination/tourism marketing organizations and their common characteristics with a convention and visitors bureau
- The site selection and inspection process
- Why a familiarization destination and facility tour is critical

In this chapter we discuss the many hospitality- and tourism-based resources available at the meeting destinations under consideration. Additionally we'll explore the site selection process in which these destination organizations often coordinate or participate.

CONVENTION AND VISITORS BUREAUS

Over the years convention and visitors bureaus (CVBs), also known as housing bureaus, have evolved to service their markets more effectively. Originally, bureaus were created in large U.S. cities to promote their destination to convention groups needing hotel guest rooms and meeting facilities. As the name implies, the term visitors refers more to the tourism promotion.

Convention bureaus can be funded through different sources. Some are organizations to which local hotels, attractions, convention facilities, and services become members and pay fees. Some are funded through local room tax proceeds, which are paid by tourists (or anyone else) staying in the hotels. Yet, another funding source can be from publicly funded and built exhibition halls. In the 1980s and 1990s, many smaller cities were able to get convention centers built primarily through this method.

Regardless of the funding sources, the main mission of the convention bureau is to promote and market that destination and its visitor services. The visitors can be convention delegates, tourists, or both. If, after the meeting, some attendees stay a day or two and visit local tourist attractions, the CVB has accomplished one of its objectives.

Figure 5.1 is an example of an organizational chart from a membership structured bureau. In this type of organization the members are on top. This model illustrates the decision and policy-making structure for the board of directors and CEO. There are usually two or three different operational departments. A bureau's primary program is that of marketing a destination as a meeting and vacation venue. The sales and marketing department is primarily responsible for identifying, developing, and obtaining commitments and then providing servicing and support.

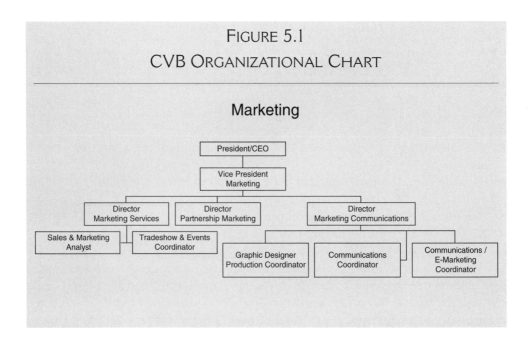

FIGURE 5.1

CVB ORGANIZATIONAL CHART

The marketing and communications department has a multitude of responsibilities directly related to the development of bureau publications and the writing of news stories and press releases. Other key areas include telling the bureau's story not only to its own community, but also to the trade and consumer markets.

Figure 5.2 shows the marketing department of a CVB with the same organizational structure.

Site Inspections and Familiarization Tours

In recent years, site inspections have become an industry standard. Conducted by the meeting planner, it is an in-depth tour and evaluation of a hotel under consideration for an event. Examples of site inspection standard guidelines and recommended facilities and services to be evaluated are included in the addendum. The site inspection typically occurs after there has been a confirmation that accommodations and event space are available for the dates

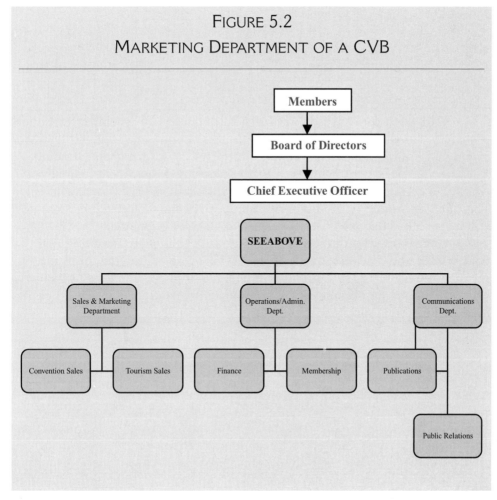

FIGURE 5.2
MARKETING DEPARTMENT OF A CVB

Source: Gartnell, R. (2004).

sought by the group. The hotel sales manager, along with the convention services coordinator, will conduct the inspection. If the CVB was the first point of contact for the meeting planner, it will usually coordinate the inspections at each hotel. A CVB should always be involved in planning the inspection itinerary when it is anticipated that multiple hotels will be utilized for citywide conventions. With this type of planner the CVB representative will most probably pick up the planner at the airport and escort him or her for the entire tour.

On the other hand, a familiarization (or "fam") tour is often the first introduction to the destination, whether hotels or tourism attractions or both. Originally a tool used by destination marketing organizations to familiarize travel agents, now group meeting/event planners are being offered fams.

Figure 5.3 is an example of a promotion advertisement, in the form of an invitation. The invitation was placed in a monthly trade publication that many professional meeting planners read. The fam is for all types of meeting and event planners to attend in Jamaica. Events such as this often are jointly sponsored by the publication, destination marketing organization, and area hotels and meeting facilities.

Destination Marketing Organizations

The other category of destination marketing organization (DMO) is a tourism or travel office. Their promotional focus is primarily on developing the leisure visitor, but we will briefly discuss these organizations here, as they work closely with a CVB.

Many of these tourism organizations throughout the world operate independently from each other. Scope and jurisdiction vary widely. The one common thread is that each receives some level of governmental funding. As many travel tourism professionals know, many regions of the United States (and other countries) have a hotel room or so-called "tourist tax" law in place. This funding source is rapidly diminishing or being redirected as local governments seek viable alternatives to their own state budget cuts.

The current situation at many destinations is that there may no longer be both a CVB and a separate tourism or DMO office. Therefore, both meeting planners and hotel sales and convention services professionals must research which local tourism organization can provide the materials and resources they need to ensure the success of each event.

Industry Insider

How buyers and sellers "find each other" . . . it's no secret that meeting planners get frustrated with hotel sales managers who don't do their homework. Qualifying the lead *before* you contact them means you have hotel rooms and event facilities large enough to accommodate their needs. On the other hand, a lead from a CVB is prequalified and a streamlined way for the buyer and seller to find each other.

FIGURE 5.3
SAMPLE PROMOTION ADVERTISEMENT

Qualified Meeting Planners — Join us...

and see what JAMAICA can do for meetings, incentives and events...

Jamaica Meetings Exchange
June 21 - 25, 2003 • Half Moon Golf, Tennis & Beach Club • Montego Bay, Jamaica

If you're looking for an ideal weather destination for your corporate, incentive, golf or association meetings — join us in Jamaica.

This special program brings resorts, boutique hotels and other local suppliers from Jamaica together to meet you.

Our Marketplace combines professional development, networking activities and one-on-one supplier meetings in a relaxed business environment — giving you all the tools you need to plan inspired meetings, conventions or incentive programs. Come see how easy doing business in Jamaica can be at JAMEX.

Our program for qualified planners includes:
• Airfare
• Hotel accommodations
• All meals
• Activities
• Meetings with suppliers of your choice
• Professional development sessions
• Site inspections of Jamaican properties

To be considered for participation:
E-mail John Mulvey at
jmulvey@successmtgs.com

Source: Successful Meetings Magazine (2003).

LEADS PROGRAMS

In some cities the convention and visitors bureau will offer a *leads* program. Leads generated by their own convention sales department will be sent to member hotels and related services, that pay to receive them. Any of the recipient hotels that subsequently book rooms from this lead in turn will pay a fee or percentage to the convention bureau on the total rooms utilized.

THE MISSION OF CONVENTION AND VISITORS BUREAUS

Convention and visitors bureaus have one fundamental mission. Perhaps the most complete description of the services provided by a CVB is from Richard B. Gartrell, in his book, *Destination Marketing for Convention and Visitors Bureaus*.

"To solicit and service conventions and other related group business and to engage in visitor promotion, which generate overnight stays for a destination, thereby enhancing and developing the economic fabric of the community."

KEY BENEFITS OFFERED BY A CVB

The following key benefits can be an extension of the hotel's group sales department:

- They represent area hotels at trade shows, which smaller properties may not have in their marketing budget.
- They promote the destination as a whole to group market segments through marketing efforts and advertising placements.
- They act as a liaison between the meeting planner who may be considering multiple hotels at multiple destinations.
- They offer cooperative advertising with hotels. Costs are shared so larger ads can be placed.

Promoting Your Destination through a CVB

The advertisement in Figure 5.4 is a testimonial given by an independent meeting planner and site selection firm. It was placed by the Hawaii CVB and promotes the destination, facilities, and ease of planning for groups.

The meeting planner pictured and quoted in the HCB advertisement is Laura Bohannon of Bohannon and Associates. Figure 5.5 is a interview in which Ms. Bohannon discussed how that particular testimonial came about.

FIGURE 5.4
HAWAII CONVENTION AND VISITORS BUREAU

Courtesy: Hawaii Convention and Visitors Bureau.

FIGURE 5.5

LAURA BOHANNON TESTIMONIAL

Q. Describe the main services that your company provides to meeting groups and planners.
R. Our agency takes the clients needs and works quickly to find the right venue for their program. We negotiate the rates for their program and we review the contract prior to the client signing it. We also step in and act as the clients agent when there are any disputes that the client feels they cannot handle alone. Having worked in the hotel business for 12 years and as a planner for the past 11 years I feel that I can easily remedy most challenges because I know where both sides can afford to bend and where they cannot afford to lose.

Q. How did the idea for the Hawaii CV Bureau advertisement come about?
R. One of my favorite partners in this industry is the Director of Sales for the Hawaii CVB. She originally introduced me to the various islands and the resorts about 10 years ago. We now do a great deal of business together and she thought that I would make a good testimonial for them.

Q. How/Why were you selected to give this testimonial?
R. I believe there were five high volume clients asked to participate in this ad campaign although the shoot cost a great deal and turned out well so they only used mine. I feel so strongly that Hawaii does such a great job servicing their visitors that I was only too happy to share my opinion in their advertisement which they called a testimonial ad campaign.

Q. On average how many events do you plan or conduct resort site inspections for in the Ha. Islands?
I plan anywhere from 3-5 programs a year in Hawaii. I generally travel to the islands three times in a year with clients or on actual programs that occur. I assist in the management of many of the programs that we do sites for.

Q. Do you think this kind of advertising is effective? In what way has your company benefited? (I already have feedback from the HCVB ad agency on this)
I am not sure that I have personally derived new business from this campaign but it sure does help my credibility with the hotel sales people who may not have previously known me.

Q. Please briefly summarize your hospitality industry background, prior to forming your present company.
R. I started in the industry in 1983 as a Sales Manager for the Sheraton Hotel in Beaumont, Texas. I left to become a Director of Sales of a small suite hotel after the first year and stayed in that position, in Austin, Texas for the next three years. Marriott's Regional Office in Dallas recruited me to help open more than 10 Courtyard by Marriott hotels, as a Regional Sales Mgr., for the following two years. After vacationing in beautiful Monterey, California I decided to move there and stayed in one place for nearly seven years as an associate Director of Sales at The Monterey Plaza. Once my first daughter was born it was time for me to slow down a bit and work at my own pace. I had a strong rapport with my long-term clients who entrusted me with their business once I became an independent site selection, third party planner. After three years in business I started taking managing full service conventions and now, nearly 11 years later my company handles all aspects of meeting planning services from managing very large trade shows to designing and implementing large public events.

Source: Interview conducted by author.

INTERNATIONAL ASSOCIATION OF CONVENTION AND VISITORS BUREAUS (IACVB)

As discussed earlier, the lack of standardization within the convention-travel-visitors promotion industry creates confusion for both buyer and seller. Founded in 1915, the IACVB is the *only* CVB-based member organization. The IACVB also belongs to the CLC, referred to throughout this text for the glossary terms. In other words, the IACVB helped to standardize the industry definitions. Additionally, almost all major U.S. city CVBs are members of the IACVB, which is based in Washington, D.C.

Meeting planners are encouraged to use their vast resources directly for convention and event planning at no charge. The following information is from the IACVB Web site and answers most initial questions planners may have.

IACVB Name Change

The IACVB changed its name to Destination Marketing Association International (DMAI). According to an article in the August 2005, *Meetings West* publication, the new name is intended to improve public understanding of the organization's mission: destination marketing. Additionally, it will be more inclusive and appealing to potential members outside the United States. Please note this is an association in transition. Many convention trade organizations are still using the IACVB name when referring to DMAI. As of the time of publication, the website for DMAI is www.iacvb.org.

Frequently Asked Questions about CVBs

The following are FAQs are from www.IACVB.org:

What is a Convention and Visitors Bureau?

Convention and visitor bureaus are not-for-profit organizations charged with representing a specific destination and helping the long-term development of communities through a travel and tourism strategy. Convention and visitor bureaus are usually membership organizations bringing together businesses that rely on tourism and meetings for revenue.

For visitors, CVBs are like a key to the city. As an unbiased resource, CVBs can serve as a broker or an official point of contact for convention and meeting planners, tour operators, and visitors. They assist planners with meeting preparation and encourage business travelers and visitors alike to visit local historic, cultural, and recreational sites.

Why Is a Convention and Visitors Bureau Valuable to a Visitor, a Business Traveler, or a Meeting Planner?

- CVBs offer unbiased information about a destination's services and facilities.
- CVBs save visitors time and energy, as they are a one-stop shop for local tourism interests.

Continued

- CVBs can provide the full range of information about a destination.
- Most services provided by CVBs cost nothing.

If CVBs Don't Charge for Their Services, How Do They Make Money?

For most services, convention and visitor bureaus do not charge their clients—the visitor, the business traveler, and the meeting planner. Instead, most CVBs are funded through a combination of hotel occupancy taxes and membership dues.

Why are Meetings and Tourism Important?

Travel and tourism enhances the quality of life for a local community by providing jobs; bringing in tax dollars for improvement of services and infrastructure; and attracting facilities like restaurants, shops, festivals, and cultural and sporting venues that cater to both visitors and locals.

Travel and tourism is one of the world's largest service exports and largest employers. In the United States, for example, travel and tourism is the third biggest retail sales sector. The industry contributes more than $545 billion annually to the nation's economy and generates $94 billion in tax revenues (2001 figures). Indeed, travel and tourism is an economic engine and CVBs are the key drivers.

How Can You Find Out More about Convention and Visitors Bureaus?

Visit www.iacvb.org, the official Web site of the International Association of Convention and Visitors Bureau (DMAI) for more information on CVBs. Also, visit www.OfficialTravelGuide.com for a listing of CVBs around the world, along with contacts and hyperlinks to more than 1200 local CVB Web sites.

How Do CVBs Help Meeting Planners?

Convention and visitor bureaus make planning and implementing a meeting less time-consuming and more streamlined. They give meeting planners access to a range of services, packages, and value-added extras. Before a meeting begins, CVB sales professionals can help locate meeting space, check hotel availability, and arrange for site inspections. CVBs can also link planners with the suppliers, from motorcoach companies and caterers to off-site entertainment venues, that can help meet the prerequisites of any event.

No matter the size of the meeting being organized, from 50 to 50,000, all planners are encouraged to use a bureau's services. In fact, some larger bureaus even have staff members dedicated to small meetings.

Among the advantages of going through a CVB to plan a meeting are:

- CVBs can assist planners in all areas of meeting preparation and provide planners with detailed reference material.
- CVBs can establish room blocks at local hotels.
- CVBs will market the destination to attendees via promotional material, thereby encouraging attendance.
- CVBs can act as a liaison between the planner and community officials, thus clearing the way for special permits, street closures, and such.
- CVBs can obtain special letters of welcome from high-ranking government officials and in some cases, can bring officials to speak at a meeting.
- CVBs can offer suggestions about ways meeting attendees can maximize free time, along with helping to develop spouse programs and pre- and post-convention tours.

What Are Some of the Specific Services CVBs Can Offer the Meeting Planner?

- They can assist in the creation of collateral material.
- They can assist with on-site logistics and registration.
- They can provide housing bureau services.
- They can develop pre- and post-conference activities, spouse tours, and special events.
- They can assist with site inspections and familiarization tours, as well as site selection.
- They can provide speakers and local educational opportunities.
- They can help secure special venues.
- They can assist in the coordination of local transportation.

What Information Do CVBs Have on Hotels?

Convention and visitors bureaus keep track of room counts, as well as other meetings coming to the area. In this way, they can help planners avoid conflicts with other events. Moreover, as CVBs have first-hand familiarity with the hotels and with meeting space in the area, they can help planners match properties to specific meeting requirements and budgets.

What Services Does DMAI Offer to Meeting Professionals Via its Web Site?

By visiting www.iacvb.org, planners can connect to all IACVB member Web sites worldwide. Additionally, the IACVB site allows planners to submit Requests for Proposals (RFPs) to any CVB worldwide at no charge.

Source: www.iacvb.org

SUMMARY

This chapter has been written as a resource, to both the buyer and the seller, on services available from convention and visitors bureaus (CVB) or destination management organizations (DMO). All related industry trade organizations, Web sites, and some published relevant industry forms have been included either in this chapter or in the addendum. Only the documents that are available at no charge and don't require a membership to access are included herein. For additional information, please contact each organization directly by going to its respective Web site.

REVIEW QUESTIONS

1. What is the role of destination/tourism marketing organizations, and what characteristics do they have in common with a CVB?
2. List and describe three ways a CVB can assist the meeting planner.
3. Define the term familiarization trip. How can this be a sales tool for a destination marketing organization?
4. Describe the main responsibilities of the CVB sales and marketing departments.
5. List and describe three ways a CVB can assist a hotel's sales and marketing efforts.

REFERENCES

Bohannon, Laura. Personal interview with author.
Gartnell, R. B. (1994) *Destination Marketing for Convention & Visitor Bureaus*, Dubuque, IA: Kendall Hunt Publishing Company.
Hawaii Convention and Visitor Bureau, (2005) Advertisement.
San Jose Convention and Visitors Bureau. (2004).

ADDITIONAL RESOURCES AND WEB SITES

www.iacvb.org	Destination Marketing Association International (DMAI)
www.sjcvb.org	San Jose Convention and Visitors Bureau
www.OfficialTravelGuide.com	Official Travel Guide

GLOSSARY

Congress: 1) The regular coming together of large groups of individuals, generally to discuss a particular subject. A congress will often last several days and have several simultaneous sessions. The length of time between congresses usually is established in advance of the implementation stage, and can be either pluri-annual or annual. Most international or world congresses are of the former type; national congresses more frequently are held annually. 2) Meeting of an association of delegates or representatives from constituent organizations. 3) European term for convention.

Convention Center: A facility that combines an exhibition space with a substantial number of smaller event spaces. The purpose of these buildings is to host trade shows, public shows, conventions, large food functions, and other functions related to the convention industry. They may be purposely built or converted, and municipally or privately owned.

Convention Rate: Rates assigned for a particular group. This is usually a discounted rate.

Convention and Visitors Bureau (CVB): Convention and visitors bureaus are not-for-profit organizations charged with representing a specific destination and helping the long-term development of communities through a travel and tourism strategy. Convention and visitors bureaus are usually membership organizations bringing together businesses that rely on tourism and events for revenue. For visitors, CVBs are like a key to the city. As an unbiased resource, CVBs can serve as a broker or an official point of contact for convention and event planners, tour operators, and visitors. They assist planners with event preparation and encourage business travelers and visitors alike to visit local historic, cultural, and recreational sites.

Destination Management Company (DMC): A professional services company possessing extensive local knowledge, expertise, and resources, specializing in the design and implementation of events, activities, tours, transportation, and program logistics. Depending on the company and the staff specialists in the company, they offer, but are not limited to, the following: creative proposals for special events within the meeting; guest tours; VIP amenities and transportation; shuttle services; staffing within convention centers and hotels; teambuilding, golf outings and other activities; entertainment, including sound and lighting; décor and theme development; ancillary meetings and management professionals; and advance meetings and onsite registration services and housing.

Destination Manager: Local on-site coordinator.

International Association of Convention and Visitors Bureaus (IACVB): A member of the Convention Industry Council. In 2005 renamed the Destination Marketing Association International.

Inspection Trip: See Familiarization Trip (Fam Trip). See also Site Inspection.

APPENDIX

The following documents are provided as a resource. Reprinted with permission.

Executive Mission Statement of the San José Convention and Visitors Bureau

EXECUTIVE SUMMARY

The Mission Statement of the San Jose Convention and Visitors bureau states the direction of the bureau and serves as the focus of our marketing plan. The mission is:

Mission Statement
The San Jose Convention & Visitors Bureau's mission is to enhance the image and economic well being of San Jose by taking the leadership role in marketing San Jose as a globally recognized destination.

The marketing efforts of the bureau are segregated into two areas: 1) meetings and conventions, and 2) event and leisure. In each of those areas, market segments have been established on a broad basis in order to focus the priorities of the bureau's marketing resources. The primary emphasis of SJCVB is on meetings and conventions, with more than half of the bureau's resources for FY 03-04 dedicated to that purpose. The event and leisure area is concentrated on producing group room business, as well as individual reservations, around the various events/festivals in San Jose. In fact, as the bureau begins the 2003 calendar year, three recent manpower changes have been made that reflect this emphasis:

- A new position, entitled Director of Community Support has been created (see Letter to the Stakeholders), The job function is designed to develop grass roots efforts in the community to solicit national and regional association meetings. The resources for this position were made possible due to the elimination of the Partnership Marketing position that was focused more on the event and leisure marketing efforts.
- The travel industry sales position has been combined with one of the two small-groups sales manager positions. This reflects the need to emphasize filling short-term meetings and conventions business while de-emphasizing the sales efforts towards groups related to events and festivals. This reflects the overall decrease in dollars while focusing the current resources to meetings and conventions.
- The Film, Video and Entertainment sales position has been eliminated due to the determination that dedicated efforts to generate proactive group business have not been productive. The future direction in this market will be more of a service-provider as opposed to dedicated sales effort.

MEETINGS AND CONVENTIONS

The current economic downturn has affected the SJCVB marketing efforts during the past two years and will continue to do so in FY 03-04. Therefore, improving on the current economic conditions and increasing occupancies means establishing a focused marketing effort on two key initiatives. Those initiatives are 1) diversification of markets and 2) improved understanding of the customer's needs through database management.

1) Diversification of Markets. The sales emphasis during the past two years has been to diversify the group business and direct sales efforts beyond just the high tech and tradeshow markets that San Jose used to thrive on into non-tech related tradeshows, national associations, California state associations, and the SMERF markets. As SJCVB continues to diversify its business mix into the non-corporate meeting and convention market segments, additional resources are required. The higher costs associated with securing this type of business are due to a longer, more complex decision-making process. This has led to the shift of manpower and bureau resources to better support the association selling process.

This diversification initiative will be one the SJCVB will champion hereafter, in good and bad economies, to prevent the current occupancy shortfall the city is experiencing. This will also mean continued support from the hotel community for this initiative.

2) Improved Understanding of the Customer's Needs (Database Management).
Understanding the meeting and convention markets means a better understanding of the customer's needs. It also means expanding upon the resource of the database of customers that SJCVB maintains to determine the universe of each market segment. As noted above, the change in emphasis to address niche markets outside of the high tech industry has led to creating new data on potential customers.

This emphasis on the customer has also led to the creation of positioning statements for each market segment within the two areas of marketing. These statements incorporate our customer knowledge; the destination's strengths, weaknesses, opportunities and threats; and the knowledge of our competition for each market segment. The objective is to tailor the marketing message to reflect the uniqueness of each segment. The chart at the end of this section presents the market segments and positioning statements for each.

The room night goals for the meetings and convention markets are less than FY 02-03 (210,000 as compared to 251,000). However, based on the current production volume, they are aggressive. The actions that have been established to implement the plan are reflective of the need to increase room night production in FY 03-04.

EVENT AND LEISURE
Research and results have shown that San Jose suffers from a low economic impact in regards to leisure market travel. It has been determined that the best way for San Jose to increase its market share on the leisure side is through product development and direct sales efforts focused on events and festivals.

The marketing effort for direct sales is a two-prong approach focused on specific events/festivals. One approach is in driving individual room night production from visitors that will attend the event/festival either calling the 888 toll-free phone line or booking through sanjose.org. The other approach is focused around tour operators and organizers that have special interests in the many events and festivals held in the city during the calendar year.

On the product development side, SJCVB is working in partnership with all of the event and festival organizers to assure that the maximum economic impact is received by the city by overnight visitors staying in our hotels. Additionally, SJCVB continues to build partnerships with all of the entities that make up the San Jose visitor "experience" including hotels, Norman Y. Mineta San Jose International Airport, airlines, car rentals, AMTRAK, restaurants, and attractions. The bureau also continues to advocate for public policy decisions designed to move the downtown and uptown products forward (i.e. further development). The Downtown Marketing Collaborative described in the Letter to the Stakeholders is one such effort.

FISCAL YEAR 03-04 OUTLOOK/NEW OBJECTIVES
The SJCVB will continue to focus most efforts and resources on converting group business for the city as it has for the past two years. The expectation is that the economic situation will improve and the overall occupancies and average daily rates will increase. However, the most critical issue will be recognizing that in the long term, a more diverse market mix is the antidote to protecting San Jose's hotel community from experiencing such a deep valley in occupancy. More details on the sales and marketing outlook, as well as the target markets, positioning to those markets, and strategies/tactics to reach those markets are included throughout the remainder of this plan. The last section of this plan focuses on a monthly flow chart of actions that will serve as the road map during the next fiscal year with strategically planned activities and initiatives referenced.

Position Statements for Each Market Segment

Market Segment	Position Statement
Meetings and Conventions Segments	
Trade Show Companies	As the "Capital of Silicon Valley", San Jose is in the best proximity to the largest concentration of high tech companies and workers in the country. For tech shows and new product launches, San Jose offers the best destination to make a tradeshow successful and generate ROI.
National Associations	San Jose is a city offering a high-quality, national brand hotel package, the best weather in Northern California, safest city for attendees to meet, and an easily accessible location with direct flights from all major hubs in the country. The city also offers a group requiring 1500-2000 rooms on peak an opportunity to own the city versus being one of many groups in a city with larger hotel alternatives. The "Virtual San Jose" product also serves as a unique offering to all groups that allows them to "meet outside of the box."
California Associations	San Jose is an easily accessible Bay Area/Northern California destination via train through Amtrak and Caltrain, plane (with a major presence of Southwest Airlines), or automobile through the freeway system to all points within the State that will attract attendance. We also have strong community support to provide local hosts and can provide meeting planning assistance through our Destination Services department. The city's hotel package and overall feel of the downtown is unique and definable for attracting and securing this business.
SMERF	San Jose offers great value in Northern California/Bay Area with close proximity to all points of interest and it's a safe, clean city. The HP Pavilion is also an outstanding facility for large, general sessions with proximity to downtown hotels. Plus, we have the ability to provide meeting and event planning assistance through our Destination Services.
National Corporate	San Jose is a destination with easy access via all types of transportation with national brand, quality hotel products. The city's Bay Area locale within Northern California offers corporate groups an ideal alternative when focusing on education and intensive product training or education. We are also a city that understands how business gets done, as we are the "Capital of Silicon Valley."
Silicon Valley Corporate	San Jose is a destination with easy access via all types of transportation, with national brand, quality hotel products. The city's largest corporate-based clientele include Adobe and Cisco, with additional large corporate headquarters based in the Valley including Sun Microsystems, Intel, and HP. The proximity of San Jose to these companies offers the city a distinct and competitive advantage when handling these local programs. So, the emphasis on buying locally is important. The city's Bay Area locale offers corporate groups an ideal alternative when focusing on education and intensive product training or education. All of this makes us a city that understands how business gets done, as we are the "Capital of Silicon Valley."

Event and Leisure Segments	
Event driven groups in conjunction with a festival or event occurring in the city	Each event will have its own positioning statement. However, the overall position will be that San Jose's event is an unique opportunity to share a special interest with others in an easily accessible location to all that Northern California and the Bay Area has to offer as a leisure experience.
Event driven individual visitors staying overnight with a festival or event occurring in the city	Again, each event will have its own positioning statement. However, the overall position will be that San Jose's event is an unique opportunity to share a special interest with others in an easily accessible location to all that Northern California and the Bay Area has to offer as a leisure experience.
Student/Youth Traveler Market	San Jose represents a great opportunity for student and youth groups to combine travel to the Bay Area with educational experiences due to its proximity to higher education institutions and its affordable hotel rates on weekends.
Senior Market	San Jose presents a great starting and/or ending point for a tour based on its easy access to transportation via air, rail and automobile, as well as its central location to the attractions of the Northern California and Bay Area experience. It is also the safest city in America.
Domestic and International tour operators, organizers, wholesalers, brokers and receptive operators	San Jose represents a great starting and/or ending point for a tour based on its easy access to transportation via air, rail and automobile, as well as its central location to the attractions of the Northern California and Bay Area experience.
Film, Video & Entertainment	San Jose offers a unique and alternate Northern California / Bay Area site serving as an ideal location for any project requiring multiple settings. Our weather guarantees blue sky and sunshine more than 300 days a year which is attractive for shooting movies, training videos, commercials, and other print advertising requiring photography and model shoots.

MARKETING AND ADVERTISING STRATEGIES

LEARNING OBJECTIVES

After studying this chapter, you will be able to discuss:

- The 4 Ps of marketing—the marketing mix
- The difference between marketing and sales as related to the hospitality industry
- The terms tangible and intangible
- Product- and service-based marketing
- Market segmentation, marketing plan, collateral materials, and advertising to the market segments
- The concept of AIDA and advertisements for each applicable part of this formula

INTRODUCTION

To become and remain financially successful, every hospitality industry-based business must have effective marketing strategies and programs. In this chapter we discuss the similarities and differences between service- and product-based marketing. We will examine the traditional marketing concepts and terms; along with samples of target advertising created specifically for the leisure and group markets. Finally, we will identify current advertising trends and consider where future growth opportunities may exist.

The Difference between Marketing and Sales

Both marketing and sales are critically important, but marketing involves more than sales. Sales is part of the marketing process, whereas marketing is strategic and long term. The marketing plan will include sales activities for specific target markets. One of the most common forms of tangible marketing strategies are advertisements. When advertisements (marketing) are effective, they can help lay the groundwork for the sales department to book the piece of business. However, advertising is just one, albeit large, component of marketing.

THE FOUR PS OF MARKETING— THE MARKETING MIX

The marketing mix often is defined as each factor that influences the sales effort. Combined, they become strategic, controllable marketing tools designed to create a demand for the product or service.

Product: Design/features of both the physical (tangible) and the intangible aspects (service).
Place: The accessibility of the hospitality product (or destination) to the market.
Promotion: The effectiveness of the advertising, or sales ability (communication, persuasiveness).
Price: The rates the target market will pay for the hotel product: rooms, banquet meals, meeting rooms, other negotiable areas (yield management practices).

Figure 6.1 illustrates the variety of ways these four Ps (Product, Price, Place, and Promotion) can be used to achieve the stated marketing objectives for a specific target market.

THE MARKETING PLAN

The marketing plan can be written by a variety of people in positions of hotel marketing management. I have held positions at hotels as both director of sales and director of marketing; often combined into one position. Many hotel corporations have organizations charts that have this position combined at the individual property level. In this case, the DOS & M (director of sales and marketing) usually reports to a regional- or corporate-level vice president of marketing who can provide marketing plan development for the novice.

The marketing plan is a comprehensive document that will guide and monitor the sales, advertising, and promotional programs developed to attract business to each revenue center. The marketing plan can help management to be proactive and make adjustments needed as a result of market changes or

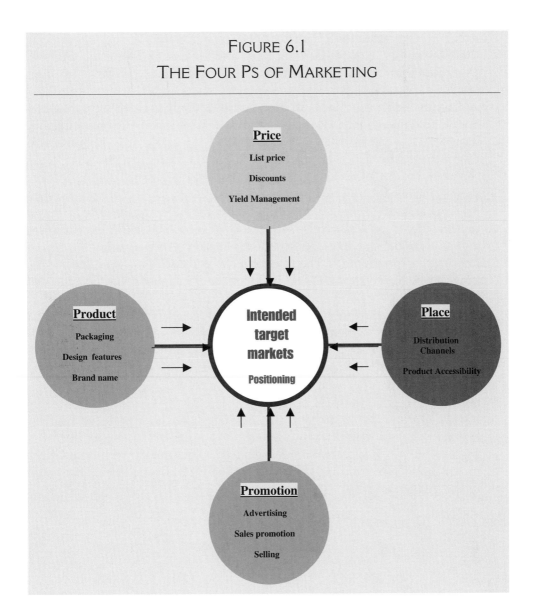

FIGURE 6.1
THE FOUR PS OF MARKETING

Price

List price

Discounts

Yield Management

Product

Packaging

Design features

Brand name

Intended target markets

Positioning

Place

Distribution Channels

Product Accessibility

Promotion

Advertising

Sales promotion

Selling

customer needs. It makes management think ahead by coordinating efforts and dividing up responsibilities. It should include concepts and programs to attract new business; as well as increase sales revenue goals from established accounts.

Some marketing consultants recommend that the marketing plan cover a three-year period. However, it is my opinion, as well as that of many hotel directors of sales and marketing, that the plan should cover only one year. Since the marketplace is constantly changing, it can be a waste of time to keep revising a marketing plan that covers a longer period of time.

Regardless of the length of time covered, the well-written marketing plan must include the following sections and subject areas:

Executive summary: Brief summary and overview of the main goals of the plan, including recommendations for a management review. Includes a table of contents before the next section.

Current market situation: Describes the current target markets, property (hotel) analysis, competition analysis, and specific marketplace analysis. Determines strengths and weaknesses of competition in relation to your hotel.

Opportunity analysis: Alerts to any possible challenges or opportunities anticipated during the period covered by the plan that would have a major impact.

Establishment of marketing objectives: States the desired objectives during the period of the plan in specific terms, and any key issues that may affect their achievement.

Marketing strategy: Outlines specifically how the objectives will be achieved in each target market, along with the corresponding dollar expenditures and advertising schedules. Specifies the planned response to any threats or opportunity presented in the opportunity analysis. Describes specifically how the projected room nights, banquets, and meeting room revenue will be met.

Action programs: Explains how each "plan of attack" will be implemented for each market segment, who will be responsible for it, and the associated marketing costs and proposed budgets. The budget section should include projected revenues and ROI (return on investment) for each action program. Once approved by management, this will become the final budget.

Controls: Outlines the controls to be used to review and monitor progress. Sets guidelines for implementation of any needed corrections, due to a poor results ROI or critical market changes. The traditional measurement includes analysis of the actual room nights/rates booked versus projected in the budget.

Putting a Marketing Plan into Action

Figure 6.2 lists the three key phases that are necessary to put the marketing plan into action. Once the plan is approved, the marketing department will begin to implement each part of the plan on an ongoing basis. Each program must then have a control to evaluate its effectiveness and ROI.

Market Positioning

The following two hotel advertisements are each attempting to position their product in the highly competitive and segmented print media. Both ran in monthly meeting planner trade publications. In Figure 6.3, The Westin South Coast Plaza positions on *luxury*, targeting those consumers or meeting groups who expect a certain level of service, with ad copy, pictures, and images that suggest that the upscale amenities and services they require are standard.

On the other hand, in Figure 6.4, the Sheraton Four Points is focusing on *value and convenience*. They are targeting the planner, near the LAX (Los Angeles, CA.) airport, who is seeking both. In addition to the obvious message, there is a more subtle one; the ad ran in black and white, surrounded by color

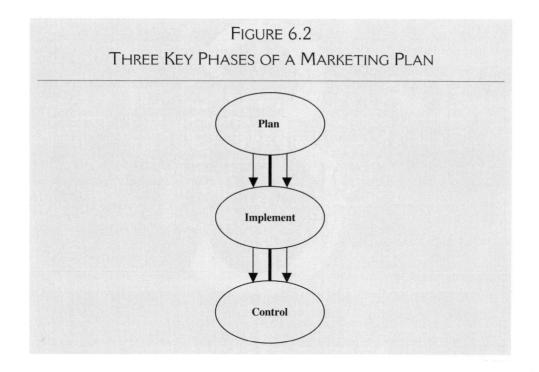

FIGURE 6.2
THREE KEY PHASES OF A MARKETING PLAN

ads. Since black and white ads are much less expensive than color, the Sheraton has also saved money. The decision to create this type of ad, and place it in this manner, is also part of the positioning process. By doing so, the original message of value will be reinforced.

Delivering the Goods

However the product is *intentionally* positioned, it must then actually provide what is promised. To be effective in positioning the product, it must be clearly differentiated. The true measure of this is whether the goods are *delivered* or not.

Remember also that whatever the chosen position strategy, the hotels' entire marketing program must support it. Additionally, a consistent positioned message will only truly be effective when advertisements are placed in the right media to reach the desired target audience.

ADVERTISING TO THE GROUP MEETING PLANNER

As discussed in previous chapters, corporate, association, and other meeting planners each have different needs in selecting a meeting facility. Though each has a different budget to guide them, they each seek a good value that is ultimately determined by the group room rate they can negotiate. As you've learned, association planners must have a room rate that their members

FIGURE 6.3
WESTIN SOUTH COAST PLAZA AD

modern
luxury

Our best effort will bring out the best in all of you. Whether it's a small meeting or a much larger function, nothing is ever ordinary at Westin. Let us plan something no one will soon forget.

Let us reserve your stay.
Call 1-714-540-2500 or your travel planner. Best rates, guaranteed, at westin.com/southcoastplaza

Costa Mesa
The Best Of Southern California

THE WESTIN
SOUTH COAST PLAZA
Orange County

MEMBER OF STARWOOD PREFERRED GUEST®

Not responsible for typographical errors. © 2004 Starwood Hotels & Resorts Worldwide, Inc.

CIRCLE NUMBER 278 FOR MORE INFORMATION

Courtesy: The Westin South Coast Plaza.

FIGURE 6.4
SHERATON FOUR POINTS LAX HOTEL AD

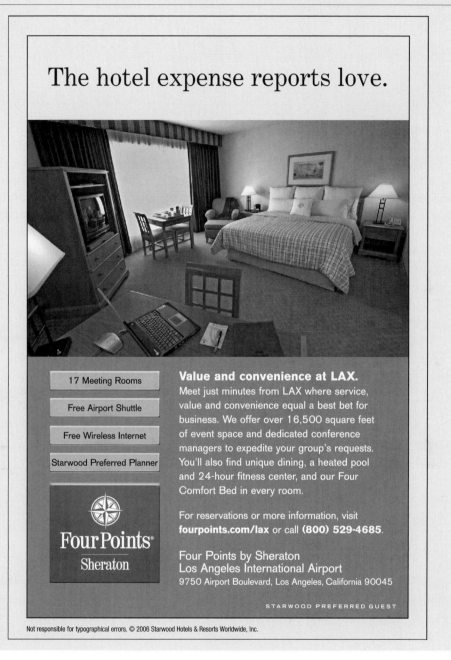

The hotel expense reports love.

17 Meeting Rooms

Free Airport Shuttle

Free Wireless Internet

Starwood Preferred Planner

Four Points
Sheraton

Value and convenience at LAX.
Meet just minutes from LAX where service, value and convenience equal a best bet for business. We offer over 16,500 square feet of event space and dedicated conference managers to expedite your group's requests. You'll also find unique dining, a heated pool and 24-hour fitness center, and our Four Comfort Bed in every room.

For reservations or more information, visit **fourpoints.com/lax** or call **(800) 529-4685**.

Four Points by Sheraton
Los Angeles International Airport
9750 Airport Boulevard, Los Angeles, California 90045

STARWOOD PREFERRED GUEST

Not responsible for typographical errors. © 2006 Starwood Hotels & Resorts Worldwide, Inc.

Courtesy: Sheraton Four Points LAX hotel/MMGWorldWide.

perceive as a good value, since they usually pay out of their own pocket. But the corporate planner can give more consideration to resort amenities, because the room rate is not as much of a deciding force in site selection. Today, all these group planners have many, many monthly trade publications sent to them *usually* free of charge, in which quality hotels and resorts pay large sums to advertise. Let's look at a few different print ads targeted to this audience and try to answer that age-old question, what do meeting planners want, anyway?

Features and Benefits of the Meeting Planners Target Market

The ad in Figure 6.5 was also placed in a meeting planner trade publication. It emphasizes the combination of tangible and intangible services offered. The Crowne Plaza is seeking to distinguish from all the other hotel brands that offer frequent hotel/airline points, yet the planner can choose from another set of enticing services that will solve the other stressful planning challenges they may encounter.

I chose this ad primarily because it is unique and distinguished itself from the ads commonly found for this target market. In the sea of meeting-planners targeted ads with a similar message, the Harrah's & Harveys Lake Tahoe ad series, in Figures 6.6 through 6.8, are also memorable. These ads are part of a strategic marketing campaign that features the resorts' well-known director of sales and marketing, Steve Lowe, in different roles or costumes.

INTERVIEW WITH STEVE LOWE

The following is an interview conducted with Steve Lowe, Director of Sales and marketing at Harrah's & Harveys Lake Tahoe, a position he has held for over 20 years.

Q. What are the strategies and goals of the recent ad campaign targeted at meetings groups?

A. The primary concept for the campaign was to create a unique advertising and direct mail program that supports our sales strategy and differentiates us with our competition locally, regionally, and nationally. This would be accomplished through personalization, humor that contains a deliberate ad focus (e.g., value season offerings, destination, new product intro, sales manager introduction, recreation). The direct mail campaign will mirror the trade ad campaign, providing greater visibility both from a broad-based shotgun approach as well as focused to current accounts.

Q. Today planners are inundated with ads and solicitations from every group facility. How does Harrah's & Harveys distinguish itself from either (1) other Lake Tahoe group meeting hotels and (2) other destinations that can accommodate their needs?

A. Through humor with a deliberate message, sales tenure, destination/recreation appeal, quality facilities with an element of "choice."

Q. Please discuss whether the above-mentioned campaign has been successful and how your department and advertising agency measure the response generated versus confirmed bookings.

A. When putting a sales marketing program together; advertising is only one component to the entire program and must link to every process. It

Continued

FIGURE 6.5
CROWNE PLAZA HOTELS & RESORTS AD

Courtesy: Crowne Plaza Hotels.

FIGURE 6.6

HARRAH'S & HARVEYS LAKE TAHOE: NO BORING MEETINGS

Courtesy: Harrah's & Harveys Lake Tahoe.

Figure 6.7

Harrah's & Harveys Lake Tahoe: Spring and Fall Value

Courtesy: Harrah's & Harveys Lake Tahoe.

FIGURE 6.8

HARRAH'S & HARVEYS LAKE TAHOE: DREAM TEAM

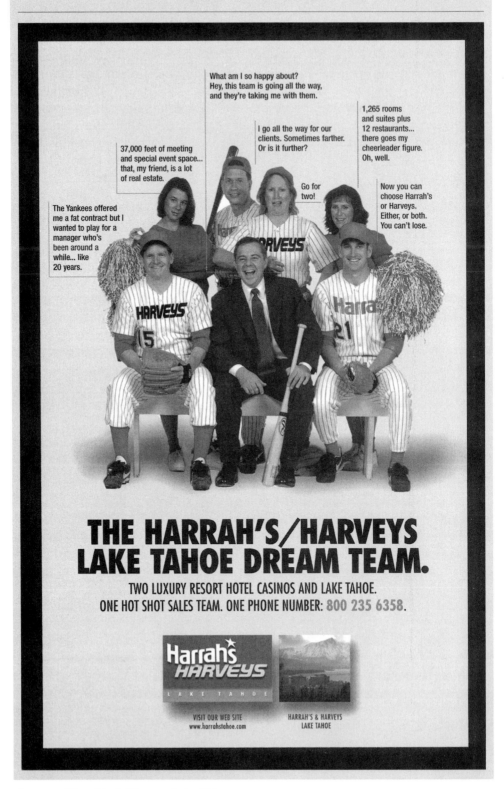

Courtesy: Harrah's & Harveys Lake Tahoe.

cannot be taken out and dissected on its own effectively. One would say that making *yourself* stand out above the pack is a strong testimonial to the success of this campaign. We have enjoyed the responses from our clients to this campaign, both new and repeat as witnessed by the many letters, calls, and trade show acknowledgments we have received. Now ROI (return on investment) . . . I believe that by being visible both in terms of your advertising and direct mail, you create a top of mind awareness to planners and will get the call to book. Relationship building and conversion now becomes the responsibility of the sales managers. *Meetings Media Publication* did a great article on ROI in their July 2004 magazine.

DISTINGUISHING THE ADVERTISEMENT

Figure 6.9 is a (Reno, Nevada) Hilton ad that was placed in a planner trade publication, *Meetings West Guide*. This type of advertisement is called a double truck, which is known in layman's terms as a centerfold. The layout is typically an ad that spans two facing pages.

The director of sales worked with their advertising agency to develop a new ad that would distinguish them and create recognition. Here is what Jeanne Corey, Director of Sales, Reno Hilton, had to say about accomplishing that objective:

"We have found that the double truck ad seems to get more attention than the standard format. But keep in mind that the convention ads generally don't generate leads; they create a front of mind presence for us. It's the recognition at trade shows with clients coming to us, as a result of the ad, and in calling on clients who have seen these ads, which helps both our credibility and in their willingness to meet with us, that seems to be the most telling."

As part of the campaign, the ad also was placed in other trade publications targeted to this market. Now that you've read the client's (Reno Hilton) comments on their needs for this advertising campaign, here's the rationale of this campaign from the perspective of the advertising agency. The following is provided by Lisa Blauth, Account Leader, R&R Partners.

Not a Campaign, a Conversation

Most advertisers would simply refer to this audience as "meeting planners." But the Reno Hilton sought a more original and personal tone for communicating with this important audience. So it was with empathy and irreverence that they set out to connect with a target best-described as "the overworked, the over-stressed, the value-seeking stagers of vital human gatherings."

Continued

FIGURE 6.9
A DOUBLE TRUCK ADVERTISEMENT

it's **possible**

Courtesy: Reno Hilton.

Easier Said than Done

It takes more than a refreshing point of view to resonate with these over-loaded people-pleasers. Every city, hotel, and convention facility on the planet wants their attention and their business. Today's meeting professional is communication-saturated, over-sold-to, and buried in forgettable marketing propaganda. Nothing stands out. Alternatives and advantages are indistinguishable amidst the clutter. Everyone's talking, but no one is listening. A great planner demands a leg up, seeks partnership with destination that will make a compelling difference in the quality of their event and the experience their clients will enjoy.

So, Why Reno? Why the Reno Hilton?

Within the industry, Reno typically is seen as a second-tier destination. A notch below the first-tier giants like Las Vegas, Orlando, Chicago, and the

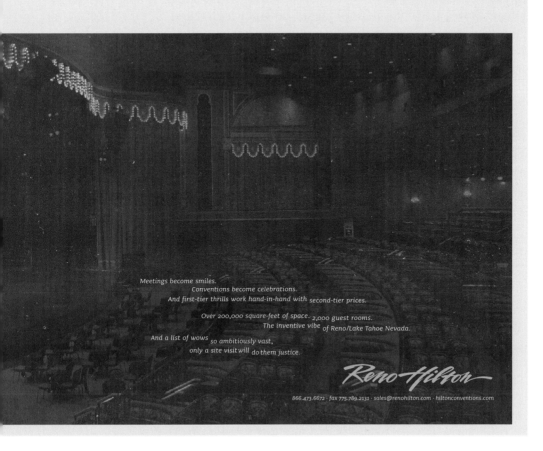

Meetings become smiles.
Conventions become celebrations.
And first-tier thrills work hand-in-hand with second-tier prices.

Over 200,000 square-feet of space. 2,000 guest rooms.
The inventive vibe of Reno/Lake Tahoe Nevada.

And a list of wows so ambitiously vast,
only a site visit will do them justice.

Reno Hilton

866.473.6672 · fax 775.789.2131 · sales@renohilton.com · hiltonconventions.com

like. Handled correctly, this perceived weakness might actually become a strength. The Reno Hilton offers most of the major amenities, dining, and entertainment options as the category leaders, but at a greatly reduced cost. As a result of this insight, it was decided to position the Reno Hilton as a best-kept-secret destination. "Somewhere just off your radar screen, there's an exuberant, can-do property that will rock your world."

A Beautiful Disruption

The Reno Hilton set forth a simple but bold creative mission: "To create a beautiful disruption in meeting and convention category, to have the absolute best, most original, most true-to-self ads in every publication we run in. To illustrate our belief in big dreams and top-drawer service in a way that provokes someone to pick up the phone, log onto the Web, and come for a site visit."

Courtesy: Reno Hilton.

As previously stated, the Reno Hilton wanted to be true to their soul, to reflect the true nature of their unique assets. And that nature just so happens to include such over-the-top offerings as 2,000-plus guest rooms, the world's largest stage, a 50-lane championship bowling center, and a vast property-side lake featuring a floating driving range. Big dreams, indeed. Big possibilities. Iconic, jaw-dropping features that represent the tip of the iceberg in terms of what an inspired planner might achieve here.

And the disruption continued when it came to media strategies. According to Jeanne Corey, to make the most of the magazine medium, it was decided to place half-page spreads (spanning the bottom half of two facing pages) as opposed to the industry boiler plate of full, half, and quarter page ad units. This attention-getting horizontal orientation gave the Reno Hilton spectacular page dominance and allowed them to literally own the idea of "big dreams made possible."

SUMMARY

To conclude our discussion of marketing strategy, let's briefly examine why such emphasis has been placed on the potential of the group market.

We certainly don't wish to minimize the impact of the individual family and leisure market. For many years this market segment, composed of vacationing individuals and families, has provided significant revenue to all types of hotels. There are many, many fine hotels and resorts for the leisure market to choose from with stiff competition from other destinations as other types of accommodations and vacations concepts, such as cruises. Therefore, hotels have had to evaluate where to focus their marketing plan to receive the best ROI on their advertising dollars.

So, back in the 1970s it became clear to growing hotel brands—like Holiday Inns, Sheraton, Hilton Hotels, and others—that developing group meeting and convention business was going to be more fruitful at filling hotel rooms than the individual vacationing family. Ideally, full-service hotels focus on developing a marketing mix, which includes different rate structures for each of these market segments. However, the way to *capture* this potential business wasn't quite as clear.

To illustrate the disparity between these two market segments, let's take a very general example at the potential revenue of each, as shown in Table 6.1.

As you can see, **B** generates $24,600 more in revenue than **A**. Though the revenue generated by meeting groups widely varies, the majority will also have potential for rebooking.

Remember that the marketing plan is a working tool that will not be effective sitting on a bookshelf. The marketing and sales department must work with management to implement the plan and strategies throughout the hotel. Every employee who interacts with the potential guest is a salesperson. Congratulations! The effective marketing plan has brought the customer to you, perhaps for an inquiry to reservations or group sales. However, all your marketing efforts can go down the drain if the service delivery falters. As men-

TABLE 6.1
FAMILY MARKET VS BUSINESS MARKET

A. Typical Family Average Needs	Revenue
Individual family of 4 (2 adults/2 children) 1 room with sleeper sofa	1 room @ $100 × 3 nights = $300.00
Food (onsite restaurant: 3 meals for 4 people)	$450.00
Total revenue generated	$750.00

B. Typical Business Group Average Needs	Revenue
Meeting group of 70 people	70 rooms @ $85.00 × 3 nights = $17,850.00
Food/Beverage (onsite banquet/restaurant: 4 meals for 70 people)	$7,500.00
Total revenue generated	$25,350.00

tioned earlier in this chapter, only marketing and advertising mediums that focus on the group meeting market have been presented here. Public relations and other forms of advertising, such as outdoor and billboard, are covered in other hospitality textbooks.

REVIEW QUESTIONS

1. What is the marketing mix?
2. Define and explain each part of the four Ps.
3. According to the chapter, who are the *salespeople* of the hotel? Who is responsible for coordinating efforts, setting responsibilities, and evaluating the results of marketing and sales efforts?
4. Describe the marketing strategy used by Harrah's & Harveys Lake Tahoe. How successful has it been?
5. List two reasons why it is more cost effective for some hotels to market to the group meeting and convention business. Be specific in describing the services and amenities hotels must have to effectively target this market.
6. Explain the positioning process. Provide two example of strategy in positioning a hotel.
7. Discuss at least two differences between the individual leisure and group markets in relation to ROI.

REFERENCES

Blauth, L. (2005) R&R Partners.
Corey, J. (2005) Reno, Hilton.
Lowe, S. (2004) Interview, Harrah's & Harveys Lake Tahoe, Nevada.

GLOSSARY

Advertising: Information about an event that the organizer pays to have printed or announced in various forms of media (e.g., press, TV, radio, cinema, outdoor).

Advertising Specialties: Promotional items that include a firm's name and/or marketing message.

Collateral: Assets that can be pledged to guarantee a loan. The promotional material used by the salespeople to support or corroborate the features and benefits of the item being sold.

Market Life Cycle: The period of time that a substantial segment of the buying public is interested in purchasing a given product or service.

Market Penetration Pricing Strategy: Method by which cost of an item is derived, based on whether or not near term income is critical, and rapid market penetration for eventual market control is desired.

Market Segments: Categorization of people, organizations, or businesses by professional discipline or primary areas of interest for the purposes of sales analysis or assignment.

Marketing: A process of identifying human wants and needs, and developing a plan to meet those wants and needs. Refers to everything involved with convincing an attendee to come to the event. Also refers to providing information to support the exhibit sales function.

Room Nights: Number of rooms blocked or occupied multiplied by number of nights each room is reserved or occupied.

Room Occupancy Pattern: Number of single and double rooms used.

APPENDIXES

The following is provided as a resource to the reader. Reprinted with permission provided by Harrah's & Harveys Lake Tahoe.

Appendix A: "Blue World" Campaign

The following advertising plan and series was used by Harrah's & Harveys Lake Tahoe in a print campaign. The slogan "Blue World" was created by an advertising agency for the Lake Tahoe Visitors Authority (LTVA).

Objective:
Create a trade advertising campaign that will support the imagery of Lake Tahoe, support brand identity, differentiate our product through relationship and humor while providing an element of "choice" for Harrah's and Harveys.

Rationale:

Advertising within the trade publications represents a very specific niche market should not be confused with a retail branding advertising campaign. One size does not fit all approach is not always the most effective method of branding products. To accomplish results within our niche market we need to provide product differentiation within our specific geographical location. Of course, a brand message needs to be incorporated but not necessarily through a pre formatted look. As noted in the Harvard Business School document "Branding is a strategic point of view, not a select set of activities" Our brand cultural message can be demonstrated through many marketing and advertising messages.
We additionally have the challenge of marketing and selling to our group segments the element of choice between Harrah's and Harveys within one message. This process needs to be carefully orchestrated while maintaining the identity of each product.

Action:

- Feature Lake Tahoe supporting community "Blue Campaign"
- Differentiate Harrah's and Harveys within the market through product uniqueness,creativity, humor, relationship imagery, and element of "Choice between Harrah's and Harveys.
- Use logo's to support the branding process along with tags
- Feature a message of destination, product identification and quality with the destination and the element of choice.
- Keep message simple and concise that stand apart from competitive advertising.
- Dramatic double ½ page trucks Lake.

Summation:
Retail advertising and trade advertising are not the same. Brand imagery and graphics indigenous to retail advertising are not necessarily appropriate for this targeted market. Group business needs to be seduced by the beauty of Lake Tahoe.

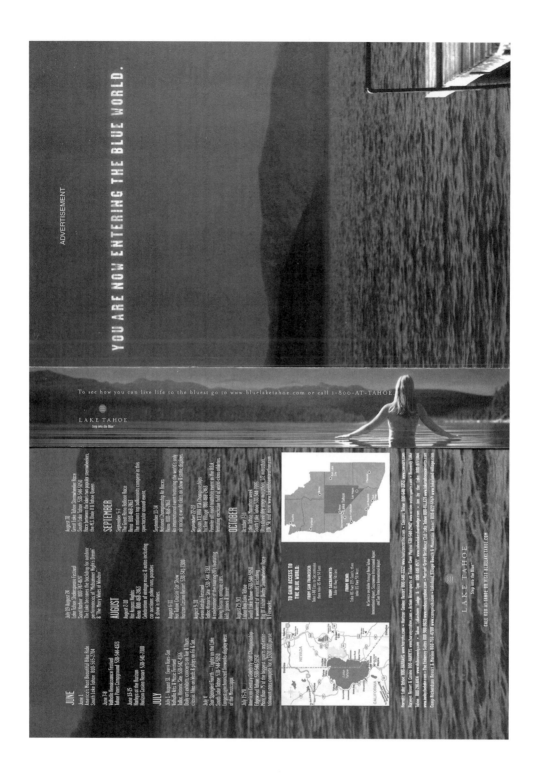

POPULATION : HAPPY

Imagine blue.

Now imagine the bluest of blues, really. Blue that's buzzing because it's just pounded a triple espresso. Can you see it? Yes. You can. Because this blue we're talking about is not only a color. It's something more.

Blue.

It's a place unlike any other. Where the landscape is as awesome as your options. Where the beauty is as stunning as your adventures.

Blue.

You can see it. You can feel it. Heck, some say you can even taste it. Welcome to the Blue World – Lake Tahoe. The deepest, clearest, bluest lake you may ever experience. Because (as the lucky ones now know) it is an experience.

Blue.

A breath-taking hike in the mile-high wilderness. Playing all night in world-class casinos. A heart-pounding ride atop the glassy water. Lake Tahoe is more than a spectacular backdrop. It's the reason you're here. It's the reason you stay. It's the reason you come back year after year.

LAKE TAHOE
Step into the Blue

Appendix B: Marconi Conference Center CD

CD/DVDs are now used by most all hotels to market their facilities to groups. The Marconi Conference Center in Marshall CA., created this CD to send to meeting planners who requested information.

Instructions:

1) Place the CD in your CD-ROM drive. (The Auto Run feature should launch your internet browser. If your CD does not run, follow the instructions printed on the CD.)

2) If this is your first time click on Introduction. (If the Intro or Exit animations do not run install Shockwave)

3) Close the introduction window and start your exploration of Marconi. (The Explore Marconi page works just like a web page with active links to information, history, photos and the forms you need.)

4) The Meeting Planner Guide has the Fill-in Forms. Click on the link in red and select the form you would like to complete. Use your Tab key to move from field to field.

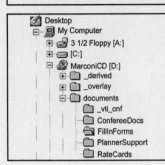

IMPORTANT NOTE:

The **Contract** and **Planning Document A** must be filled out, signed and the originals mailed to Marconi to confirm your reservation.

Helpful Hints

Q) How do I go directly to the **Contract** and **Planning Documents A, B, and C**?

A) Close the browser window that opens when you put the CD in your drive. Open your Windows Explore under My Computer. On the file tree to the left double click the Marconi CD. Open the documents folder. Open the FillInForms folder.

Q) I do not have enough room to type all the information. How do I make more room?

A) Some of the forms are expandable. (example: Planning Document B: section B1 only has 6 lines. To add another line, place your cursor in the last box of the last line and hit Tab. MS Word will add another line.)

Q) How do I save my work?

A) After you have typed in the information in the available fields, print a copy and choose File, Save As. Save the file on your hard drive for easy access if you need to make any changes.

Q) How do I activate the automatic calculation features?

A) Go to Tools on the menu bar, click on Options and select the Print tab. Make sure the Update Fields check box is checked and click OK. The forms will automatically calculate when you print.

CONVENTION SALES NEGOTIATIONS AND CONTRACTS

LEARNING OBJECTIVES

After studying this chapter, you will be able to discuss:

- Group event planning and negotiation between the buyer and the seller
- Attrition, and its meaning and impact on both buyer and seller
- Differences between tentative/definite, and letter of agreement/proposal letter
- The process of contract room block development and enforcement

INTRODUCTION

Today, it would be considered an unwise business practice to plan an event without a contract for the facilities and each service to be utilized. Not so long ago contracts of this type were only one or two pages in length and usually written by the director of sales. The art of negotiation has always been an important skill to master, but it became much more of a challenge as revenue management entered our vocabulary. In this chapter we will examine all of these important subjects, and review some samples of current contracts in use.

PROCEDURES

As discussed in Chapter 6, the initial contact or inquiry is made between the facility (hotel) sales department and the group planner. The negotiation may begin at that time or commence after collateral information has been exchanged: a sales kit, Web site, or whatever.

We will examine the general order of correspondence that leads up to a contract. Keep in mind that hotels have seen the lead time (when the initial inquiry is made) for corporate meetings dramatically reduced in recent years. Seven to nine months in advance is now more like two to four months, or even less. The association market, on the other hand, hasn't deviated from its standard annual convention pattern:

1. Proposal Letter
2. Letter of Agreement
3. Contract

If the lead time is short, the proposal letter and letter of agreement might be combined into one document. In that case, the following information would be included:

- Dates for which hotel rooms will be held
- Dates for which meeting function space will be held
- Room rates for each room type to be held
- All arrangements negotiated and agreed to and date of expiration on offer extended
- Signature may be optional
- Yield or revenue management

Regardless of whether these two documents are combined, it is essential that all arrangements are listed and restated as agreed. This protects both the client and the facility and alleviates any potential misunderstandings. All changes and amendments to the proposal normally are written in here and then initialed by both parties. Unfortunately, verbal agreements or handshakes are not practical, as people often will recall words differently when memory fades.

OTHER FORMS OF A PROPOSAL

A request for a proposal (RFP) is a fairly new document that quickly has become an industry standard utilized by hotels companies. The RFP can usually be found on its Web site, under Groups, "Plan a Meeting" or similar menu tab. It is often promoted as a tool to make the inquiry for meeting and hotel room space much easier for the group planner. The typical request for a proposal includes much of the same information as a proposal letter, with an expected faster response to the electronic inquiry.

It should be noted that prior to that development many large associations and organizations with multiple meetings and annual conventions had RFPs. They were sent to all sites under consideration. The DMAI or IACVB (International Association of Convention and Visitors Bureaus) has developed a comprehensive database of RFPs that lists group requirements that are available to all member convention and visitor bureaus.

Online Request for Proposals

Figure 7.1 is an example of an RFP sample from EventClicks, a site selection and planning organization. By completing this streamlined form online, the planner can quickly receive information about available facilities.

Figure 7.2 is an example of an RFP created by a hotel company—in this case, Holiday Inn. It is posted on their homepage Web site (www .holidayinnco.com) and accessed via a menu area for planners.

The Usefulness of an Online RFP

Here is an excerpt from an article written by Corbin Ball, a hospitality and convention industry visionary. To read the entire article, as published in *Successful Meetings*, refer to Appendix C at the end of this chapter. Corbin Ball posts many helpful resources and articles on his Web site (www.corbinball.com).

CHECKING OUT THE ONLINE SITE SELECTION AND RFPS OPTIONS

Throw out the meeting facility guides and dusty stacks of hotel brochures. Forget about faxing or express mailing your RFPs (requests for proposals) to many individual hotels. These inefficient paper-based means of finding and booking meeting facilities are falling way to web-based products that provide richer detail in faster, more convenient, and, sometimes, completely new ways.

The first online RFP site appeared in January 1996 with the Radisson Miyako Hotel San Francisco, offering a simple online meeting space request form. In four short years, a plethora of Web sites have sprung up offering everything from extensive, searchable meeting facility databases, automated RFP forms that can be sent to multiple facilities with a click, Hot Dates, and, most recently, online auctions. These sites vary considerably in the size of their databases, the richness of meeting facility detail, and how they generate revenue.

This article will help sort them out. It includes all of the major and some of the minor sites with detailed information regarding database size/usefulness, pricing models and special features, to help choose which will be the best one(s) for you.

© 2000 Corbin Ball Associates.

FIGURE 7.1

EVENTCLICKS HOME PAGE

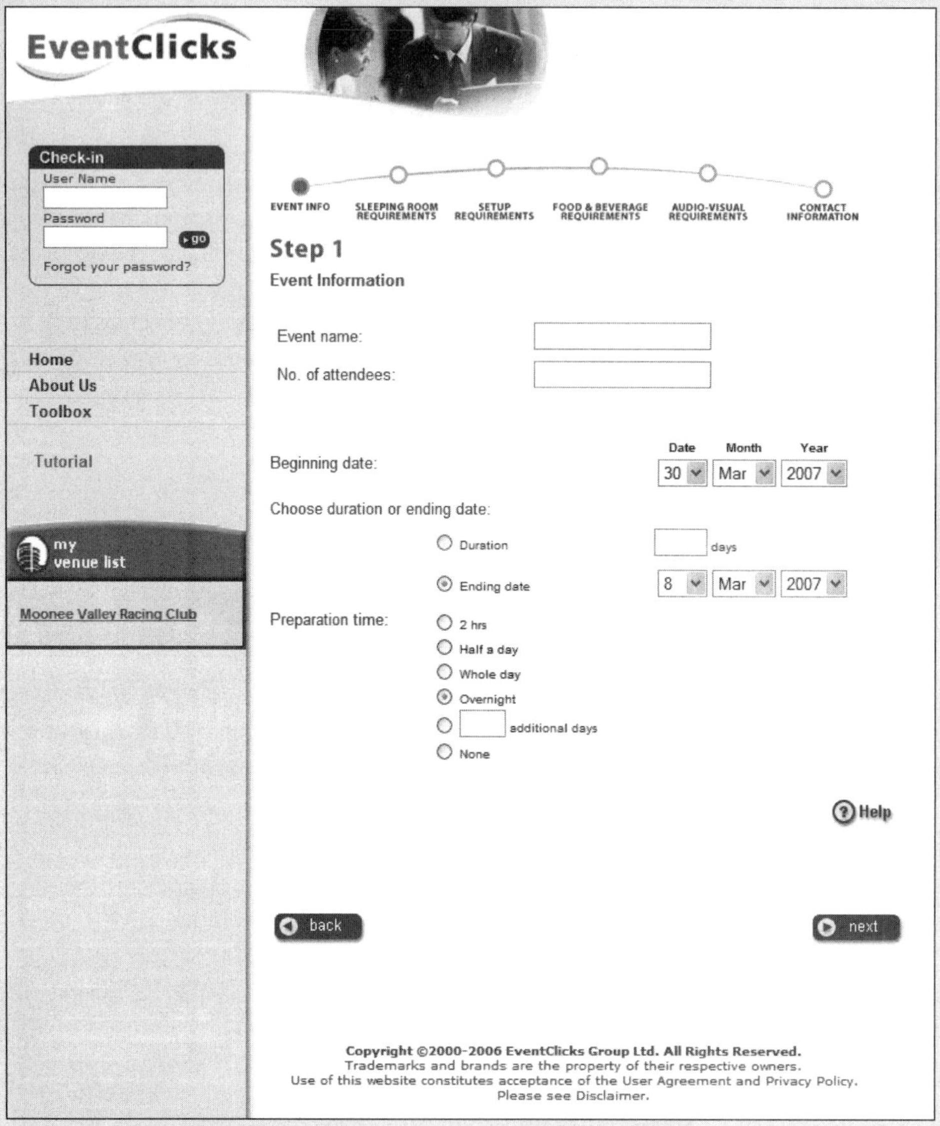

Source: EventClicks home page.

FIGURE 7.2
RFP, HOLIDAY INN

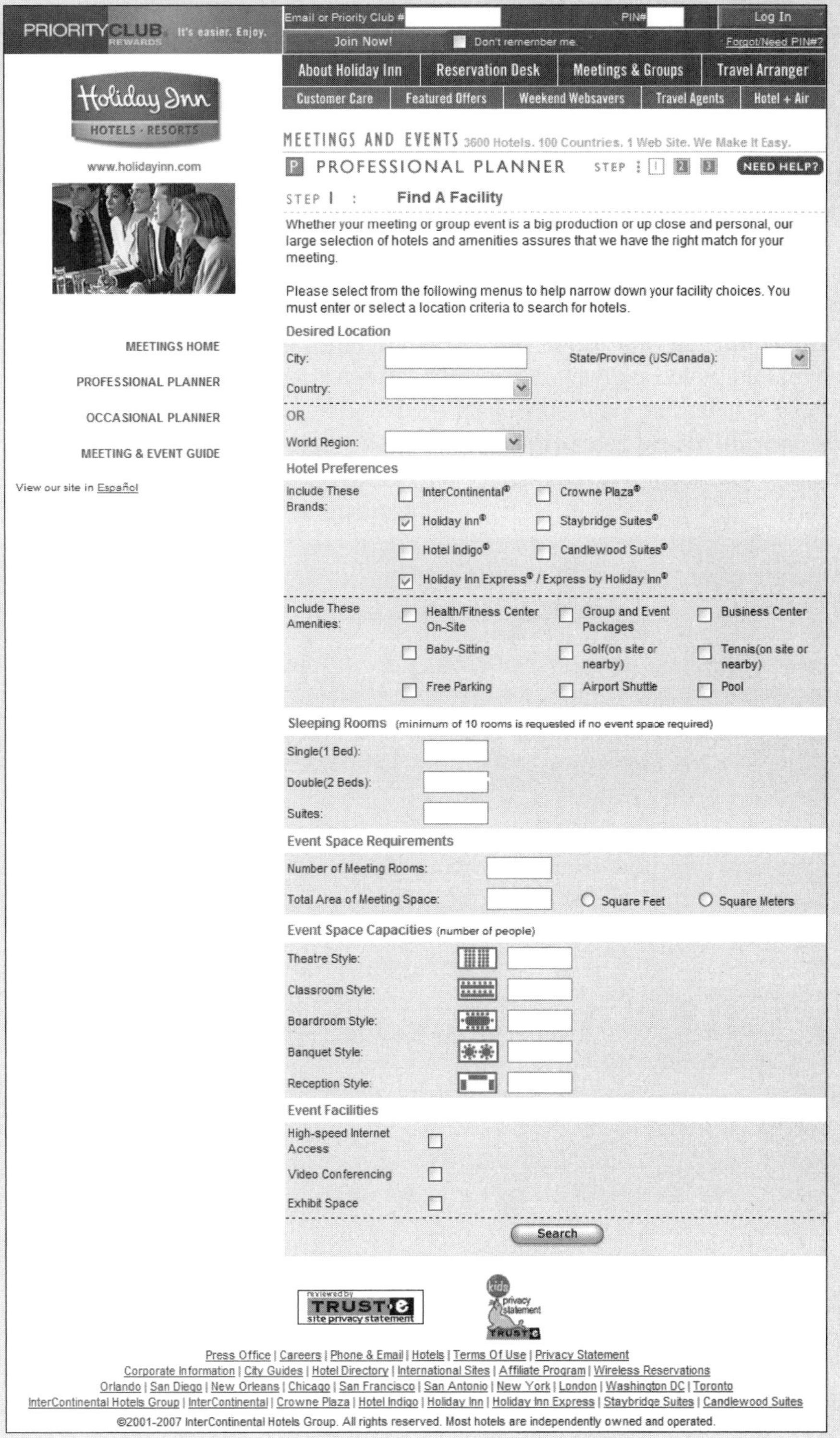

PRIORITY CLUB REWARDS It's easier. Enjoy.

Email or Priority Club # PIN# Log In

Join Now! Don't remember me Forgot/Need PIN#?

About Holiday Inn | Reservation Desk | Meetings & Groups | Travel Arranger

Customer Care | Featured Offers | Weekend Websavers | Travel Agents | Hotel + Air

Holiday Inn HOTELS · RESORTS

www.holidayinn.com

MEETINGS HOME

PROFESSIONAL PLANNER

OCCASIONAL PLANNER

MEETING & EVENT GUIDE

View our site in Español

MEETINGS AND EVENTS 3600 Hotels. 100 Countries. 1 Web Site. We Make It Easy.

P PROFESSIONAL PLANNER STEP : 1 2 3 NEED HELP?

STEP 1 : Find A Facility

Whether your meeting or group event is a big production or up close and personal, our large selection of hotels and amenities assures that we have the right match for your meeting.

Please select from the following menus to help narrow down your facility choices. You must enter or select a location criteria to search for hotels.

Desired Location

City: State/Province (US/Canada):

Country:

OR

World Region:

Hotel Preferences

Include These Brands: InterContinental® Crowne Plaza® Holiday Inn® Staybridge Suites® Hotel Indigo® Candlewood Suites® Holiday Inn Express® / Express by Holiday Inn®

Include These Amenities: Health/Fitness Center On-Site; Group and Event Packages; Business Center; Baby-Sitting; Golf(on site or nearby); Tennis(on site or nearby); Free Parking; Airport Shuttle; Pool

Sleeping Rooms (minimum of 10 rooms is requested if no event space required)

Single(1 Bed):

Double(2 Beds):

Suites:

Event Space Requirements

Number of Meeting Rooms:

Total Area of Meeting Space: Square Feet Square Meters

Event Space Capacities (number of people)

Theatre Style:

Classroom Style:

Boardroom Style:

Banquet Style:

Reception Style:

Event Facilities

High-speed Internet Access

Video Conferencing

Exhibit Space

Search

reviewed by TRUSTe site privacy statement

kids privacy statement TRUSTe

Press Office | Careers | Phone & Email | Hotels | Terms Of Use | Privacy Statement

Corporate Information | City Guides | Hotel Directory | International Sites | Affiliate Program | Wireless Reservations

Orlando | San Diego | New Orleans | Chicago | San Francisco | San Antonio | New York | London | Washington DC | Toronto

InterContinental Hotels Group | InterContinental | Crowne Plaza | Hotel Indigo | Holiday Inn | Holiday Inn Express | Staybridge Suites | Candlewood Suites

©2001-2007 InterContinental Hotels Group. All rights reserved. Most hotels are independently owned and operated.

Source: www.holiday-inn.com

CONTRACTS

In many cases one or both of the original parties who drew up the agreement may no longer be employed by those companies. Job turnover in the hotel industry is very high. Remember also that large associations must book their conventions up to five or eight years in advance. These and other concerns—especially failure to perform—necessitate that the contract be written with legal guidance.

Today, all hotel and convention facilities have legal departments that do just that. In recent years the numbers of lawsuits brought by hotels against groups that fail to fully utilize their room block has escalated. This is known as attrition (more on this subject later in this chapter).

Therefore, experts recommend today that contract language and contents be standardized throughout the organization. The four required elements are

- The offer
- The acceptance
- The obligation
- The consideration (usually monetary)

The following subjects areas or sections should be addressed and spelled out in complete detail:

- Name of the organization and hotel
- Dates hotel rooms are being held
- Dates meeting/function space is being held
- Room rates for each room type being held (room block)
- Number of each type of room being held (room block)
- Date room block will be released (rate no longer available)
- All meeting and function space being held
- Scheduled food and beverage functions and guarantees with required time notification and amount percent of food to be prepared over guarantee
- Names of representatives from the organization and hotel (their signatures required)
- Complimentary room arrangements ratio agreed to, or any discounts
- Reservations procedures
- Exhibit space registration policies
- Attrition clauses or penalties
- All arrangements negotiated and agreed to and date of expiration on offer extended

DIFFERENCES BETWEEN A TENTATIVE PROPOSAL AND A FINAL CONTRACT

The initial requirements will be itemized in the tentative proposal. All negotiated written and verbal amendments agreed to by the parties will now be drawn up into a new document—a contract. The final contract will have language predetermined by the legal department, which clearly spells out the enforceable obligations required by each party.

In the contract all additional changes are initialed and signed. Figure 7.3 is a sample of a hotel group contract, with sections that cover many key negotiated areas of concern to both buyer and seller.

FIGURE 7.3

HYATT LAKE TAHOE SAMPLE GROUP CONTRACT

The Hotel agrees to hold the space listed below on a tentative basis until October 8, 1999. If the Hotel and the Group do not have a fully executed Contract on October 8, 1999, the Hotel will release the space for sale to the public. If a request is received more than seventy-two (72) hours in advance of this date by another party, the Hotel will notify the Group and the Group will have seventy-two (72) hours from the time of notification by the Hotel to confirm by signature of this Agreement or release the space.

ROOM BLOCK

Day	Date	# & Type of Rooms
Monday	April 24, 2000	50 Run of House
Tuesday	April 25, 2000	150 Run of House
Wednesday	April 26, 2000	150 Run of House
Thursday	April 27, 2000	Check-out

The Hotel and the Group agree that the above room block shall be reserved for the Group at the guest room rates agreed to by the parties in this Contract subject to the terms and conditions of this Contract.

ROOM AND SPACE BLOCK REVIEW

The Group and the Hotel agree to review the room and space commitment on or before the following dates:

        a.   January 20, 2000

On these dates the parties will evaluate the room and space commitments based on research of the Group's previous usage, current pick-up to date and other relevant factors. If necessary, and subject to availability, the Hotel and the Group shall mutually agree to any adjustments to the room and space block. All room and space commitments will be finalized on the date set forth in (a) above. The Hotel shall confirm in writing any changes to the Contract which result from the review by the Group and the Hotel of the room and space commitments agreed to and outlined in the Program of Events, which is attached and made part of this Agreement. Any adjustments to the room block will result in a proportionate adjustment in the Group's meeting and function space block.

GROUP COMMITMENT

The Hotel will provide all of the outlined function and meeting space on a complimentary basis based on the Group's actual use of at least ninety percent (90%) of the total room block commitment detailed in the original room block provision. If the Group and the Hotel have mutually agreed to adjust the room block, then the Group will receive complimentary meeting space if the Group utilizes at least ninety percent (90%) of the adjusted room block. In the event that the total room nights fall below ninety percent (90%) of that total room block, a one-time fee for all meeting space requirements for the entire event will be assessed according to the following scale:

Source: Hyatt Lake Tahoe.

Figure 7.3

Hyatt Lake Tahoe Sample Group Contract—*Continued*

In the event that the Group wishes to set up direct billing for the Master Account, a credit application must be completed and returned no later than October 29, 1999 in order to be processed for approval. Credit procedures are provided by the Hotel upon the request of the Group for a credit application.

In the event that credit is not requested or is not approved, payment of the Group's total estimated Master Account will be due to the Hotel on March 24, 2000. Failure to remit the appropriate payment on a timely basis will result in cancellation of all arrangements outlined in this Contract and the Group shall be liable for amounts as described in the Cancellation Option provision.

CANCELLATION OPTION

Either the Hotel or the Group may cancel this Contract without cause upon written notice to the other party at any time prior to the event and upon payment of an amount based on the following scale:

More than eight (8) months from arrival date	$ 7,500.00
Eight (8) months to three (3) months from arrival date	$ 12,000.00
Three (3) months or less from arrival date	$ 20,000.00

The exercise by the canceling party of the option to cancel is agreed by the parties to constitute the exercise of a contractual option and not a default, and in no event shall the canceling party be liable for more than the option price paid hereunder.

Payment due as a result of cancellation of this Contract under this provision shall be made by the canceling party to the non-canceling party at the time the Contract is canceled by written notice.

RIGHTS OF TERMINATION FOR CAUSE

Except as otherwise provided in the Contract, neither party shall have the right to terminate their obligations under this Contract. This Contract is, however, subject to termination for cause without liability to the terminating party, under any of the following conditions:

a. The parties' performance under this Contract is subject to acts of God, war, government regulation, terrorism, disaster, strikes, civil disorder, curtailment of transportation facilities, or any other emergency beyond the parties' control, making it inadvisable, illegal or which materially affects a party's ability to perform its obligations under this Contract. Either party may terminate this Contract for any one or more of such reasons upon written notice to the other party within three (3) days of such occurrence or receipt of notice of any of the above occurrences.

FIGURE 7.3
HYATT LAKE TAHOE SAMPLE GROUP CONTRACT—*Continued*

b.   In the event that either party shall make a voluntary or involuntary assignment for the benefit of creditors, enter into bankruptcy proceedings, become insolvent or subject to foreclosure, or take any other action for the benefit of creditors or relief of debtors prior to the date of the Group's meeting, the other party shall have the right to cancel this Contract without liability upon written notice to the other.

c.   Hyatt Regency Lake Tahoe shall promptly notify the Group if there is a change in the management company which operates Hyatt Regency Lake Tahoe prior to the meeting, and the Group shall have the right to terminate this Contract without liability upon written notice to the Hyatt Regency Lake Tahoe.

d.   The phrase "without liability" wherever used in this Contract shall be deemed to include a refund by Hyatt Regency Lake Tahoe of all deposits and prepayments made within thirty (30) days of the notice of termination.

Nothing contained in the above section is intended to allow the Group the right to cancel for the purpose of holding the same meeting in another facility or city.

INDEMNIFICATION AND HOLD HARMLESS

Hotel and Group each agree to defend, indemnify and hold harmless the other party from and against all claims, actions or causes of action, liabilities, including attorneys' fees, and costs arising from the defense of any claim, action, cause of action or liabilities arising out of or resulting from any act taken or committed by Hotel or Group pursuant to the performance of each party's obligations hereunder. Hotel and Group each agree to defend, indemnify and hold harmless the other party for any claim, action, cause of action and liabilities which may be asserted by third parties arising out of the performance of either party's obligations pursuant to this Contract, except for the willful misconduct or gross negligence of the other party.

AMERICANS WITH DISABILITIES ACT

Compliance by the Hotel - The Hotel shall be responsible for complying with the public accommodations requirements of the Americans with Disabilities Act ("ADA") not otherwise allocated to the Group in this Agreement, including: (i) the "readily achievable" removal of physical barriers to access to the meeting rooms (e.g., speakers' platform and public address systems), sleeping rooms, and common areas (e.g., restaurants, rest rooms, and public telephones); (ii) the provision of auxiliary aids and services where necessary to ensure that no disabled individual is treated differently by the Hotel than other individuals (e.g., braille room service menus or reader); and (iii) the modification of the Hotel's policies, practices and procedures applicable to all guests and/or Groups as necessary to provide goods and services to disabled individuals (e.g., emergency procedures and policy of holding accessible rooms for hearing and mobility impaired open for disabled individuals until all remaining rooms are occupied).

FIGURE 7.3

HYATT LAKE TAHOE SAMPLE GROUP CONTRACT—*Continued*

CUT-OFF DATE

The "cut-off date" is March 30, 2000. Reservation requests received after the cut-off date will be accepted on a space and rate availability basis up to the Group block. If the Group rate is not available after the cut-off date, the prevailing rack rates will apply for any reservations confirmed.

CHECK-IN AND CHECK-OUT PROCEDURES

Our check-in time is 3:00PM and our check-out time is 11:00AM. For earlier arrivals, guests will be accommodated to the best of our ability.

PORTERAGE CHARGES

Should the entire Group arrive and depart at the same time, a charge of $5.00 per person for the handling of porterage will be applicable. This covers the handling of baggage in and out of the Hotel based on two (2) bags per person. This is a 1999 tariff and is subject to change.

HOUSEKEEPER GRATUITY

Although housekeeper gratuities are up to the individual's discretion, we recommend two dollars ($2.00) per day per room, double occupancy.

DEPOSITS

A deposit of $201.60 representing first and last night's room and tax for each of the confirmed rooms will be due from individuals attending the meeting/event fourteen (14) days after room is confirmed by the Hotel but no later than the cut-off date specified above. All deposits for individual room reservations are fully refundable if a room is canceled fourteen (14) days or more prior to the arrival date. Personal checks, money orders or a valid American Express, Diners Club, Visa or Mastercard number and expiration date will be needed for the deposit. The Group remains bound, however, by any cancellation fee or liquidated damages provision of this Agreement.

Checks or money orders should be sent to:

> Hyatt Regency Lake Tahoe
> P.O. Box 98536
> Las Vegas, NV 89193-8536

CREDIT ARRANGEMENTS

Individuals shall be responsible for their own room, tax, incidental charges, and any other charges not authorized by the Group to be billed to the Master Account. All charges incurred are to be paid upon check-out. The Group's Master Account is limited to charges for meeting/function room rental, food and beverage functions and other requested services.

FIGURE 7.3
HYATT LAKE TAHOE SAMPLE GROUP CONTRACT—*Continued*

Compliance by the Group - The Group shall be responsible for complying with the following public accommodations requirements of ADA: (i) the "readily achievable" removal of physical barriers within the meeting rooms utilized by the Group which the Group would otherwise create (e.g., set-up of exhibits in an accessible manner) and not controlled or mandated by the Hotel; (ii) the provision of auxiliary aids and services where necessary to ensure effective communication of the Group's program to disabled participants (e.g., braille or enlarged print handouts, interpreter or simultaneous videotext display); and (iii) the modification of the Group's policies, practices and procedures applicable to participants as required to enable disabled individuals to participate equally in the program.

Mutual Cooperation in Identifying Special Needs - The Group shall attempt to identify in advance any special needs of disabled registrants, faculty and guests requiring accommodation by the Hotel, and will notify the Hotel of such needs for accommodation as soon as they are identified to the Group. Whenever possible, the Group shall copy the Hotel on correspondence with attendees who indicate special needs as covered by ADA. The Hotel shall notify the Group of requests for accommodation which it may receive otherwise than through the Group to facilitate identification by the Group of its own accommodation obligations or needs as required by ADA.

INSURANCE

The Hotel and the Group shall obtain and maintain and provide evidence of insurance upon request in amounts sufficient to provide coverage for any liabilities arising out of or resulting from the respective obligations pursuant to this Contract.

BINDING AGREEMENT

The Group Sales Contract, along with the attachments called "Program of Events," are all of the terms agreed to by the parties. Any changes to these terms must be made in writing and signed by both parties to be effective. All prior agreements, verbal or written, are no longer effective once this Contract is signed by the parties.

NOTICE

Any notice required or permitted by the terms of this Contract should be made in writing. Notice must be delivered through one of the following methods in order to be deemed given:

1) Certified Mail, return receipt requested.
2) Registered Mail, return receipt requested.
3) Overnight Delivery, with a signature signifying receipt.

All notices must be addressed to the person named on the first page of this Contract as that party's contact/representative. The notice shall be deemed effective as of the date shown on the receipt signifying delivery of such notice to the party to whom it is addressed.

FIGURE 7.3
HYATT LAKE TAHOE SAMPLE GROUP CONTRACT—*Continued*

ATTORNEYS' FEES

In the event any legal action is taken by either party against the other party to enforce any of the terms and conditions of this Contract, it is agreed that the unsuccessful party to such action shall pay to the prevailing party therein all court costs, attorneys' fees and expenses incurred by the prevailing party. In addition, the Group shall be responsible for payment of attorneys' fees and interest associated with the Hotel's efforts to collect monies owed under the terms of this Agreement.

ADDENDA

If there are any terms and conditions contained in any attachment to this Contract hereto which are inconsistent with the terms and conditions contained in the body of this Contract, the terms and conditions of this Contract shall prevail.

HEADINGS

The headings appearing in this Contract have been inserted as a matter of convenience. If there is any conflict between the headings and the text of this Contract, the text will control.

WAIVER

If one party agrees to waive its right to enforce any term of this Contract, it does not waive its right to enforce such term or any or all other terms of this Contract at any other time.

GOVERNING LAW

This Contract shall be governed by and construed under the laws of the State of Nevada. If any provision of the Contract is unenforceable under applicable law, the remaining provisions shall continue in full force and effect.

When signed by representatives of both parties, this Contract, which includes the Program of Events, and the Hotel's Policies and Procedures, which are incorporated by reference, will constitute a binding agreement between the Group and the Hotel.

By the Group's Authorized Representative	By the Hotel's Authorized Representative
By: _____	By: _____
Name:	Name:
Title:	Title: Sales Manager
Date:	Date:

ROOM BLOCKS

The CIC defined a block as (1) the total number of sleeping rooms reserved for an event, (2) the number of rooms, seats, or space reserved in advance for a group, and (3) to assign space. The room pickup is defined as the number of facility guest rooms actually used out of a room block.

The group room block commitment is included as part of the final contract. This section of the form should always include the following:

- Dates the meeting function space is being held
- Room rates for each room type being held (room block)
- Number of each type of room being held (room block)
- Date the room block will be released (rate no longer available)
- Penalties, fees resulting from unused rooms in block—not released
- Sliding scale of charges applicable for each time period block not utilized

Decades ago, hotels began to make meeting room rental fees directly tied to the number of guest (sleeping) rooms utilized by the group hotel. Both large and small meeting convention groups agreed to this method, primarily because they did not want to pay for meeting space rental. However, years ago, when attendees began to book "outside the room block" (for a variety of reasons—see following) and stay at less expensive properties, failure to fulfill contractual obligations began.

Throughout this chapter and in articles in the appendixes, many examples of effective strategies for this issue have also been provided for your consideration.

NEGOTIATION

The objective of a negotiation is for two or more parties to try to reach an agreement for mutual benefit. A common business phrase used stated that the outcome of a successful negotiation was a "win-win situation." In other words, each party benefited. This would seem to indicate that both parties have some areas where they may be more flexible, while others are mostly nonnegotiable, depending on whether it is a buyer's or seller's market.

The following is from an trade industry article on the subject of negotiation.

> While the hospitality industry is just starting to catch its breath after more than a year of sliding occupancy rates and empty meeting space, meeting planners are in the somewhat peculiar position of dictating terms to suppliers that have abandoned their stubborn streak of the late '90s.
>
> "All of the sales strategies of the past are out the window," says Bret Matteson, vice president of Seattle-based Columbia Hospitality, which operates Seattle's Bell Harbor International Conference Center and Aljoya

Continued

Source: Davidson, T. *Meetings West*, (2002).

The seller or supplier (hotel, facility, vendor for outside or off premise services) and the buyer (group planner) have different "hot buttons." Knowing whether it is a *buyer's* or *seller's* market will also put you at an advantage. Also, compare the proposals of three or more hotels to get a truer picture of the current market.

ATTRITION

Planner and facility negotiations center on each part of the final deal and contract content. Today, almost all contracts mention the terms *attrition* and *attrition clause*.

These are the CLC definitions:

Attrition: The difference between the actual number of sleeping rooms picked up (or food-and-beverage covers or revenue projections) and the number or formulas agreed to in the terms of the facility's contract. Usually there is an allowable shortfall before damages are assessed.

Attrition Clause: Contract wording that outlines potential damages or fees that a party may be required to pay in the event that it does not fulfill minimum commitments in the contract.

In recent years, attrition has become *the* main topic of concern among both corporate and association meeting planners. Industry leaders say that there are two reasons why:

- Many contracts were written during a strong economy when meeting attendance was high; large room locks were justified by past attendance history. However, the convention actually occurred during a "recession," when attendance is down.
- The rates are likely also too high, compared not only to current hotel group rates but also the cheap rates often found on the same hotels' own Web site.

Figure 7.4 provides insight for both planners and hoteliers to facilitate contract development.

As these seven secrets show, the industry is constantly evolving and trying new strategies against which they gauge their attendees' responses. For associations especially, their success is measured in the actual convention attendance by their members.

FIGURE 7.4
SEVEN ATTRITION SECRETS REVEALED

1. **If attrition is not mentioned in the contract, you don't owe attrition penalties.**
   Simply put, "You don't owe for attrition if you don't have a clause or any other language in the contract that specifies that attrition charges may be assessed," says John Foster, an Atlanta-based attorney who helped litigate *Hyatt Hotels Corp. vs. Women's International Bowling Congress*, a landmark attrition case that was settled in 1999. Hyatt tried unsuccessfully to bring a lawsuit against the WIBC for breach of contract when the group failed to purchase almost half the 4,735 room-nights it blocked for its annual convention, even though the contract between the two parties contained nothing covering attrition. Still, Foster says, the case dragged on for almost two years before a federal court threw it out.

2. **"Double dipping" by hotels is legal.**
   Though unethical, it is legal for hotels to "double dip" by charging attrition penalties on rooms that were resold to guests outside the meeting group. Planners can detect instances of double dipping by conducting an audit of the hotel's sales, and planners should refuse to pay full attrition penalties on rooms that were resold. Though it may be legal, double dipping spells disaster for supplier-planner relationships. In instances of double dipping. "Hotels use the attrition to pad their profit margins," says Tom Carrier, an independent planner based in Centreville, VA. "It's no wonder that many meeting managers would like to see attrition penalties removed."

3. **Hotels may legally charge taxes on attrition penalties.**
   In certain states, including Florida, California, and New York, hotels may add a tax of up to 15 percent to attrition penalties, because the attrition penalties are considered a sale, and are thus subject to sales tax. "It is not easy to find out if the states charge taxes on attrition," says industry attorney John Foster, "because there is no specific statute that says whether a state will charge a tax on attrition." To find out if your attrition fees are subject to sales tax, Foster suggests looking up sales-tax codes in the laws of the state in which you're doing business. In any case, he says, "Put it in the contract that sales taxes will be paid on this only if required by state and local law."

4. **For hotel salespeople, stricter room-blocks mean higher pay.**
   In many cases, hotel sales managers are paid commission on only the guaranteed portion of the room-block. If a contract is for 100 room-nights, with an allowed attrition rate of 20 percent, the salesperson receives commission on 80 rooms. If the attrition rate is 10 percent, the salesperson receives commission on 90 rooms "That's a hidden factor that drives attrition," says InterContinental's Jeff Senior. "Whatever the attrition cutoff is, that's what the sales manager gets credit for."

5. **Planners can charge hotels reverse attrition.**
   "Meeting planners can include clauses for reverse attrition in contracts," according to industry attorney Mark Roysner. A reverse-attrition clause specifies that if the room-nights used by attendees exceed a specified percentage, the hotel will compensate the group, usually with a credit to the master account. "The hotel may not agree to it," says Roysner, "but it can be used as a bargaining chip for something else." If the hotel does not have rooms available that it had promised as part of the original room-block, that can be grounds for a "reverse attrition" payment as well.

6. **Years later, hotels can legally assess attrition penalties.**
   If you walk away from a meeting having negotiated down your attrition charges, make sure to create a document that specifies the terms of compensation and the fact that you are not liable for any further charges. Otherwise the past could come back to haunt you. "In one case, the meeting was awful. The food & beverage counts were terrible, and the client did not pick up the room-block," remembers the decorated attrition veteran Roysner. "The hotel told the planner to forget about attrition penalties, and they all walked away. But nobody got a letter waiving the charges." Two years later the group got a letter from the hotel asking for a $10,000 attrition payment. Since the statute of limitations on the contract was four years, the hotel was within its rights to ask for payment.

7. **Going blockless is OK.**
   Lately, more and more planners are circumventing the housing hassles and the threat of attrition by eliminating room-blocks altogether. Hotels often balk at this, but if you are willing to pay a premium for meeting space and food & beverage, you may find that blockless meeting planning is a workable solution for ever-infensifying housing woes. "I call it the death of the room-block. What used to be a convenience to attendees and a cost savings is now a problem," says Eric McNulty, managing director of conferences for Harvard Business School Publishing in Boston, who this spring is hosting his first conference without a room-block. "I'm happy to be out of housing my attendees," he says. "Depending on how the event goes, I'll either be a genius or a dope."

Source: Ben Chapman, *Successful Meetings*, (April 2003).

The CIC Project Attrition

For the Convention Industry Council (creators of the APEX glossary of industry standards terminology), the subject of understanding attrition became a full-scale project. The following press release is from Smith Bucklin & Associates, a large hotel representation firm whose client had a situation reflective of today's climate.

In 1999, a Smith Bucklin & Associates (SBA) client contract was signed for 2003 and 2005. Since then, there have been a number of changes in the client's industry segment—and overall event attendance numbers have decreased. Nine to twelve months out, the association found itself facing approximately $1 million in attrition potential (inclusive of room revenue as well as food & beverage) because of the need to reduce their room nights by approximately 48%.

Ms. Anita O'Boyle, Convention Director, notes that strong relationships, constant communication between the association staff, the hotel, the association board, and the organization's executive director, all contributed to solving the challenges and making an outstanding meeting.

The meeting was scheduled for April 2003 at a hotel in Orlando, Florida. Anita worked with the hotel Director of Sales, General Manager, and with the hotel company's corporate office. The association board understood the severity of the problem and supported the strategy put together by Anita and her team. The strategy was to cut the room block, and cover as much of the food & beverage guarantee as possible.

Everyone's focus was on problem solving. All were totally honest with each other and they conducted weekly (sometimes daily/hourly) conversations to come to an agreeable solution. One solution was for the association to release some of its contracted meeting space, and when the hotel had an opportunity to book another group three months prior to the meeting— the association released even more meeting space. The association ended up with extremely tight space—but a great meeting where everyone worked together.

Furthermore, the group (hotel sales and association meeting staff) met to discuss the current status (3 weeks out) and the final ramifications for the group. Three weeks out the options were:

- Cut the hotel a check;
- Sign a contract with the hotel for the same meeting in a future year; or
- Sign a contract with the hotel for another SBA client for a future year meeting.

The association staff marketed more than ever to the membership to bring in as many people as possible. They also worked with hotel marketing and SBA's marketing team to devise messaging that would focus on booking hotel rooms at the property, as well as promotions to draw the largest crowd. They also watched Internet rates to make sure the hotel was not selling guest rooms at a lower rate than the convention rate. The staff continually communicated with the hotel and Anita notes that the staff's collaboration was something she had never seen before.

The collaboration continued on-site, where the hotel and meeting planning staff worked together to address problems (like walked guests on oversold nights, etc.) and solve them together. The hotel made it evident that they wanted this group to return to their hotel.

Anita's staff surveyed their event attendees who responded that it was the best meeting ever. In the end, the association agreed to conduct the meeting with the hotel in 2005, and will definitely consider the hotel again for 2007.

Source: Smith Bucklin & Associates Web site.

SUMMARY

Today, the final signed agreement *must* be the result of years of meeting management experience and knowledge of contract law. Hotel companies all have standard clauses and language that has been written (or at least approved) by legal counsel. The financial impact of attrition, on both buyer and seller, necessitates that it will remain a critical concern, especially as groups discuss solutions with their peers during industry conferences. Additional related articles are provided in the appendixes at the conclusion of this chapter.

REVIEW QUESTIONS

1. Define the term RFP. At what stage of the negotiation process is this used by hotels? Select Web sites for two hotel companies and go to their Group Meeting area. List and describe the information the RFP offered to planners by each hotel. Did you find it user-friendly or not? Why?
2. Define the terms *attrition* and *attrition clause* (in your own words). List a few ways suggested in the chapter articles for effectively dealing with this subject.
3. Describe the steps a hotel sales manager should take to effectively negotiate his or her hotel to the best position and rate.
4. Read the two articles at the end of this chapter on attrition, negotiation, and room block management. List and describe some effective strategies for effectively managing these areas today.
5. How does a strong or weak economy impact the meetings industry?

REFERENCES

Ball, C. (2000) *Checking Out the Online Site Selection and RFPs Options*, Corbin Ball Associates.

Chapman, B. (April 2000) The war of attrition, *Successful Meetings*.

Chapman, B. (April 2000) Seven attrition secrets revealed declassified. *Successful Meetings*.

Convention Industry Council (CIC). (2005) CIC Request for Proposal (RFP) APEX Report.

Davidson, T. (May 2002) The art of negotiation: A buyer's market has planners haggling hard, *Meetings West*.

Hill, R. A. (July 2002) Controlling your room block: Planners find corralling outside-the-block bookings akin to herding cats, *Meetings West*.

Smith Bucklin & Associates. (www.smithbucklin.com).

GLOSSARY

Attrition: The difference between the actual number of sleeping rooms picked up (or food-and-beverage covers or revenue projections) and the number or formulas agreed to in the terms of the facility's contract. Usually there is an allowable shortfall before damages are assessed.

Attrition Clause: Contract wording that outlines potential damages or fees that a party may be required to pay in the event that it does not fulfill minimum commitments in the contract.

Bid: 1) A statement of what one will give or take in return for something else (a price); proposal. 2) Proposal submitted by a convention and visitors bureau and/or hotel(s) to an event organizer that includes defined dates and room blocks.

Block: 1) Total number of sleeping rooms reserved for an event. 2) A number of rooms, seats, or space reserved in advance for a group. 3) To assign space.

Booking: 1) An arrangement with a company for use of facilities, goods, or services. 2) For a hotel event, a future event contracted in writing by an event organizer with a hotel. According to guidelines from the International Association of Convention and Visitors Bureaus, the local CVB should receive a copy of the contract, or a written communication from an authorized agent of the hotel that a contract has been signed. The communication should detail dates, space requirements, and estimated room block. The CVB should track estimated attendance and attendee spending for the event. 3) For a citywide or convention center event, according to guidelines from the International Association of Convention and Visitors Bureaus, given the long-time frame often involved in such an event, the booking process generally takes two steps. The first is a "confirmed booking," where a future event is confirmed in writing (letter, booking notice), signed by an authorized agent of the event organizer and the convention center (if applicable). The written communication should detail dates, space requirements, and estimated room block. The local CVB should track estimated attendance and attendee spending. The second step is a "contracted booking," where a future event is contracted in writing by the event organizer with the event facility (e.g., convention center). The local CVB should receive communication of this stage in writing from an authorized agent of the convention center.

Cancellation Clause: Provision in a contract that outlines damages to be paid to the noncanceling party if cancellation occurs, due to the canceling party's breach of the contract.

Cancellation or Interruption Insurance: Insurance that protects a event organizer against financial loss or expenses incurred when contractually specified perils necessitate canceling or relocating a event, or cause a reduction in attendance.

Cut-Off Date: Designated date when the facility will release a block of sleeping rooms to the general public. The date is typically three to four weeks before the event.

Check-In: Procedure for hotel guest arrival and registration.

Check-In Time: Time at which hotel guests may check in and occupy sleeping rooms.

Check-Out: Procedure for hotel guest departure of their sleeping room including account settlement.

Check-Out Time: Time set by facility when hotel guests are required to vacate sleeping rooms.

Group Arrivals/Departures: Information included in the specifications guide for an event that outlines approximate dates and times at which groups of event attendees can be expected to arrive at a facility (hotel) for check-in or check-out. This is intended to give the facility notice in order to prepare for front desk staffing.

Group Booking: Reservation for a block of sleeping rooms specifically for a group.

Group Rate: Confirmed rate extended to attendees booking their sleeping room accommodations as part of a group room block.

Lead: 1) According to the International Association of Convention and Visitors Bureaus, when an inquiry by a corporation/association/organization/independent event organizer that includes a request for a minimum of 10 sleeping rooms over a specific set/range of dates is forwarded by the CVB sales staff only to those hotels that meet the event organizer's event criteria. A lead is more formalized than just exchanging/forwarding business cards to hotels. For convention center events, if the CVB sends a lead first to the convention center for date availability and then to the hotel(s) for room blocks as a matter of policy, this process should be counted as one lead for reporting purposes.

Master Account: A record of transactions during an event where the resulting balance is paid directly by the group. May include room, tax, incidentals, food and beverage, audiovisual equipment, and décor. Also called *Master Bill.*

Pick-Up: Number of facility guest rooms actually used out of a room block.

Proposal: 1) Plan put forth for consideration or acceptance. 2) Communication sent by a supplier to a potential customer detailing the supplier's offerings and prices.

Rental Charges: Cost of hiring a piece of equipment or an exhibit space for a specified period of time. It may or may not include ancillary services (security, connections to water, electricity, gas, etc.).

Reservation: An arrangement to have a sleeping room (at a hotel or other housing facility) held for one's use. Process by which an individual or group secures space at a facility.

Reservation Center: Telephone reservation sales office.

Reservation Form: See *Housing Form.*

Reservation Method: Manner by which sleeping room reservations are to be made for attendees of a specific event.

Reservation Request: A communication by which a guest indicates sleeping room requirements; these are forwarded to the hotel to secure a reservation.

Reservation Review Date: Designated day when the facility will release a block of sleeping rooms to the general public.

Release Date: Date beyond which a facility is free to rent the unused sleeping rooms or function space to other groups.

Request for Proposals: RFP. A document that stipulates what services the organization wants from an outside contractor, and requests a bid to perform such services.

RevPAR Revenue per Available Room: A performance measurement commonly used in the hotel industry. It is calculated by dividing a hotel's net rooms revenue by the total number of available rooms, or by multiplying a hotel's average daily room rate (ADR) by its occupancy.

Revenue Management System: A sophisticated computer-based pricing system that vendors use to adjust prices based on anticipated demand. Also referred to as *Yield Management.*

Room Block: Total number of sleeping rooms reserved for an event.

Shoulder: The beginning and ending days of a room block when fewer rooms are contracted.

Special Block: Small block within the event's room block reserved for dignitaries or people with special needs.

Tentative Hold: A space temporarily held by a facility or venue for a specific date pending a definite booking. There are no consequences for cancellation.

Yield Management: Computer program that uses variable pricing models to maximize the return on a fixed (perishable) inventory, such as hotel rooms, based on supply-and-demand theory.

APPENDIXES

Appendix A: The Art of Negotiation: A buyer's market has planners haggling hard

The following complete article on negotiation is provided as a resource. *Source: Meetings West*, May 2002. Reprinted with permission.

While the hospitality industry is just starting to catch its breath after more than a year of sliding occupancy rates and empty meeting space, meeting planners are in the somewhat peculiar position of dictating terms to suppliers that have abandoned their stubborn streak of the late '90s.

"All of the sales strategies of the past are out the window," says Bret Matteson, vice president of Seattle-based Columbia Hospitality, which operates Seattle's Bell Harbor International Conference Center and Aljoya Conference Center at Laurelhurst. "It was a seller's market, and all of the properties I encountered yielded maximum rates. We would normally let business walk away before we'd negotiate down. From '95 on it was typically a non-negotiated situation. The general feeling I saw in hotels was if someone wasn't willing to pay your rack rate, there was someone right behind them ready to come in.

"Today the marketplace is very volatile," Matteson continues. "There's all sorts of evidence that show declines in hotel rates, REVPAR and occupancy. You're seeing a complete flip in all of these financial measurements."

Jonathan T. Howe, a top meetings industry attorney who is a senior partner in the Chicago- and Washington, D.C.-based firm of Howe & Hutton, Ltd., confirms suppliers are conceding everything from contract clauses to 'hard-money' items.

"Right now it's more of a buyer's market because you have capacity that's available to be used, and because of that people are anxious to put heads in beds," Howe says. "Pretty much everything is on the table—There's been more give and take and more concern than just the dates, the rates and the block. Planners are asking for more things than they might have asked for: concessions on food and beverage, amenities, staff room comps—Certainly, attrition and cancellation are two key areas, and since 9/11, *force majeure* clauses."

According to Tim Brown, a partner with Newport Beach, Calif.-based Meeting Site Resource, which specializes in hotel contract negotiation, negotiators on both sides now have to be more creative, and planners have an increasing obligation to protect the liability of their client companies by playing hardball with contract issues.

"We're shifting from the phenomenal, giant growth of the '90s of being order takers to being more creative, 'due diligent' buyers and sellers," he says.

In today's climate, suppliers are willing to give a little to get a little, Brown believes.

"They're budging, they're not drawing a hard line," Brown says of meeting facility negotiators. "There's an attitude of getting deals done in this environment.

"Clearly the emphasis is on value now," he adds, "because companies have been hammered from every perspective, from earnings to layoffs, but also on contract performance clauses, room pickup, cancellation, food and beverage guarantees, and revenue guarantees. In the past a lot of planners focused on dates, rates and space, but now you're seeing more attention paid to the contract portion of the negotiation."

Brown says there is currently a lot of short-term activity in the 90- to 120-day booking window range, and sees the current market holding at least through the end of this year and well into 2003.

"I'm seeing hotels holding the line a little better for rates and services for 2003, but I still think 2002 and 2003 will be soft years, and I think the advantage will definitely be on the buyer's side," he predicts.

Planner Tactics

When it comes to the nuts and bolts of negotiation strategy, it pays untold dividends for planners to develop a database that logs their meetings history with properties, detailing how much has been spent for room nights, food and beverage and audiovisual services, and other expenses. After all, if a planner can demonstrate his or her past dollar value to a supplier, the skids will be greased for the current negotiation process.

Arlene Sheff, senior meeting and event planner in Space and Communications for The Boeing Company, subscribes to the relatively common wisdom of negotiating around holes in a facility's schedule, when planners have more buying power by being flexible with dates.

The Seal Beach, Calif.-based Sheff, who also teaches a class in negotiation and contracts for California State University, Fullerton, confirms that the negotiating pendulum has swung to the side of the planners for the moment, which translates into better deals.

"I'm probably negotiating more—negotiating better [contract] clauses because of cancellations or acts of God, and how to limit the liability of the company [regarding] attrition rate," Sheff says.

"In case my attendance is really low, I want to commit to a certain dollar amount to the hotel," she continues. "I'll commit to 'x' number of dollars to a hotel and I'll disperse it to all of the meals over the day. Instead of planning for 100 and paying for 90 people for breakfast, 90 people for lunch and 90 people for dinner, I will say, 'I can do a normal breakfast, do a normal lunch, and do a fabulous dinner.' The hotel will still make the same profit as they were going to make, but I get to disperse it any way I see fit."

Other Sheff tactics include negotiating for guest room discounts for speakers and meetings support and audiovisual staff; decor items such as colored table cloths, upgraded linens or the use of any props the hotel may have in storage; a staffed lemonade station for delegates at check-in; the same room rate for pre- and post-date stays; a reduced rate for the ballroom setup day; a complimentary microphone in each meeting room; or arranging for the health club to open earlier or late for early- or late-arriving guests.

Sheff says properties might even reluctantly budge on in-house A/V costs, with a little planner prodding.

"It's amazing that the minute you put A/V out to bid, the hotel A/V company sure comes back with a better price," Sheff says.

Sheff will sometimes bargain for buffer space—especially for confidential meetings—by asking the hotel to not sell the space next to the hard-wall space she's using.

"The question becomes, 'What's it going to take to get you in the hotel," attorney Howe says. "The planner just has to see how far they're going to push the envelope."

Suppliers' Side

Hal Powell, director of sales and marketing for Lansdowne Resort, in Leesburg, Va., says his property is offering add-ons to its CMP during certain periods, including complimentary pool parties and airport transportation. Powell also is willing to deviate further from the CMP if the need arises.

"If they don't want to have dinner here every night, we'll certainly move off the CMP," he says, adding that room comps and staff upgrades are also on the table.

Powell says that planners of all stripes are using more addendums in contract negotiations, which previously was the providence of planners booking pharmaceutical and consulting firm meetings.

Popular addendums include the ubiquitous *force majeure*, as well as no-walk policies, change of ownership and bankruptcy clauses, conflict of interest stipulations, and Americans with Disabilities Act provisions.

Beyond contract haggling, planners have also fixed a steady gaze on the bottom line.

"We're seeing that rate is definitely an issue for a lot of planners, and that they are more than ever willing to talk about what will work to get them the best rate, from the standpoint of patterns, time of year and the time between booking date and actualization date," Powell says. "The biggest change is that customers are doing their comparison shopping even on short-term meetings. We're getting a lot of calls saying, 'You're our preferred property, but here's the other properties we're looking at and their rates."

Even the industry's big fish are starting to jump, such as the International Association of Conference Centers, which added the use of LCD projectors to its standard CMP.

"Conference centers have felt the pinch like the rest of the hotel industry," says IACC Executive Vice President Tom Bolman, who says the conference center segment is starting to show signs of recovery. "We had to be a little more forgiving on attrition and cancellation fees, and had to be more flexible with the CMP package."

Columbia Hospitality's Matteson says many planners are negotiating to bring subcontractors in to reduce costs, and are being much more aggressive in asking for complimentary items and enhancements to the meeting package.

"They're looking to get the pre-convention reception for hundreds for free," Matteson says of some of the more over-the-top planner requests. "I'll be honest with you, we may do it—that's the reality of it."

Even though the scales have tilted in favor of planners, Howe and many others advise planners to maintain good relationships with suppliers—including maintaining the lines of communication open after the contract is signed—because, as the saying goes, what comes around, goes around.

"It's going to be a tight market in the not to distant future because fewer hotels are being constructed," Howe says, "and we can be right back into the economy we were in before the market shifted."

Source: Davidson, T. *Meetings West*, (May 2002).

Appendix B: Controlling Your Room Block: Planners find corralling outside the block bookings akin to herding cats

The following complete article on room block control is provided as a resource. *Source: Meetings West*, May 2002. Reprinted with permission.

If wavering or weak hotel room bookings keep you up at night, you may find comfort in misery with Valerie J. Jensen, regional vice president of HelmsBriscoe, the Scottsdale, Ariz.-based global site selection firm. After two years of negotiating with a major Las Vegas property on behalf of her association client for a show that carried almost a full week of 800-room nights, Jensen found herself staring at a client attrition bill.

"We had negotiated a rate of $165, then the September 11 attacks hit and everything went to hell," Jensen says. "When everyone in Vegas dropped their rates, the hotel dropped our rate to $135 three months out. But we had a problem meeting our block because attendees found they could book $99 rooms for the same dates on the property's Web site. In addition, they found a $79 rate at sister properties in Vegas for the same dates."

The group came up short by only eight rooms on one peak night and three on another, she said, but the wash on the other sides was really bad. "We weren't able to pick up our full block, but they were able to fill the hotel on those nights. Two weeks after the show, they sent us a bill for over $60,000."

Even though the hotel gave her company a credit for attendee rooms that booked outside the block, there were still problems. "In doing an audit, we found room nights the property didn't credit to us," she says. "The match was possible because we had every attendee fill out an emergency contact card at registration, and we compared them with the hotel roster. Our big problem is that we had probably missed 217 people because for one reason or another they didn't fill out a card. And, the hotel won't credit us for all the attendees who booked into their sister properties. I know they are not the same hotels and same budgets, but we feel we are getting unfair treatment."

Jensen says her case is not unique to Vegas. She is seeing similar scenarios in other cities. Though attrition clauses and occasional bills for missing the contracted booking mark have been around for ages, group performance shortfall has become a more significant problem for many planners, their clients and hoteliers in the current economic climate. New time-consuming negotiation phases are being opened up long after contracts are signed because of group performance issues.

Fueling the misery is the rise in Internet buys of deeply discounted rooms that hotels typically offer for short-term bookings. Attendees have always discovered methods to find better room deals: billboard promotions, hotel newspaper ads and front-desk deal making, for instance. But myriad Web sites now make it easier than ever to beat the event contract rate.

Associations whose members pay their own expenses and may book rooms anywhere are having the greatest difficulty controlling room blocks. Planners blame their room block blues on properties that release inventory "for sale" on the same dates as their group's event and still expect them to pay the higher contracted rate. On the other side, hotels say buyers purchase rooms at the rate they signed off for in contracts and are bound to honor the agreements, which direct hotels to reserve inventory for a specific buyer. Hotels contract group room rates to support a bigger property-use commitment, they say, a deal that includes the use of other hotel facilities and services such as meeting rooms, F&B, sales staff time, and so on. Contract rates reflect that commitment, and are a two-way street in that they protect both parties against loss.

As for deeply discounted rates on the Internet and elsewhere, hoteliers argue they place unsold rooms on sale whenever they must, just as a department store discounts dresses or any other consumer products to move them out the door. One buyer gets the room at one price; another gets lucky in a promotional sale. The Web is just one more distribution channel. *a la* toll-free numbers and travel agents.

Groups and planners get into attrition hot water mostly because they often don't understand contract performance clauses, say industry attorneys and others. Room blocks rarely fall apart when all parties (including attendees) understand their responsibilities, and good communication between hotel and planner flows at all stages of negotiating, planning and followup. The key to room block integrity falls to group buyers, who are in the best position to control their members and avoid room block fallout (see sidebar.)

"Attrition is not new," says attorney Lisa Sommer Devlin of the Phoenix-based law firm Kurtz Sommer Devlin. "There is more complaining now because the economic climate has changed, and group planners are seeing more occasions where they get attrition bills. Planners fail to realize that when you contract, you are buying a future, an option. That means you are guaranteeing a price, whether they go up or even down."

Jonathan Howe of Howe & Hutton, Ltd., in Chicago, agrees. "Planners often don't understand the attrition clause, don't evaluate their blocks regularly, and don't communicate with the hotel along the way. Block review dates should be in the contract for verifying and cross-matching registrants," he advises. "Hotels are sometimes reluctant to release what they call private information about guests, but planners need to know their pickup and get credit for any of their attendees who are in the hotel no matter how they got there."

As for instances when hotels offer room prices lower than those in a group contract, Howe defends hoteliers. "A hotel room is a perishable product if it goes unused and unpaid for," he contends. "There is no opportunity to sell it the next day."

"Hotels have a fiduciary responsibility to owners and managers," he continues, "and they sign off on contract rates that predict what a particular group will bring to the party and how much revenue they will generate. It is also important for planners to understand the nature of the property they are buying. For instance, a resort probably has more difficulty re-selling rooms a group doesn't use on a weekday than does a transient airport hotel."

In most situations, Howe says, a well-drafted attrition clause works well for all parties. It should provide for periodic review of the room block so the group doesn't get hit with any surprise.

Trust and Verify

"Beyond that, we operate on the Ronald Reagan theory of trust and verify," Howe says. "There should be a contractual obligation for the hotel to submit a house list so planners can crosscheck their registration lists. Names and other information are subject to human error."

Bob Hope, CMP, and managing director of housing, registration and travel services for the Chicago-based Radiological Society of North America, says attendee hotel information should not only be available to planners, it should be available at any time.

"Having the ability to go online at any time and check hotel pickup is an excellent thing," he says. "But today, the majority of hotels don't have that capability, mostly because they have concerns about privacy. There are already tech tools to give password-protected access to information. As it is now, we have to call the hotel staff to ask for a printout. Nine times out of 10, I don't get my report, and there is a lot of back-and-forth wasted time between our staff and the hotel."

Online verification capability might eliminate a situation Annette Hoel, CMP, director of the meetings and convention division of Kansas City-based American Academy of Family Physicians, recently encountered.

"We have an annual meeting here that almost got into attrition recently," she says. "We were on the hook for between $5,000 and $10,000. Our staff ended up having to go down to the hotel to spend half a day matching names. We found double bookings in the system that could have been a hotel error or people who made two reservations."

Accurate records are essential, Hoel says, but the planner is often at the mercy of hotel staff for information. "Hotels need to keep more accurate records so you don't have to argue with them about your rights," Hoel contends. "Our pickup reports often have problems— we almost always find discrepancies, and sometimes even 15 room nights can make the difference in whether you pay $10,000 or $15,000."

Hoel and her staff attempt to protect their position at the front end. "On many of our recent contracts, we have reserved the right to buy up to the percentage we block," Hoel says. "If you have an 80 percent cutoff, and you pick up 70 to 79 percent, you are probably better off buying the unsold rooms than paying the attrition fee. I have always been bothered by the fact that we might owe a lot of money just by missing 10 rooms."

Reference the Past

Meetings histories are important, too, Hoel added, because they help you know at contract time what happened in the past and how the percentages went. "With a good history, we can take the total number of bodies at the meeting—everyone has to sleep somewhere—and compare that number with the number of rooms on peak nights. Invariably, it's about 60 percent to 65 percent of the total registrants. That way we can contract our block based on the last meeting."

Fred Shea, vice president of sales for Hyatt Hotels Corporation, joins Hoel in espousing the merits of referencing meetings histories. In this economy, he says, it is especially important to conduct business with the past in mind.

"We recommend that planners book their blocks conservatively, because that lessens the opportunities for attrition problems," he advises. "What happens with some of these blocks is that the group's history doesn't support them, so that makes hotels reluctant to give much on the attrition side. It's not usually a good idea to overbook a hotel."

Shea, who is a former professional meeting planner, says that when decisions on blocks are made several years prior to the event, nobody knows where the economy will stand at event time. Blocking rooms must therefore be a shared risk, he said, because the planner is directing the hotel to take rooms out of inventory. "A few years ago, hotels took the entire risk, but owners decided after the 1991–'92 period that there had to be some middle ground," he says. "That was when we began to control inventory more. Customers can't book willy-nilly.

"When a planner has a realistic history on the group and books rooms conservatively," Shea continues, "the hotel is most often more willing to work with them to reduce attrition liability should the group fall short. But if they want special treatment and a lot more rooms than the hotel is comfortable in giving, the opposite is true. There must be risk for everyone."

Rate Integrity Issues

Shea acknowledges that attrition issues are among the industry's hottest topics, and that rate integrity—i.e., controlling rates—is also a major matter in Hyatt's new training program for its director of sales positions. Discussions surround the need to keep the whole picture of client relations and revenue yields in balance, he explains.

"The wholesale business has been around for years and years. What has been surprising is how fast it has shifted to the Internet," he says. "We know there has been some panic selling of unused inventory in this economic readjustment period, and we are moving to get better control on this. If I post a rate on www.hyatt.com there should be nowhere else to find a cheaper price. Also, we are moving to make sure people can't resell rooms and asking our hotels to reconsider how they forecast. We must control our use of the Internet. We can't let it control us." Shea acknowledges that Hyatt knows it creates problems when the convention pays one rate and an interloper buys unused room inventory at the last minute. In cases in which planners can show their people are coming into the hotel outside the contract channel, Hyatt will credit the groups, he says.

"Groups are 50 percent of our business and we want to protect them against risk," he says. "But sometimes the only way we have to attract other guests is by promotional rates. We have to look at the whole picture."

The planner also has a role to play in controlling their group blocks, Shea says. One of his recommendations to planners is to shift the burden of purchase back to the individual attendee. Then, if they want to book outside channels, they'll pay a different fee from those who book with the group.

"The bottom line is, we book thousands of groups and very few even get into the attrition box," Shea says. "This is not a business we want to be in."

Source: Hill, R. *Meetings West*, (July 2002).

Appendix C: CIC Request for Proposal (RFP)

The following report was created to establish accepted practices in the meetings, convention, and exhibitions industry. It is provided as a resource. *Source*: CIC Convention Industry Council 2003. Reprinted with permission.

REPORT CONTENTS

REQUESTS FOR PROPOSALS (RFPS) PANEL CHARGE

The purpose of the APEX RFPs Panel is to develop recommended industry accepted practices for consistent and thorough Requests for Proposals (RFPs) that address core information and unique needs.

INSTRUCTIONS FOR THE USE OF THIS REPORT

This preliminary report of the APEX Requests for Proposals (RFPs) Panel is presented to the industry at the mid-point in the panel's planned work. In order to develop accepted practices regarding requests for proposals (RFPs) for the meetings, conventions and exhibitions industry, members of all facets of the industry are asked to review the preliminary findings and provide input. This input can be:

- Comments ratifying and endorsing the suggestions of the panel.
- Constructive criticism of the preliminary recommendations, including a rationale and suggested solution.
- Other comments that enhance the process and/or the product of this panel.

The panel will consider all comments from industry members. All comments must be submitted via one of the following methods using the outlined format. All comments should be constructive to the process of developing feedback. Therefore, any criticism of a panel recommendation should be accompanied by a rationale and suggested solution.

PREFERRED METHOD - Submitting Comments Via the APEX Web Site:

Complete the form at http://www.conventionindustry.org/rfps_prelim_comments.htm

Sending Comments Via Email:

Send comments, in the following format, to ccote@conventionindustry.org:

Full Name:
Title:
Employer:
Address, City, State & Zip:
Telephone Number:
Email Address:
Comment/Suggestion:

Sending Comments Via Postal Mail or Fax:

Send comments, in the following format, to:

Convention Industry Council's APEX Initiative
8201 Greensboro Drive, Suite 300, McLean, Virginia 22102 ▪ Fax: (703) 610-9005

Full Name:
Title:
Employer:
Address, City, State & Zip:
Telephone Number:
Email Address:
Comment/Suggestion:

I: CONTACT INFORMATION

Event Host: _____   Event Organizer (if different from Host): _____

Event Name: _____

Key Contact:

Personal Title *(Mr., Ms., Dr., etc.)*: _____   First Name/Initial: _____

Middle Name/Initial: _____   Surname: _____

Suffix/Professional Designations *(Ph.D., Esq., CPA, etc.)*: _____   Preferred Name: _____

Job Title: _____   Employer: _____

Mailing Address Line 1: _____   Mailing Address Line 2: _____

City: _____   State/Province: _____

Postal/Zip Code: _____   Country: _____

Phone: _____   Mobile Phone: _____   Fax: _____

Email: _____   Web Address: _____

Contact Type: *Drop Down Options:*
                       ❑   Employee of Association Management Company
                       ❑   Employee of Event Management Company
                       ❑   Employee of Event Host
                       ❑   Employee of Event Organizer
                       ❑   Exhibit Manager
                       ❑   Independent/Third Party
                       ❑   Other: _____

Contact Role   *Drop Down Options:*
(check all that apply):   ❑   Event Organizer (Planner)
                       ❑   Informational Contact
                       ❑   Staff
                       ❑   Volunteer
                       ❑   Other: _____

Repeat for additional contacts as necessary.

II: EVENT PROFILE

Event Name: _____ *(populated from Section I)*   Event Host: _____ *(populated from Section I)*

Event Organizer (if different from Host): _____ *(populated from Section I)*

Event Type: *Drop Down Options:*
    ❑ Board Meeting   ❑ Incentive Travel   ❑ Special Event
    ❑ City-Wide Convention   ❑ Local Employee Gathering   ❑ Team-Building Event
    ❑ Committee Meeting   ❑ Product Launch   ❑ Trade Show
    ❑ Customer Event   ❑ Public Show   ❑ Training Meeting
    ❑ Educational Meeting   ❑ Sales Meeting   ❑ Video Conference
    ❑ General Business Meeting   ❑ Shareholders Meeting   ❑ Other: _____

Event Status: *Drop Down Options:*
    ❑ Anticipated
    ❑ Confirmed
    ❑ Tentative

Event Host Overview *(mission, philosophy, etc.)*: _____

Event Objectives: _____

Event Web Address: _____

Anticipated Number of Attendees: _____

Demographics Profile (Attendees & Exhibitors): _____

ADA Accessibility/Special Needs: _____

Event History:
- Most Recently Past Date & Venue for this event: _____ *(date)*, _____ *(venue)*
- Most Recent Total Attendance for this event: _____
- Next Date & Venue for this event: _____ *(date)*, _____ *(venue)*
- *Attach appropriate APEX Post-Event Reports*

Event Frequency: *Drop Down Options:*
    ❑ One Time Only   ❑ Bi-Annual
    ❑ Annual   ❑ Semi-Annual
    ❑ Quarterly   ❑ Monthly   ❑ Other: _____

The event is or includes an exhibition: ❑ Yes ❑ No
- *If Yes,*
    Type of Exhibits   ❑ Constructed ❑ Pipe & Drape
    choose all that apply: ❑ Table Tops ❑ Other: _____

    Number of Exhibits Expected: _____   Number of Exhibiting Companies Expected: _____

    General Service Contractor (GSC) Selected: ❑ Yes ❑ No
- *If Yes,*
    Company Name: _____   GSC Contact Name: _____
    GSC Contact Phone: _____   GSC Contact Email: _____ GSC Contact Fax: _____

Future Open Dates For This Event:
- Published Start Date: _____   Published End Date: _____
- *Additional future dates as necessary*

III: REQUIREMENTS

Statement of Need: *General description of the types of facility and/or services for which this RFP is soliciting proposals.*

Date Requirements

The event must occur on a specific date: ❑ Yes ❑ No
- *If Yes:*
  Start Date: _____   End date: _____
- *If No:*
  Preferred times for the event are *(choose all that apply)*:

Season	Month	Start Day	End Day	Other
❑ Winter (Jan. - March)	❑ January	❑ Monday	❑ Monday	❑ ____
	❑ February	❑ Tuesday	❑ Tuesday	❑ ____
❑ Spring (April - June)	❑ March	❑ Wednesday	❑ Wednesday	❑ ____
	❑ April	❑ Thursday	❑ Thursday	
❑ Summer (July - Sept.)	❑ May	❑ Friday	❑ Friday	
	❑ June	❑ Saturday	❑ Saturday	
❑ Fall (Oct. - Dec.)	❑ July	❑ Sunday	❑ Sunday	
	❑ August			
	❑ September			
	❑ October			
	❑ November			
	❑ December			

There are specific dates on which this event *cannot* occur: ❑ Yes ❑ No
- *If Yes:*
  Start Date: _____   End date: _____
- *If No:*
  Times during which the event cannot occur are *(choose all that apply)*:

Season	Month	Start Day	End Day	Other
❑ Winter (Jan. - March)	❑ January	❑ Monday	❑ Monday	❑ ____
	❑ February	❑ Tuesday	❑ Tuesday	❑ ____
❑ Spring (April - June)	❑ March	❑ Wednesday	❑ Wednesday	❑ ____
	❑ April	❑ Thursday	❑ Thursday	
❑ Summer (July - Sept.)	❑ May	❑ Friday	❑ Friday	
	❑ June	❑ Saturday	❑ Saturday	
❑ Fall (Oct. - Dec.)	❑ July	❑ Sunday	❑ Sunday	
	❑ August			
	❑ September			
	❑ October			
	❑ November			
	❑ December			

The event organizer is willing to accept alternate dates for lower rates: ❑ Yes ❑ No

Facility Requirements:

Minimum # of Guest Rooms: _____

Minimum Ballroom Capacity: _____

Minimum Exhibit Hall Square Footage: _____

Other: _____

170   HOTEL CONVENTION SALES, SERVICES, AND OPERATIONS

Location Requirements:

The event must take place in a specific location: ❑ Yes   ❑ No
- *If Yes:*
  City: _____   State/Province: _____   Country: _____
- *If No:*
  Preferred locations for the event are *(choose all that apply)*:

❑ United States	❑ Canada	❑ Africa – Eastern	❑ Europe – Eastern
❑ North Central	❑ Central	❑ Africa – Southern	❑ Europe – Western
❑ Northeast	❑ Eastern	❑ Africa – Northern	❑ India
❑ Northwest	❑ Western	❑ Africa – Western	❑ Indian Ocean
❑ South Central		❑ Asia – Eastern	❑ Mediterranean
❑ Southeast		❑ Asia – Southeast	❑ Mexico
❑ Southwest		❑ Asia – Western	❑ Middle East
		❑ Australia/New Zealand	❑ Oceania
		❑ Caribbean	❑ South America
		❑ Central America	❑ South Pacific
			❑ Other: _____

Other Location Requirements *(i.e., proximity to a convention center, etc.)*: _____

Guest Room Block Requirements:

Guest Rooms are Required for this Event: ❑ Yes   ❑ No
- *If Yes,*
  The following chart outlines guest room requirements for the event. It begins with the first day of attendee/staff arrival and ends with the final departure day:

Day & Date (i.e., Monday, mm/dd/yyyy)	# of Single Rooms Required	# of Double Rooms Required	# of Suites Required	Total # of Rooms & Suites Required
Day 1				
Day 2				
Day 3				
Day 4				
Day 5				
Day 6				
Day 7				
Repeat for additional days as necessary.				
TOTALS				

Room Rate Must Be No More Than: _____ *(indicate currency type)*

Room Rate Must Be No Less Than: _____ *(indicate currency type)*

Government Per Diem Rates Required: ❑ Yes   ❑ No

Reduced Staff Room Rates Required: ❑ Yes   ❑ No

Handicapped Accessible Rooms Required: ❑ Yes   ❑ No

Complimentary Rooms Required: ❑ Yes   ❑ No
- *If Yes,* Required Ratio of ___ (#) room night(s) for every ___ (#) room nights used on an accumulated basis.

Rebates, Assessments, or Commissions Will Be Paid on Room Rates: ❑ Yes   ❑ No

Function Space Requirements:

Function Space is Required for this Event: ❑ Yes ❑ No
- *If Yes,*

The following chart/schedule outlines function space requirements for the event.

Day & Date	Function Type	Start Time	End Time	# of Attendees	Setup	24-Hour Hold Required
	Drop Down Options: ❑ Breakfast ❑ Lunch ❑ Reception ❑ Dinner ❑ General Session ❑ Breakout Session ❑ Other: _____				*Drop Down Options:* ❑ Theatre ❑ Conference Style ❑ U-Shaped ❑ Classroom ❑ Hollow Square ❑ Rounds for 8 ❑ Rounds for 10 ❑ Reception ❑ Table Top Exhibits ❑ 8' x 10' Exhibits ❑ 10' x 10' Exhibits ❑ Other: _____	❑ Yes ❑ No
	Repeat for additional functions as necessary.					

Function Space/Audio Visual Comments: _____

Food & Beverage Requirements:

Food & Beverage is Required for this Event: ❑ Yes ❑ No
- *If Yes,*

F&B Function Types Required *Choose all that apply*	Amount Budgeted Per Person *(Complete only if Function Type is Selected)*
❑ Coffee Break	_____ *(indicate currency type)*
❑ Reception	_____ *(indicate currency type)*
❑ Plated Breakfast	_____ *(indicate currency type)*
❑ Buffet Breakfast	_____ *(indicate currency type)*
❑ Continental Breakfast	_____ *(indicate currency type)*
❑ Hot Plated Lunch	_____ *(indicate currency type)*
❑ Cold Plated Lunch	_____ *(indicate currency type)*
❑ Buffet Lunch	_____ *(indicate currency type)*
❑ Plated Dinner	_____ *(indicate currency type)*
❑ Buffet Dinner	_____ *(indicate currency type)*

Other Specific Requirements:

Description of any particular requirements for this event.

V: PROPOSAL CONTENT

Each proposal responding to this RFP must include the following information (in the order presented here).

Name of Property: _____

   Mailing Address Line 1: _____   Mailing Address Line 2: _____

   City: _____   State/Province: _____   Postal/Zip Code: _____   Country: _____

Primary Sales Contact:

   Personal Title: _____   First Name/Initial: _____   Middle Name/Initial: _____

   Surname: _____   Suffix/Professional Designations: _____   Preferred Name: _____

   Job Title: _____   Employer: _____

   Mailing Address Line 1: _____   Mailing Address Line 2: _____

   City: _____   State/Province: _____   Postal/Zip Code: _____   Country: _____

   Phone: _____   Mobile Phone: _____   Fax: _____

   Email: _____   Web Address: _____

Experience:

   For how many events has the property provided event services in the past year? _____

   Of which industry association(s) is the property (or its employees) a member *(choose all that apply)*?
- ❑ American Hotel & Lodging Association (AH&LA)
- ❑ American Society of Association Executives (ASAE)
- ❑ Association for Convention Operations Management (ACOM)
- ❑ Hospitality Sales and Marketing Association International (HSMAI)
- ❑ Insurance Conference Planners Association (ICPA)
- ❑ International Association of Assembly Managers (IAAM)
- ❑ International Association of Conference Centers (IACC)
- ❑ International Association for Exhibition Management (IAEM)
- ❑ International Special Events Society (ISES)
- ❑ Meeting Professionals International (MPI)
- ❑ National Association of Catering Executives (NACE)
- ❑ National Coalition of Black Meeting Planners (NCBMP)
- ❑ Professional Convention Management Association (PCMA)
- ❑ Religious Conference Management Association (RCMA)
- ❑ Society of Government Meeting Professionals (SGMP)
- ❑ Society of Incentive & Travel Executives (SITE)
- ❑ Other _____

Response to Requirements:

   Dates & Guest Rooms Available for the _____ (Event Name)

Start Day & Date	End Day & Date	# of Single Rooms Available	Single Room Rate~	# of Double Rooms Available	Double Room Rate~	# of Suites Available	Suite Rate~
Option 1	Option 1	#	_____ ~	#	~	#	~
Option 2	Option 2	#	_____ ~	#	_____ ~	#	_____ ~
Additional Options as Necessary							

~indicate currency type

IV: PROPOSAL SPECIFICATIONS

(Event Host) expects that all work will be performed in a professional manner. All information provided in this RFP is proprietary for this purpose only. Information cannot be released without written permission from (Event Host).

Questions:
Direct all questions and requests for additional information regarding this RFP to the contact person designated in Section I (Contact Information).

Decision Making Process:
Final Decision Maker *(i.e., staff, board of directors, etc.)*: _____

There will be a preliminary cut with a second review of finalists: ❑ Yes ❑ No

Timeline:
- Response Deadline: _____
- Proposal Presentation Dates & Location, if required: _____
- Decision Date: _____
- Approximate Date of Site Inspection (if required): _____
- Number of Site Inspection Attendees: _____

Notification Method *(choose all that apply)*:
❑ Telephone Call   ❑ Email   ❑ Letter   ❑ Fax   ❑ Other: _____

Key Decision Factors:
Selection is based on the following criteria *(choose all that apply)*:
❑ Ability of vendor to provide high level of service
❑ Airlift to destination
❑ Hotel and/or convention center rates
❑ Information provided in the response to the RFP
❑ Proposal in the response to the RFP is in the proper sequence
❑ Inventory of guest rooms near convention center – quality
❑ Inventory of guest rooms near convention center – quantity
❑ Meeting space requirements and/or layout
❑ Overall cost of service
❑ Preferred dates
❑ Proximity of hotel facility to off-site venues
❑ Public safety record for last 5 years
❑ Recommendations from previous and existing clients
❑ Union/non-union
❑ Other: _____

Instructions for Responding:
- Each proposal responding to this RFP must include the information requested in Section V *(Proposal Content)* of this RFP (in the order presented).
- Expenses related to the preparation and completion of a response to this RFP are the sole responsibility of the vendor.
- The proposal with the lowest dollar amount will not necessarily be considered as the best proposal.
- Incomplete and/or late responses will not be considered.
- Other instructions: _____

Competition:
All companies listed below will be sent this RFP:
- _____ (Company Name 1)
- _____ (Company Name 2)
- _____ (Company Name 3)
- *Additional Company Names As Necessary*

If Complimentary Rooms Required in Section III:
___ (#) complementary room night(s) will be provided for every ___ (#) room nights used on an accumulated basis.

Function Space Available for the _____ (Event Name)
Complete the following chart for each function outlined in Section III:

Day & Date	Function Type	Start Time	End Time	Setup	Function Room Name	Maximum Capacity for Setup Indicated	24-Hour Hold Available
							☐ Yes ☐ No
	Repeat for additional functions as necessary.						

Food & Beverage Available for the _____ (Event Name)
Complete the following chart for each type of F&B outlined in Section III:

F&B Function Type	Average Per Person Price
Coffee Break	_____ *(indicate currency type)*
Reception	_____ *(indicate currency type)*
Plated Breakfast	_____ *(indicate currency type)*
Buffet Breakfast	_____ *(indicate currency type)*
Continental Breakfast	_____ *(indicate currency type)*
Hot Plated Lunch	_____ *(indicate currency type)*
Cold Plated Lunch	_____ *(indicate currency type)*
Buffet Lunch	_____ *(indicate currency type)*
Plated Dinner	_____ *(indicate currency type)*
Buffet Dinner	_____ *(indicate currency type)*

Insurance Coverage:

Indicate the types and levels of insurance the company carries:
- ☐ Errors & Omissions Insurance: _____ *(indicate currency type)*
- ☐ Workers Compensation Insurance: _____ *(indicate currency type)*
- ☐ Liability Insurance: _____ *(indicate currency type)*
- ☐ Other - _____: _____ *(indicate currency type)*

References:

Provide three references for events similar in size and scope to the one outlined in Section II *(Event Profile)* of this RFP:

	Reference 1	Reference 2	Reference 3
Reference Event Name			
Reference Event Host			
Reference First Name/Initial			
Reference Middle Name/Initial			
Reference Last Name			
Reference Title			
Reference Employer			
Reference Phone			
Reference Email			

Attachments:

The following documents should be attached to this proposal:
- ☐ The property's APEX Site Profile with the proposal
  *To be finalized in 2004, this will address general Information (location, etc.), guest services information (guest room types, features, on-site amenities such as pool, gym, etc.), space and food & beverage information (function space details, average food & beverage prices, etc.), other services information (audio/visual services, transportation, parking, etc.).
- ☐ Standard sales kit for the property
- ☐ Other attachments *(list all)*:
  - _____
  - _____
  - _____

FOOD AND BEVERAGE FUNCTION PLANNING

LEARNING OBJECTIVES

After studying this chapter, you will be able to discuss:

- The main types of food and beverage functions and services held during meetings and conventions
- How to effectively create these functions and work with the facility in planning menus
- Beverage cost control and potential liquor liability issues
- The most common menu pricing methods used for groups

INTRODUCTION

In this chapter we will discuss the important role food and beverage functions play in the overall success of the meeting or convention. Think of the meetings you've attended in the past. Food and beverage functions provide the perfect relaxed environment to interact with other attendees. All meetings or functions have some type of food and or beverage service. Since the 1990s, many prominent trade organizations have donated leftover (edible) food to the local food bank or homeless shelter. Therefore, all aspects of the planning process require close communications between the catering, convention services, and culinary staff, with a group planner to ensure each function is a success.

Rely on the hotel group servicing department for planning of the menu and room setup. Some hotels are large enough to warrant a separate catering and convention services department. Other hotels may call this the event planning department. Regardless of the job title and organizational structure, for many years planners have voiced frustration over having two hotel contacts for menu and function planning. Consequently, hotel corporations periodically have developed systems that are designed to streamline the process and reduce redundancy.

One such system, *uniserve*, was created by Sheraton Hotels, and first gained recognition in the 1980s. Their definition is "a meeting system service where the CSM (convention services manager) or event manager handles all aspects of planning the event, including the catering, food, and beverage functions."

While naming this system, a term also was created to describe the previous method that many hotels and group facilities still continue to use: *duoserve*. This is defined as a meeting system service where the planning procedures are for the catering department to coordinate *primarily* the food and beverage events and menus. Other responsibilities, including meeting and convention serving, are planned by the convention services manager. This system often is viewed as requiring more work and repetitive time for the group planner, since multiple hotel contacts are required.

For planners, the main benefits of uniserve are the following:

- Work with one hotel contact for all arrangements, not two
- Decision-making authority to plan all events

According to the majority of the Sheraton convention services managers (CSMs) I spoke to, this system is still used at some Sheraton hotels and resorts; however, it is not standardized throughout Sheratons. In developing the APEX Glossary of Terms, the CLC decided to include the following terms as they are recognized. Note that they refer to hotel locations (properties) that have this system. It is generic and not credited to a particular hotel company for having creating the system.

Uniserve property: A hotel property in which the CSM handles all aspects of the event, including catering.

Duoserve property: A hotel property in which logistics are handled by the CSM, with catering handled by a separate manager.

The CLC recognizes these terms, in part, because many other well-known hotel companies have developed their own variation on this concept. Over the years, these programs with similar objectives have been touted and advertised to meeting planners. Though these slogans may come and go, planners must ask their initial contact, the sales person, who first booked the group.

Who Will I Be Working with to Plan Our Food and Beverage Functions?

There are always exceptions because the standard procedures may change. Sound confusing? Well, keep this in mind: The ownership and management of an individual hotel property can change every few years. You may have already learned that this can result in a name or brand change. Expect that change to also bring new:

- Procedures/policies in group function space holds and servicing
- Job titles and responsibilities: organizational chart structure
- Management and possibly new contacts in catering or convention services

Therefore, all arrangements should be confirmed in writing. As mentioned previously, e-mail communications aren't legally binding contracts.

A closing comment on this subject: food and beverage planning for meeting groups (with guest rooms) has varied at each hotel I have worked for or with as a planner. Expect any and all of the job titles previously mentioned. Some job descriptions samples have been included in this chapter to facilitate your understanding.

We will now focus on the planning process and steps as they relate to Food and Beverage. Planners should always be sure to review all details on each event function sheet before signing it, regardless of the hotel contact and his or her job title.

BANQUET MENU PRICING

Hotels or facilities usually will not guarantee group menu prices more than six to eight months in advance. The seasonal availability and constant fluctuation of food costs prevent pricing guarantees from being feasible beyond that timeframe. Therefore, when planning for future events, experts suggest building a 10 to 15 percent cushion into their food budgets. If contacted in advance, the executive chef often is willing to customize a menu that may actually be lower in cost than those listed on the standard banquet menus. All agreements on menus, prices, and terms should *always* be in writing.

Banquets can yield a profit margin of 30 to 40 percent, as opposed to hotel restaurants, which have higher labor costs and typically much lower profit. Therefore, banquets are largely responsible for the food and beverage department being the second largest source of income for the hotel. Figure 8.1 is a sample of a hotel banquet and buffet lunch menu.

Types of Food Functions

It is important to remember that the planning for the food and beverage functions should relate to the overall objectives and theme of the conference;

FIGURE 8.1

MENU SAMPLE

BUFFET LUNCHES
Lunch Buffet Service 1 (One) Hour

DELI STYLE BUFFET
Minimum of 30 guests
(If less than 30 guests add $2.00 Per Person)

Selection of Ham, Turkey, Salami, Roast Beef
Cheddar and Swiss Cheeses,
Lettuce, Tomatoes, Olives and Pickles
Potato Salad
Cole Slaw
Pasta Salad
Seasonal Green Salad with an
Assortment of Dressings
Fresh Vegetable Tray with
Roasted Red Pepper Ranch Dip
Assorted Breads
Complimentary House Dessert Selection
Appropriate Condiments
Coffee, Decaf, Tea or Milk

$12.95

HOT LUNCHEON BUFFET
Minimum of 60 guests
(If less than 60 guests add $2.00 Per Person)

Choice of 3 Salads   *Choice of 2 Entrees*
Seasonal Green Salad   *Hickory Smoked Baby Back Ribs*
Potato Salad   *Sliced Roast Beef with*
Cole Slaw   *Mushroom Demi Glaze*
Potato Salad   *Mesquite Grilled*
3 Bean Salad   *Breast of Chicken*
Fresh Vegetable and Seafood Pasta Salad   *Sliced Roast Turkey Breast*
Marinated Cucumbers & Tomatoes   *Served with Gravy*
Rice Noodles, Peanut and Peas Salad   *Old Fashioned Beef Stew*
Marinated Mushrooms and Artichoke Hearts   *with Fresh Vegetables*
with Herbed Vinaigrette   *Country Style Fried Chicken*
Fruit Salad   *Meat Loaf with*
Marinated Fresh Vegetables   *Brown Gravy*
with Corn Relish

Hot Entrees served with:
House Potatoes
Fresh Vegetable
Complimentary House Dessert Selection
Rolls & Butter
Coffee, Decaf, Tea or Milk

$14.95
Additional Entree - Add $2.00 per person

Courtesy: Marriott Ontario Airport.

therefore, care should be taken in developing each and every function. Food functions fall into two categories:

- Meal (sit-down banquet or buffet style service)
- Reception (hors d'oeuvres or canapés and beverages)

Types of Service

- Banquet or "plated": This style has the assembled, preselected meal "plated" in the kitchen, kept at proper temperature, served to the guest at the table—usually a "banquet" or round table with 8 to 10 people seated. Menu selections are preordered from the banquet menus in advance, resulting in better portion cost control.
- Buffet service: Each guest proceeds through a serving line and select each food item. For large groups, this is the most expedient form of meal service. This method requires less wait staff than plated, but it is difficult to control portion size and can result in higher costs.
- French service: This style consists of the waiter placing each food item on the guest's plate from the preordered menu. This service can be very expensive and usually is limited to small VIP functions.
- Russian service: This style consists of a waiter displaying food items on a platter to guests and letting them serve themselves. This service is impressive but requires more wait and kitchen staff. Limited to small and VIP functions, as it can require more wait staff.

Figure 8.2 is a sample of a hotel banquet dinner menu.

Note: The menus shown in Figure 8.2 are examples of preset menus; customized menus can usually also be developed by the facility executive chef.

Hors d'Oeuvres Reception

These receptions fall into two distinct types. The beverage side and the setups commonly used are discussed a bit later in this chapter. When held directly prior to the meal, hors d'oeuvres (also called canapés or appetizers) may be limited to light finger foods and chilled items. These types of receptions should be kept to one hour in length. Otherwise, the meal service can be delayed from starting on time.

The other option is to not have a meal but instead a "heavy" hors d'oeuvre and cocktail reception. Many groups will plan the first evening function in this style, which is known as the *icebreaker*. Usually two hours in length, it is held during the dinner period. This is the ideal choice if people are arriving into town or at the hotel for the first time. Since they will be arriving throughout the evening, it is important to order sufficient quantities of each item. Light hors d'oeuvres or dry snacks should always be included during a reception; this cuts down on the absorption of alcohol.

Figure 8.3 is a sample of a hotel (cold) hors d'oeuvres reception menu.

FIGURE 8.2
SAMPLE DINNER MENU

DINNER ENTREES

All Entrees Include:
Choice of Salad
Chef's Choice of Starch & Fresh Vegetable
Rolls with Butter
Coffee, Decaf, Tea or Milk
Choice of Complimentary House Dessert

CHICKEN

CHICKEN KIEV

Breast of Chicken Stuffed
with Herbs and Butter
Breaded, Baked and Served on
Citrus Beurre Blanc
and Lemon Zest

$18.95

CHICKEN WELLINGTON

Puff Pastry Surrounds a Breast of
Chicken, Filled with Duxelles on a
pool of Sauce Madeira

$18.95

CHICKEN MARSALA

Chicken Breast Sauteed and Served
with Sauce of Mushroom and
Marsala Wine

$18.50

CHICKEN LANGOSTINO

Chicken Breast Stuffed with Seafood,
Laced with Lobster Saffron
Beurre Blanc

$21.95

CHIPOTLE CHICKEN

Grilled Breast of Chicken
Served on Mild California
Chili Ranchero Sauce,
Topped with Avocado Relish

$16.95

CHICKEN LORRAINE

Lightly Breaded Chicken Breast
on a Bed of Wilted Spinach, Bacon,
Onions and Mushrooms, Laced
with Chicken Veloute

$17.95

CHICKEN PICCATA

Chicken Breast, Sauteed with White
Wine, Lemon and Capers

$17.50

CHICKEN OSCAR

Chicken Breast Crowned with Fresh
Asparagus & Crab Meat, Topped with
Bearnaise Sauce

$19.95

SONOMA CHICKEN

Chicken Breast Stuffed with Shrimp
Spinach & Mushroom, Laced with
Chardonnay Beurre Blanc

$21.50

BURMESE CHICKEN

Grilled Chicken Breast on a pool
of Ginger Pineapple Sauce, Topped
with Grilled Pineapple and Toasted
Sesame Seeds and Finished with
a Plum Sauce Inlay

$17.95

Courtesy: Marriott Ontario Airport.

FIGURE 8.3
SAMPLE HORS D'OEUVRES MENU

HORS D' OEUVRES

COLD
Based per 100 pieces

Bouchees:

Seafood Salad	$125.00
Chicken and Melon Salsa	$125.00
Herbed Boursin Cheese	$100.00
Ceviche on Cucumber Wheel	$125.00
Tenderloin wrapped Asparagus with Herbed Boursin Cheese and Toasted Pinenuts	$150.00
Montrachet with Glazed Black Walnuts on Lahvosh	$100.00
Lamb Medallion with Mustard Thyme on Toasted Round	$175.00
Lobster Medallion and Herbed Cream Cheese with Spicy Cocktail Sauce on Toasted Brioche	$250.00
Smoked Salmon and Herbed Boursin Cheese, topped with Caviar on Cucumber Wheel	$225.00
Stuffed Eggs with Black Forest Ham and Feta Cheese	$125.00
Smoked Salmon Coronets with Herbed Cream Cheese on Toasted Round	$125.00
Assorted Finger Sandwiches	$125.00
Assorted Tea Sandwiches	$125.00
Deviled Eggs topped with Bay Shrimp	$100.00
Salami and Stuffed Olive Coronets	$100.00
Crab Claws on Ice with Cocktail Sauce	$225.00
Jumbo Prawns on Ice with Cocktail Sauce	$250.00
Melon wrapped with Proscuitto	$150.00
Assorted Deluxe Canapes	$150.00

8/91

Courtesy: Marriott Ontario Airport.

Event Fees

Two methods of charging are:

- By the piece (for example, 50 pieces or 75 pieces)
- By the individual platter or tray (for example, cheese and fruit platter or tray of assorted sandwiches)

Once this is a reception, the room can be set up in cocktail tables (round tables that are approximately 30 inches in diameter and 4 feet high) scattered with bar-stool-style chairs or standard banquet tables. In lieu of dinner, a sandwich deli-style buffet may be included as well. Most people are more familiar with the types of receptions used for weddings.

Changing Tastes and Choices

Today, meeting attendees expect more than basic banquet food. Meeting planners, in turn, expect the catering menus to reflect current trends toward more healthy diets, especially vegetarian meals. Smart chefs will anticipate their customers' needs and have special menus already costed out, which can then be customized quickly. Low-calorie meals, snacks, and breaks with healthy alternatives to the Cheese Danish as well as "spa cuisine" really have grown in popularity. Another trend is innovative cuisine. Many hotels have a chef on staff who has been elevated to the status of "celebrity chef." Private-prepaid cooking demonstrations for groups have regained popularity with meeting attendees.

Many of these newer food trends may initially seem too high in food and labor costs for application to group banquets. However, hotels promote these same features and benefits in their advertising to planners. Expect to make good on those delicious-looking promises!

Beverage Service

It is well known that this area can quickly break the budget, and consequently all instructions must be completely spelled out in the banquet event order (BEO) or function sheets. Here are some guidelines to consider:

- The peak bar flow is usually within the first half-hour to one hour.
- When the bar is hosted, consumption is usually higher.
- Many facilities will not allow groups to bring in their own liquor or bottles.
- Expect a "corkage" fee per bottle ($8 or more per bottle) if it is allowed.
- Customers usually know the retail liquor price; unfair markups breed ill will.

TYPES OF BEVERAGE SETUPS

There are many different types of beverage arrangements offered by hotels for group functions. In this section we will discuss the most common arrangements found and present samples of catering department setups and policies. Each hotel will have its house brands for liquor as well as individual "Well" and "Premium" brand prices.

Sample beverage menus are included in this chapter as a reference.

Cash Bar

Also known as a no-host bar, this is when each person pays for his or her own drinks. There are two methods commonly used for cash bar setups. The bartender can make drinks and collect the money, or a cashier can be provided who will issue coupons in exchange for money received from the guest. The latter method results in faster service because the bartender can focus on just making drinks. Coupons have drawbacks such as longs lines to purchase coupons, multiple coupon choices needed for drink types, and so on.

To minimize delays, catering and convention services managers recommend

- Posting numerous visible signs with drink types and prices
- Color-coding coupons with beverage types

Hosted Bar

There are several pricing methods usually available:

By the drink:
- Charge for each drink served
- Must agree on size of drink to be poured
- No bartender charge included in price (minimum time usually required)

By the hour (also known as per person):
- Flat rate charged for each person per hour
- Rate is the same for beverages with or without alcohol
- Past experience and knowledge of attendees will help determine if this method is cost effective
- Must have way of counting guests to ensure accuracy
- Must determine bartender/labor cost or dollar minimums

By the bottle:
- Pay *only* for bottles opened (some states require full charge for partially consumed bottles; however, some states allow for partials to be given to the planner to use)
- Popular for hospitality suites with small self-service groups
- Bottle count must be verified before and after function to ensure accuracy of bartender or supervisor
- Must determine bartender/labor cost or dollar minimums

Hospitality Suites

These are held mostly in a hotel parlor (living room) suite with invited guests coming and going. They can be part of a suite reserved or occupied by group representatives or sponsors, or multiple hospitality suites ongoing simultaneously either before or after scheduled group functions. Policies on liquor purchased outside of the hotel must be communicated both in print and verbally by the catering or convention services manager.

WINES

The inclusion of wines during group functions has increased greatly in recent years. In addition to cocktail service, bottles of wine often are provided during dinner and, occasionally, lunch meals. The catering manager should provide price and menu food pairing suggestions. The old rules of "red with meat" and "white with fish" no longer apply. There are too many wines with characteristics that compliment more than one food type.

In addition to the standard reds and whites, expect the group planner to ask for price quotes on Merlot, Zinfandel, Pinot Noir, Pinot Grigio, and others that are now available.

If the group has true appreciation for fine wines and spirits, ask the chef to create menus for gourmet dinners paired with complementary wines. "Meet the Winemaker" dinners and tastings may also be requested and can be affordable if the hotel is located near vineyards. The hotel may have a wine sommelier available as well. Figures 8.4 and 8.5 are samples of banquet beverage service menus from three different hotels.

BEVERAGE CONTROLS AND PROCEDURES

Many states have passed *Dram Shop Acts*, which impose liability on the dispenser of alcohol sold illegally. Illegal sales in most states include sales to intoxicated persons, a minor [all states comply with Drinking Law of 1984, which raised the age to 21], or a known alcoholic. It is the responsibility of hotel management to enforce these laws and also train food and beverage service staff. To protect themselves from potential prosecution, management must also document liquor-related incidents that involve patrons and/or employees. Each state has a liquor board that issues liquor licenses that can be revoked in the event of violations.

During the function, the banquet or event manager of duty will make the final decisions on when the bars should close. If guests must be "cut off," the manager should be professional and discreet in these matters and involve the meeting planner only when absolutely necessary.

BANQUET EVENT ORDERS (BEO) OR FUNCTION SHEETS

According to the Convention Industry Council (CIC), a Banquet Event Order (BEO) is the form most often used by hotels to provide details to personnel concerned with a specific food and beverage function or an event room setup. Increasingly, it is also being called an Event Order or a Function Sheet. Regardless of the name used, this has become a standardized form used industrywide. The form in Figure 8.6 is a sample of one used by Omni Hotels.

FIGURE 8.4
SAMPLE WINE MENU

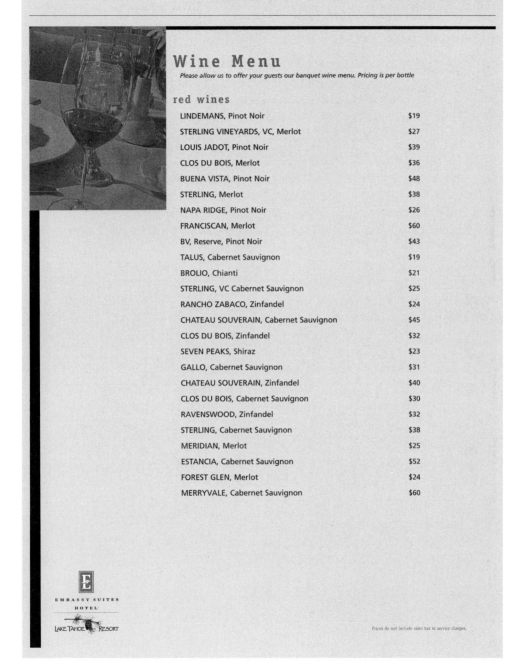

Wine Menu

Please allow us to offer your guests our banquet wine menu. Pricing is per bottle

red wines

LINDEMANS, Pinot Noir	$19
STERLING VINEYARDS, VC, Merlot	$27
LOUIS JADOT, Pinot Noir	$39
CLOS DU BOIS, Merlot	$36
BUENA VISTA, Pinot Noir	$48
STERLING, Merlot	$38
NAPA RIDGE, Pinot Noir	$26
FRANCISCAN, Merlot	$60
BV, Reserve, Pinot Noir	$43
TALUS, Cabernet Sauvignon	$19
BROLIO, Chianti	$21
STERLING, VC Cabernet Sauvignon	$25
RANCHO ZABACO, Zinfandel	$24
CHATEAU SOUVERAIN, Cabernet Sauvignon	$45
CLOS DU BOIS, Zinfandel	$32
SEVEN PEAKS, Shiraz	$23
GALLO, Cabernet Sauvignon	$31
CHATEAU SOUVERAIN, Zinfandel	$40
CLOS DU BOIS, Cabernet Sauvignon	$30
RAVENSWOOD, Zinfandel	$32
STERLING, Cabernet Sauvignon	$38
MERIDIAN, Merlot	$25
ESTANCIA, Cabernet Sauvignon	$52
FOREST GLEN, Merlot	$24
MERRYVALE, Cabernet Sauvignon	$60

EMBASSY SUITES
HOTEL
LAKE TAHOE RESORT

Prices do not include sales tax or service charges.

Courtesy: Embassy Suites, Lake Tahoe.

FIGURE 8.4
SAMPLE WINE MENU—*Continued*

BEVERAGE SERVICE
OUR PROFESSIONAL BANQUET STAFF CAN CREATE A
CUSTOM LIQUOR AND WINE MENU FOR YOUR SPECIAL EVENT.

HOSTED BAR - 3 HOUR MINIMUM (SET-UP INCLUDED)	$100.00 HOUR
NON-HOSTED BAR - SET-UP FEE (BARTENDER INCLUDED)	$125.00
MIXED COCKTAILS - CALL LIQUORS	$ 4.00 EA.
MIXED COCKTAILS - PREMIUM LIQUORS	$ 5.00 EA.
CORDIALS AND COGNACS	$ 6.00 EA.
HOUSE WINE - BY THE GLASS	$ 3.50 EA.
DOMESTIC BEER	$ 3.25 EA.
IMPORTED BEER	$ 3.50 EA.
SOFT DRINKS & BOTTLED WATER	$ 2.00 EA.
CORKAGE FEE PER BOTTLE (BEVERAGES NOT PURCHASED THROUGH THE CAL-NEVA RESORT)	$ 10.00

CAL·NEVA RESORT
SPA & CASINO
LAKE TAHOE

ALL CHARGES ARE SUBJECT TO A 7.25% SALES TAX AND AN 18% SERVICE CHARGE

Courtesy: Cal-Neva Resort, Lake Tahoe.

FIGURE 8.5
SAMPLE BANQUET BEVERAGE MENU

BANQUET BEVERAGES

BANQUET BAR SERVICE

Bar Guarantee:	A minimum of $250.00 in liquor sales per bar is required or a $50.00 bartender fee will apply.
Cash Bar:	Individual guests pay for own drinks.
Host Bar:	Organization or Designated person pays for all drinks - 17% service charge and current sales tax will be added.

PRICE PER DRINK

(Host prices are listed below. Cash prices are an additional $.25 each, except soft drinks.)
We provide 1 bartender for every 100 persons unless otherwise requested. Additional bartenders available at $50.00 each.
Cocktail servers may be requested at $35.00 per server per hour.

Well Brands - $2.75   Call Brands - $3.25   Premium Brands - $4.00   Fancy Blends - $4.50

Domestic Beer - $2.25 per bottle   Imported Beer - $2.75 per bottle

House Wine - $2.75 per glass   Soft Drinks - $1.50 per glass

1/2 kegs of Domestic Beer - $225.00   1/4 kegs of Domestic Beer - $125.00
(serves approx. 100 - 16oz. glasses)   (serves approx. 50 - 16oz. glasses)
A bartender will be required to serve kegs

Host Bar Packages (Well Brands)

1 Hour - $7.00/person
2 Hours - $11.00/person
3 Hours - $14.00/person
4 Hours - $17.00/person

CALIFORNIA WINE & CHAMPAGNE

Cooks Grand Reserve Champagne   Robert Mondavi House Wine
$14.00 per bottle   Chardonnay, White Zinfandel, Cabernet Sauvignon
$14.00 per bottle

Martinelli's Sparkling Apple Cider
$8.00 per bottle

Tropical Fruit Punch   Champagne Punch
$25.00 per gallon $40.00 per gallon

HOSPITALITY SUITES
(Self Service)

Bar Package Includes:
Plastic Glasses, Napkins, Stir Sticks, Ice and Cocktail Garnishes which include: Lemons, Limes, Cherries and Olives. $50.00 Minimum or $2.00 per person if over 25 people.

Well Brands - $28.00 per bottle   Call Brands - $35.00 per bottle

Limited Premium Brands - $45.00 per bottle

Orange and Grapefruit Juices - $7.00 per quart   Bloody Mary Mix - $7.00 per quart

Soft Drinks - $7.50 (Six-pack)

If a Bartender is requested in the Hospitality Suites, banquet bar guidelines apply.

Courtesy: Marriott Ontario Airport.

FIGURE 8.6
OMNI BANQUET EVENT ORDER

OMNI❦HOTELS®

500 Interlocken Boulevard, Broomfield CO 80021
Telephone 303-438-6600 Fax 303-464-3250

BEO #: 28041

Event Date: Tuesday, November 9, 200

Banquet Event Order

Page: 1 of 1

Date Created 11/ 5/04

Organization: Stratom, Inc.	**BEO Name:** Meeting
Post As: Stratom, Inc.	
Contact: Ted Horton	**On-Site Contact:** Ted Horton
Address: 5757 Central Avenue Ste. 88 Boulder, Colorado 80301	
Phone: 303-250-8135 **Fax:**	**Catering-Conference Mgr :** Shelby Castillo

NO TACKING, ATTACHING ITEMS TO ANY MEETING ROOM WALLS

Date	Time	Room	Function	Set-up	ATT	GTD SET	Rental
11/ 9/04	8:00 AM - 9:30 AM	Interlocken C	CBKF	EXIS	30	7	
11/ 9/04	8:00 AM - 5:00 PM	Interlocken C	MTG	CRES	30	7	$200.00
11/ 9/04	8:00 AM - 5:00 PM	Interlocken C	ABRK	EXIS	30	7	
11/ 9/04	2:00 PM - 3:00 PM	Interlocken C	PBRK	EXIS	30	7	

Menu Requirements

Room: Interlocken C

THE EXECUTIVE'S PACKAGE
Serve: 8:00 AM to 5:00 PM
Freshly Brewed Peet's Coffee, Decaffeinated, and Boulder's Celestial Seasonings Teas
Assorted Individual Soft Drinks
Bottled Spring Water

7 people @ $10.00 Per person

Room: Interlocken C

BOULDER CONTINENTAL BREAKFAST
Serve: 8:00 AM to 9:30 AM
Freshly Squeezed Orange, Grapefruit, Apple and Cranberry Juices
Almond Granola, Fruit Yogurts
Sliced Seasonal Fruit with Seasonal Berries
Bagels and Cream Cheese, Breakfast Pastries served with Preserves and Butter (Toaster Provided)
Freshly Brewed Peet's Coffee, Decaffeinated, and Boulder's Celestial Seasonings Teas

7 people @ $17.00 Per person

Room: Interlocken C

THE EXECUTIVE'S PACKAGE
Serve: 2:00 PM to 3:00 PM
Assortment of Brownies
Lemon Bars

Beverage Requirements

Miscellaneous Requirements

Room Requirements

Room: Interlocken C
Event: 8:00 AM to 5:00 PM
Head Table in Front of Room for Materials
CRESCENT STYLE SET: with 6 guests per table with Gavel Service: Water Pitchers (1 pitcher per 3 guests), Glasses, Hard Candies, Notepads and Pens
Refreshment table placed inside of room
REGISTRATION TABLE located outside of room to include: Skirted 6' table with 2 chairs, Tissues, Wastebasket, Water Pitcher, Glasses, Hard Candies, Notepads and Pens

Room: Interlocken C
Event: 8:00 AM to 5:00 PM
Refreshment table placed inside of room

Audio Visual Requirements

Room: Interlocken C
Event: 8:00 AM to 5:00 PM
Outside (Client's Own) LCD Package: including: Cart, Cabling, Power, Screen and Technical Support @ $130.00 per day

Billing Requirements
Credit Card number on File

Should this function cancel a fee equal to 100% of the value of the BEO will be due. Changes or cancelation within 24 hours prior to start of function to the menu, room set or audio visual are subject to availability and possible charges. A 20% service charge and a 7.85% tax will be applied to all Food, Beverage, and Audio Visual items
Your final guest count is due 72 business hours prior to the function date. In the event we do not receive this guarantee we will automatically use the countlisted on this BEO.

For Organization

Date

For Omni Hotels

Date

Courtesy: Omni Hotels, Broomfield, Colorado.

SPONSORS

To reduce food and beverage costs, multiple sponsoring organizations often are sought to pay for specific functions or receptions. They may work directly with the hotel or through the group contact to communicate sponsorship visibility (signage) and of billing arrangements. For new ways to secure sponsorships, see the Web site (www.meetingsfocus.com).

Figure 8.7 is an advertorial from *Meetings West*, featuring the Loew's Hotel, whose catering department has received many accolades. Each year the *Meetings Guide to the South* publication asks planners to send in their vote

FIGURE 8.7

EXAMPLE OF ADVERTORIAL FOR BEST CATERING

Planners who book the Loews Miami Beach Hotel, situated in South Beach with the Atlantic Ocean out its back door, can bank on great food and exceptional service, according to Michael Darst, director of catering and conference management at the property.

"We're known as the hotel that embraces a client's vision and delivers." he says, explaining that the property can prepare everything from a Jimmy Buffett-style feast poolside, including mini cheeseburgers and four different margaritas, to a gala beach clambake with ribs, shrimp and beer. "Planners are surprised by the depth of what we offer and that a 1,000-person event has restaurant-like service."

Prior to choosing a menu, planners can count on a tasting with the hotel's staff, which might include an introduction to Executive Chef Marc Ehrler.

"It's interactive," Darst explains. "Let us show you 10 different stations and you could choose five for your buffet. "You'll get the feeling of what it will be like for 500 people."

Source: *Meetings Media*, text reprinted with permission.

for the best in many categories. In 2004, the top spot for Best Catering went to Loew's Miami Beach Hotels. Planners cited the great food, exceptional service, and the Atlantic Ocean view (out the back door) as the areas that made them number one.

METHODS OF CONTROL AND TRACKING

The use of tickets is the preferred method of attendance and cost control for large functions. Include the event name, date, and any applicable number series on the ticket. Tickets are issued for each function included in the registration fee. Color-coding them also improves identification and helps avoid mix-ups. Ticket collections occur upon arrival at the door or during the meal function, which is used as a check against the number of meals served and subsequently charged to the customer. Another method used is to *count heads*. However, it can be difficult to ensure accuracy at receptions when people aren't seated. Most important, the agreed collection method must be communicated to the waitstaff to ensure that they answer any guests' questions correctly. It may sound simple, but you must be sure the employees involved know exactly who will be performing that task. For small events—under 50 people—it is possible to simply count plates. This can only work, though, if the chef or designated kitchen staff can ensure accuracy.

GUARANTEES

The hotel will require a guarantee of the number of people expected 48 or 72 hours prior to the function. For weekend events, the 72-hour minimum is usually the norm. Expect additional requirements if more unusual or specialty menu items are ordered. For example, 500 pastry shells personalized with the company name or first letter baked into it or in a chocolate mold will require additional labor and prep time. These standards have been established to ensure that adequate food is ordered and prepared. Additionally, the kitchen will automatically prepare anywhere from five to eight percent over the guaranteed number for food functions. This overage is built into the food cost and necessary for the "extra" attendees, who may arrive without a reservation. To cover costs, groups will usually charge a higher price when this occurs. Planners must remember, though, that the "guaranteed" number they provide is the *minimum* they will be charged, even when fewer people show up.

THE SELLER'S PERSPECTIVE

More so than ever before, a hotel or any group facility must maximize revenue. Banquets, cocktail receptions, and food and beverage functions all provide additional revenue opportunities. As discussed in Chapter 7, during this process a piece of "group business" is evaluated for guest rooms *and* food and beverage revenue. Groups that meet the criteria can help the food and beverage department meet their own budget and revenue goals each month. On a larger scale they can contribute to the overall profitability of the property.

HEAD TABLE PLANNING

A speaker's or head table is used as a form of recognition for VIPs or guests. Usually the guest or keynote speaker will be seated here along with the person responsible for introductions. The head table, usually in the front of the room, can be placed on a raised platform stage or dais. Keep in mind that the main objective is for all participants to be able to view the speaker and others at the head table. The convention services department will usually skirt it along with any food and beverage function tables. A lectern or podium with a microphone should also be set up on or adjacent to the head table. If situated directly on the table, avoid placement in front of a place setting if a meal is being served.

Table 8.1 is a checklist, which helps the novice meeting planner to be sure all key areas are discussed with the facility.

TABLE 8.1
CHECKLIST

Checklists for Food and Beverage Functions: Items to discuss			
Day_____ Time_____ Function rm. location: _____ Separate sheet for each:	Discuss: Hotel event dept. Contact: √	Outcome/Decision Action: Name	Event form issued by hotel? Y N
Menu-Fd. service			
Décor/Theme			
Beverages/Bar order			
Room set up style Head table Dance flr.			
Guarantees? Attendance estimates?			
Speaker(s) Arrangements AV Podium/Lectern			
DEPOSITS:			
Additional areas:			

CATERING GUIDELINES AND POLICIES

The sample in Figure 8.8 is used by hotels to advise the planner of their catering policies and procedures. It typically is inserted as a cover page in the banquet menu packet.

LABOR AND UNION ISSUES

In many U.S. cities, many restaurant and hotel hourly employees belong to a union. Check with the event coordinator as to the applicable local union rules, which may govern labor staffing, seating setup, or related areas. Some cities, most recently Las Vegas and San Francisco, have had strikes that have virtually shut down the meetings planned during that period. Planners should keep in close contact with the hotel management if the unionized employees there (or at that destination) currently are operating without a contract. Labor contract negotiations may be ongoing, and alternative locations may be needed if talks break down.

GRATUITIES AND TIPPING

This subject is discussed in detail in Chapter 9. The food and beverage department staff, including banquets servers, have their hourly wage based partially on a gratuity. Be sure to review that section in the chapter and confirm the applicable service charges and automatic gratuities with your event coordinator.

SUMMARY

Each food and beverage function held during a meeting or convention can contribute or detract from the overall success of the event. They represent an area where good communication and planning can make the event look effortless, impressing both the client and participants. Always remember, though, that for most planners coming in at or *under budget* is equally—if not more—important. Experienced planners recognize the profit potential of food and beverage functions to hotels. At the same time, most association and nonprofit planners must rely on sponsors to underwrite function costs. Therefore, during planning, it is important for both buyer and seller to be aware of the other negotiable areas and fixed-cost centers.

FIGURE 8.8

SAMPLE POLICIES AND PROCEDURES CAL-NEVA RESORT

CAL-NEVA RESORT
CATERING GUIDELINES AND POLIIES

Deposits and Payment

A deposit 50% of estimated food and beverage charges are due 60 days before the event. Final payment, less any credits, will be due 21 days before the event. The client agrees by signing a banquet contract for food, beverage, and or services, they acknowledge no dispute over such services. The client is solely responsible for payment of the total amount due. Any additional charges incurred at the event are doe from the client at the conclusion of the event. An Event Order will be sent to you containing all information pertinent to your event(s). This document is finalized by the client's signature and returned. Failure to return the Event Order presumes all the information is accurate and acceptable.

Guarantees

A final confirmation of the anticipated number of guests is required a minimum of 3 weeks prior to all events. If no confirmation is received, the last number of persons discussed will be used as the guarantee. Client will be charged for the guaranteed or the actual number of guests served: whichever is greater. In addition, the Cal-Neva Resort is not obligated to set or serve for more than 5% above the guaranteed number. Should guarantee increase or decrease by 20% of the guaranteed number of attendees, the Cal-Neva Resort reserves the right to cancel or relocate your group without refund or room rental fees/charges.

Food and Beverage

All listed prices are current however, are subject to change due to market fluctuations. Confirmed prices will be quoted thirty (30) days prior to be event. All food and beverage must be consumed on the premises and purchased solely through the Cal-Neva Resort. Entrée selections are limited to one, with the exception of buffets. If a split entrée is required, an additional charge per person will apply. Only one selection will be permitted on plated menu items; with the exception of vegetarian meals.

Decorations, Displays and Signs

Decorations must be of professional quality and not be used without prior Cal-Neva Resort approval. The Banquet Department must approve any decorations requiring candles or flames, three (3) weeks before the event. Affixing materials to the walls, floors, ceilings or furnishings is not permitted.

Florals, Photography & Special Services

The Cal-Neva Resort provides professional in-house florist and photographer to help you with your special event. Clients may not duplicate any services provided by the Cal-Neva Resort. Suitable ice sculptures can be created for decoration at an additional charge, with advance notice. The Cal-Neva Resort will be more than happy to coordinate a variety of entertainment offerings. We are able to provide you with a dance floor, music and entertainment. All charges will be itemized and included on the Event Order.

Loss or Damage to Property

The Cal-Neva Resort is not responsible for lost or damaged personal property (i.e. Cake Knifes, Champagne Glasses, Flowers, and Gifts) that you or your guests bring to or leave at the events' location, before, during or after the use of the facilities. The Cal-Neva Resort is not responsible for articles left overnight in the function room during multiple events. The client accepts all responsibility for damage done to equipment or facilities at the time the premises are under their control including but not limited to damage or excessive clean up may be required.

Courtesy: Cal-Neva Resort, Lake Tahoe.

REVIEW QUESTIONS

1. List and define the three common types of food service setups offered for catered group functions.
2. Describe the different options available for a cash bar. What controls should be used with each option?
3. Define and discuss the terms *duoserve* and *uniserve*. Give an example for each style as it relates to food and beverage planning and communication.
4. What is the Dram Shop Act, and why is it important to groups having food and beverage functions?
5. Explain what a *corkage fee* is and when it would be applicable.

REFERENCES

Abbey, J. and Astroff, M. (2003) Convention Sales and Services, 6e. Cranbury, NJ: Waterbury Press.
Meetings West, (March 2005).

ADDITIONAL RESOURCES AND WEB SITES

NACE: National Association of Catering Executives
Headquarters:
9881 Broken Land Parkway, Suite 101
Columbia, MD 21046
Phone: 410-290-5410 Fax: 410-290-5460
www.nace.net

National Off-Premise Caterers Roundtable Association
P.O. Box 2881
Bakersfield, CA. 93302
(805) 325-1715 ph

Publications

Catering Business
633 Third Ave.
New York, N.Y. 10017
(212) 984-2293 ph

Catering Today
P.O. Box 222
Santa Claus, IN. 47579
(812) 937-4464

GLOSSARY

Banquet: Formal, often ceremonial dinner for a select group of people, often in honor of a particular person.

Banquet Event Order (BEO): A form most often used by hotels to provide details to personnel concerned with a specific food and beverage function or event room set-up.

Banquet Manager: A person in charge of banquet service.

Bordeaux Wines: Wines from the Bordeaux region in southwest France known for richness and fragrance. Red wines (also known as Clarets) include Médoc, Margaux Saint-Emilion, Pauillac, and Pomerol; fine white Bordeaux include Sauternes, Barsac, and Graves. A Château is a wine estate in Bordeaux; some of the best are Château Latour, Château Mouton-Rothschild, Château Lafite-Rothschild, and Château Margaux.

Box Lunch: Light lunch to go, in a box or a bag. Used for an off-site catered lunch.

Break: Short interval between sessions at which time coffee, tea, and/or other refreshments are served. Also called coffee break, energy break, refreshment break.

Buffet: Assortment of foods, offered on a table, self-served.

Burgundy Wine: Wine from the Burgundy region in eastern France, which produces both red and white wines. The white wines, made from Chardonnay grapes, and the red wines, made from Pinot Noir or Gamay grapes, are considered the world's best examples of these wines. Some of the better known Burgundy wines include those from Beaujolis, Pommard, Beaune, Meursault, Chablis, Pouilly-Fuissé, Chambertin, Corton, Romanée Conti, and Echézeaux.

Butler Service: 1) Servers offer a variety of both hot and cold hors d'oeuvres on platters to guests at receptions. 2) A style of table service where guests serve themselves from platters presented by the server. 3) Specialized in-room service offered by a hotel.

By the Bottle: Liquor served and charged for by the full bottle.

By the Drink: Liquor served and charged for by the number of drinks served.

By the Piece: Food purchased by the individual piece, usually for a reception.

By the Person: A fixed price per attendee; covers all consumption of food and beverage at a function, within a given time frame; usually includes beverages, snacks, or hors d'oeuvres. In some cases, beverages are purchased by the person, and food is ordered by the piece.

Cash Bar: Bar at a reception where guests pay cash or exchange tickets for their beverage.

Caterer: 1) A food service vendor, often used to describe a vendor who specializes in banquets and theme parties. 2) An exclusive food & beverage contractor within a facility.

Catering: The provision of food and beverages.

Catering Sales Manager: Staff person responsible for selling and servicing group and local food and beverage functions.

Chef's Choice: Selection of food items to best complement the entrée. The selection is being left up to the chef.

Chef's Table: The opportunity to sample a menu in advance of the event, usually in the company of the chef. Also refers to a food event held in the kitchen where the attendees interact with the chef and kitchen staff.

Continental Breakfast: Light morning meal consisting of pastries, juices, and hot beverages. Usually served buffet style.

Continental Buffet: Buffet consisting of pastries, juices, and hot beverages.

Continental Plan: A room rate that includes a continental breakfast. Also called American plan, European plan, Modified American plan.

Cordial: A liqueur usually served after dinner (e.g., Amaretto, Chambourd, Frangelica).

Crudités: 1) Pieces of raw vegetables served as hors d'oeuvres, often with dip. 2) Raw vegetable salad, usually julienne cut.

Hors d'oeuvres: Small appetizers; hot and/or cold finger foods served at a reception.

House Brand: Brand of wine or distilled spirits selected by a hotel or restaurant as their standard when no specific brand is specified. Also called a *well brand*.

Seating Plan: Plan or other document showing where individuals should be seated for an event. Particularly applies to a banquet or on a platform at an event. Usually accompanied by an alphabetical listing showing at which tables individuals should be seated.

Service Charge: 1) A mandatory and automatic amount added to standard food and beverage charges, usually used to defray the cost of labor, such as housemen, servers, technicians, etc. The facility receives a portion of the charge; in return, the guest is relieved the responsibility for tipping. 2) A fee charged to a client by a travel agent in addition to the commissions paid to him or her by his or her principals.

Smoking Room: A designated area where smoking is allowed.

Smorgasbord: Swedish buffet of hors d' oeuvres, open-faced sandwiches, salads, hot or cold cooked vegetables, pickled or marinated fish, sliced meats, cheeses, and desserts. It may be all appetizers or an entire meal.

Snifter: A large, short-stemmed goblet used for brandy or cordials.

Social Dinner: Nonworking evening function at which a meal is served.

Social Event: 1) An event with the purpose of facilitating pleasant companionship among attendees. 2) Lifecycle celebration (e.g., a wedding, bar/bat mitzvah, anniversary, birthday, etc.).

Soft Drink: Beverage that does not contain alcohol. Soft drinks are most often thought of as carbonated, though it is not a requisite.

Sommelier: A wine steward, expected to have an extensive knowledge of wines and their suitability with various dishes.

SOP: Standard Operating Procedure (or Practice).

Sorbet: A frozen product, similar to sherbet. Designed to be a palate cleanser. Served just prior to the entree. It has a tart flavor, never sweet. It usually has a wine or champagne base.

Uniserve Property: A hotel property in which the convention services manager (CSM) handles all aspects of the event, including catering.

Welcome Cocktail: A drink served as an introductory gesture of welcome. Can refer to a single drink, or a reception where such drinks are served.

Welcome Reception: An opening event where welcome drinks and often food are served.

Well Brand: Also called *House brand*. The liquor name brands that the facility uses for food & beverage functions.

Working Lunch: Light meal for small discussion groups, without a break from working sessions.

APPENDIX

The following organizational charts are provided as a resource. In this hotel organizational chart model, the Food and Beverage and Event Management functions are in separate divisions.

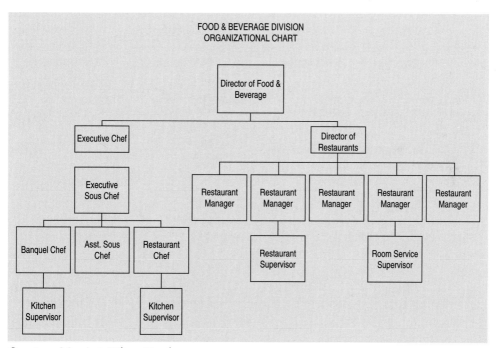

Courtesy: Marriott Hilton Head.

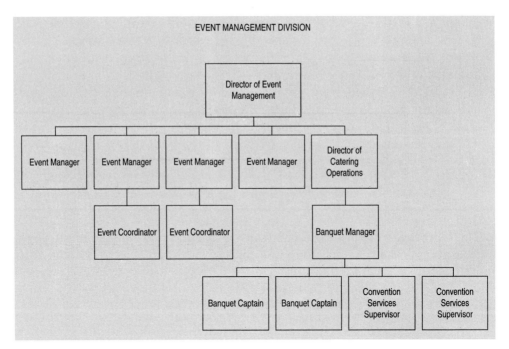

Courtesy: Marriott Hilton Head.

MEETING ROOM AND CONVENTION PLANNING

LEARNING OBJECTIVES

After studying this chapter, you will be able to discuss:

- The most common types of meeting room setups
- The manual and automated systems used by meeting facilities in blocking function space
- The audiovisual terms and terminology used for meetings and conventions
- Factors that convention service managers must consider to maximize function space assignments

INTRODUCTION

The convention sales department must work closely with the director of sales to ensure that the blocking and control of function space doesn't lose sight of the goal: maximizing revenue. In this chapter we will discuss the considerations to be made to effectively assign space. This chapter in particular has an extensive glossary from the Convention Industry Council (CIC)–APEX approved definitions list. Finally, we will discuss these terms and where they fit into the convention services meeting setup process.

THE FIRST STEP

The first contact between the convention services department and meeting planner will be between a few weeks or a few months after the event has been confirmed. This length of time will be determined by

- The size of the group and the function space needed
- The actual event date

For larger conventions, booked years in advance, contact will be minimal until approximately one year before the event. As the event approaches, the meeting planner will contact a hotel group coordinator about their guest room block needs. These areas are discussed in other chapters, but note that many properties have combined these functions to minimize frustration for the planner. Therefore, the hotel event contact assigned to this group must be completely knowledgeable, regardless of his or her title.

TYPES OF FUNCTION ROOMS

The function setup terminology has changed over the years as many more design options in furniture, lighting, and AV become standard. However, some of the most common styles and their names have not. The complete definitions from the CIC Glossary are listed at the end of this chapter.

Setup Styles

In the next sections, following each style description is the corresponding diagram with the common variations using standard hotel and convention industry terminology. These diagrams are not to scale and should be used only as a guideline. Keep in mind that room capacity and aisle sizes are regulated by local fire departments. This information is usually also listed on the Meeting room capacity guide provided in a group convention sales kit.

Figures 9.1 and 9.2 are examples of the room specifications and capacity sheets for a 100-room hotel with a 1,830 square foot (approximately) conference center.

The diagram in the bottom of Figure 9.1 shows the common table and chair setup styles.

The diagram in Figure 9.2 shows the actual dimensions of the meeting and function space, along with the room capacity chart on a two-sided brochure card.

Theater or Auditorium Style

These names are used interchangeably. This style requires only chairs, which are set up in rows. The chairs face the speaker or stage, typically in the front of the room. Theater style is used for general sessions for small or large groups, which require limited or no note-taking.

It is recommended that the first row of chairs be no less than six feet back from the stage or head table at the front of the room. The most popular setup uses a center aisle, like in a theater. However, dividing the room into three sections, with eight seats in the center row and less on the outsides is popular as well. Variations on this style include *senate*, *semicircular*, and *v-shaped*. Each

FIGURE 9.1

INN BY THE LAKE MEETING FACILITIES

SOUTH LAKE TAHOE

Meeting Facilities

INN BY THE LAKE Conference Center provides for a variety of meeting space, including the Sierra, Nevada and Lake View rooms. Convenient, full-service facilities for small to medium-sized groups. Detail focused staff, tastefully designed and fully equipped for relaxing, professional meetings.

Capacities

	Sierra	Nevada	Sierra Nevada	Lake View
Conference	20	30	54	36
Hollow Square	20	30	60	32
U-Shape	18	26	48	26
Classroom*	16/24	28/42	48/72	28/42
Theater	40	60	100	80
Banquet**	24/30	40/50	64/80	48/60

*   2 per table/3 per table
** 8 per table/10 per table

340 sq. ft. of lake view pre-function space for registration and break service. Full service business center, professional catering and audio-visual equipment are available.

Meeting Room Set-ups

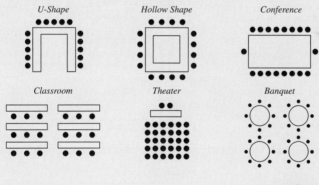

U-Shape   Hollow Shape   Conference

Classroom   Theater   Banquet

VANSAN
HOTELS RESORTS

LEXINGTON
SERVICES
A subsidiary of The Panel Company

3300 Lake Tahoe Boulevard • South Lake Tahoe, California 96150 (530) 542-0330 • FAX (530) 541-6596
E-Mail: info@innbythelake.com   Web Site: www.innbythelake.com

Courtesy: Inn by the Lake.

FIGURE 9.2

INN BY THE LAKE MEETING SPACE DIMENSIONS

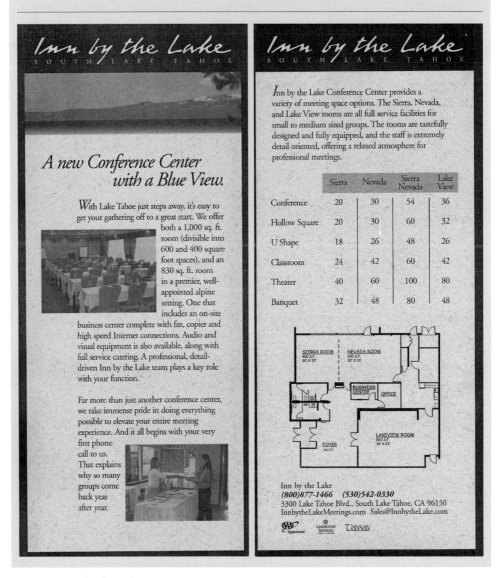

Courtesy: Inn by the Lake.

is used to increase the viewing area for attendees. As with each setup presented here, the CSM will know each room in the facility best. Inexperienced meeting planners therefore should rely on their expertise.

One big drawback of theater style is the difficulty for attendees in the rear rows to see the front stage area. If possible, the stage or head table area (used for seated speakers or a panel) should be put on risers to increase their visibility. A multimedia presentation format, using large screens and power point, is recommended for large groups in most styles of setup.

The distinguishing factor from theater style is the addition of tables. These are usually used for longer meetings or training sessions that require extensive writing or note-taking.

Setup Styles with Tables

Schoolroom or classroom: These names are used interchangeably. This style requires narrow tables, known as *classroom* tables, either six or eight feet in length, to be set up with chairs in rows that are facing the front of the room or stage. It is equally as common a style as the theater setup, but needed only for longer sessions that require note-taking. This setup is the standard for training meetings, but a big drawback is the amount of space needed. Additional table setups possible for this style include *perpendicular* or *V-shaped*.

Conference style: Also referred to as *board of directors*. This setup is so popular with smaller groups (10–20 people) that many forward-thinking hotels now have a permanent meeting room space outfitted with a rectangular "boardroom" table and comfortable seating. Hotels need function space to be flexible, so rectangular classroom or banquet tables are substituted when a permanent table isn't available.

U-shape or horseshoe: When a face-to-face design is needed for small groups, the U-shape is a common solution. It is also known as a horseshoe, because of its shape. If the group is large, an *inside and outside U-shape* may be recommended. In general the U-shape is well suited for board meetings with AV presentations.

Hollow square and hollow circular: This is similar to the U-shape, except the open end is closed. This style is a good choice when a head table area isn't necessary. This setup historically has been used with multiple monitors/VCRs/DVDs/CDs set up inside the hollow for comfortable viewing from all seats.

Figure 9.3 shows a 20,000+ convention center facility diagram with specific room capacities.

Seat Distance

The distance between each seat for each style mentioned in this section varies. Planners can obtain the complete function room equipment list, which includes table sizes, dimensions, and types from the CSM. They will know best how to set up each room to achieve the goal of comfort desired for each attendee. The recommended guideline is 24 to 36 inches of space per attendee between chairs. Function room size, layout, and any restrictions that impact the line of sight must be considered.

Table Spacing and Placement

Spacing guidelines are also contained in the complete function room equipment list. Additionally, the function layout in their collateral material will

FIGURE 9.3
HARVEYS CONVENTION CENTER

CONVENTION CENTER

OUR 20,000 SQUARE-FOOT CONVENTION CENTER IS SPECIFICALLY DESIGNED TO ALLOW A COMPLETE SPECTRUM OF ROOM LAYOUT AND CAPACITY OPTIONS. HIGH-SPEED ELEVATORS AND ESCALATORS OFFER EASY ACCESS FROM THE HOTEL LOBBY AND GUEST ROOMS TO OUR CONVENTION CENTER. WHETHER YOUR MEETING REQUIRES A SPACIOUS AND ELEGANT BALLROOM OR THE INTIMACY OF ONE OF OUR HANDSOME BOARDROOMS, HARVEYS LAKE TAHOE WILL PROVIDE YOU WITH FRIENDLY, PERSONALIZED SERVICE. OUR EXPERT CONVENTION SERVICES AND CATERING TEAM WILL ANTICIPATE YOUR EVERY NEED TO GUARANTEE YOUR COMPLETE SATISFACTION. FOR YOUR ADDED CONVENIENCE, OUR PROFESSIONALLY STAFFED BUSINESS CENTER OFFERS:

- PHOTOCOPY & FAX SERVICES
- E-MAIL & INTERNET KIOSKS
- SECRETARIAL SUPPORT
- COMPUTER EQUIPMENT & PRINTER ACCESS
- OFFICE SUPPLIES
- SHIPPING & RECEIVING ASSISTANCE

HARVEYS.

CONVENTION CENTER • THIRD LEVEL

ROOM	SQUARE FOOTAGE	ROOM SIZE	THEATER STYLE	CLASSROOM STYLE	RECEPTION	BANQUET
EMERALD BAY BALLROOM	9230	142 x 65	1000	620	1000	750
PRE-FUNCTION AREA	2666	86 x 31			300	
EMERALD BAY PROMENADE AREA	6210	138 x 45			600	
EMERALD BAY A OR B	2015	31 x 65	220	140	220	170
EMERALD BAY A AND B	4030	62 x 65	425	275	450	370
EMERALD BAY 1 + 2 + 3 A B	6630	102 x 65	700	440	675	550
EMERALD BAY 4 + 5 + 6 A B	6565	101 x 65	650	400	675	520
EMERALD BAY 1 + 2 + 3 A	4615	71 x 65	500	320	475	400
EMERALD BAY 4 + 5 + 6 B	4550	70 x 65	450	300	475	380
EMERALD BAY 1	570	30 x 19	55	35	50	30
EMERALD BAY 2	690	30 x 23	70	45	70	50
EMERALD BAY 3	600	30 x 20	60	40	60	40
EMERALD BAY 1 + 2	1260	30 x 42	135	80	125	90
EMERALD BAY 2 + 3	1290	30 x 43	135	80	125	90
EMERALD BAY 1 + 2 + 3	1860	30 x 62	200	125	180	150
EMERALD BAY 4	580	29 x 20	50	35	55	30
EMERALD BAY 5	670	29 x 23	60	40	65	40
EMERALD BAY 6	580	29 x 20	50	30	45	30
EMERALD BAY 4 + 5	1250	29 x 43	120	70	100	80
EMERALD BAY 5 + 6	1250	29 x 43	120	70	100	80
EMERALD BAY 4 + 5 + 6	1830	29 x 63	175	100	180	130
EXECUTIVE BOARDROOM	770	24 x 32	20 FIXED SEATS CONFERENCE STYLE			
TAHOE ROOM	340	12 x 28	12 FIXED SEATS CONFERENCE STYLE			
COMSTOCK ROOM	360	18 x 20	30	20	40	30

Courtesy: Harveys, Stateline, NV.

include diagrams that show examples. Planners also should check on diagrams available through the sales or catering department software used by that property. The recommended guideline is nine feet from the center of one table to the next one. Keep in mind that the size of the table will vary, based on what the hotel uses; the two sizes most commonly used are described next.

Banquet Setup Styles

Food and beverage functions can require tables, or chairs, or both, depending on the type of event being held by the planner. As with meeting functions, the CSM will know the best setup design for the particular room being used for each function. Commonly used setups include the following:

Banquet round tables: These come in two sizes, with the smaller one comfortably seating eight and the larger up to 10 people. They are used for sit-down or buffet dinners. Note: Round tables are also commonly used for meetings that are known as Round Table meetings. After the meeting, these tables can remain in the room and be used for a food function. This is an efficient way to maximize room use for small groups who need to control their meeting room rental costs. Examples of a banquet round table layout are provided in Figure 9.5, as part of a floor plan.

Buffet tables: These are used most commonly for the buffet food lines or displays. A popular variation is a circular buffet table setup. This can be achieved by using banquet rounds or serpentine tables shaped like a big S.

FUNCTION ROOM ASSIGNMENTS

The CSM or event manager is in charge of function room assignments. The exact meeting room location (name) usually is not assigned until a few months prior to arrival or later, depending on the size of the group. Some of the criteria to be considered include:

- Size and capacity under required room setup (fire code compliant)
- Type of event/presentation style
- Room location with regard to traffic
- Room location with regard to who's next door
- Move-in and move-out dates of other groups

It is important for the event or hotel CSM to be knowledgeable in audiovisual terminology and requirements. This is true regardless of whether the AV equipment is owned by the facility or an outside AV services company is used. Almost all meetings today require some AV equipment, so it is important to understand the different types available, the different sources that supply it, and what to charge for equipment. This section presents the central issues in this crucial aspect of meeting management.

Audiovisual Requirements and Equipment

When a new hotel is being built, management is faced with a large decision:

Either to purchase AV equipment and hire staff to manage and service that department, or to select an outside vendor AV company from whom they will order the equipment.

The final decision will vary, depending on the type of facility: conference center, resort destination, or convention hotel. Other issues to consider are the standard policies of that hotel or conference center chain and their philosophy and commitment to servicing groups.

Other considerations are:

- Cost of equipment. Will the use justify the purchase of many different items?
- Is there adequate, secured storage in the hotel?
- What will be the labor cost to staff an in-house AV department?
- Is there a reliable local AV vendor to contract with?
- What method are your competitors using?
- What discounts or commissions are part of the AV contract or associated costs?

One convention services manager in Lake Tahoe, Nevada, had this to say about finally deciding to go in-house: "We are in a very isolated area, so each time I need to order a single piece of equipment due to a group change, the service charge is outrageous. The AV company's office is in Reno, 35 miles away, and the weather can be a factor on equipment delivery nine months out of the year."

In evaluating whether to use an outside AV company, isolated destination resorts also have to consider "minimum orders" set by firms to cover their own costs. All properties must forecast projections for tentative/definite group meetings and future AV equipment needs.

Changing Technology

Not so long ago, AV was meant to supplement and support the actual presentation. The capabilities of the latest AV multimedia equipment now have become the news themselves. Most attendees now either bring their laptops along during the meeting or demand a "cyber computer bank" so they can quickly check their e-mail during meeting breaks.

With that in mind, the following will provide an overview of the standard AV equipment used by hotels for meeting. A list of useful Web sites is provided at the end of this chapter for additional information on the use of meeting technology. In addition to learning what is available, some sources provide a link to a Web site for a free CD demo disk so you can evaluate the technology and decide if it's right for you.

Teleconferencing

Teleconferencing first gained interest in the 1980s, but lost popularity when it was much too expensive for meeting use. As the price has been lowered through improved technology, so has its acceptance increased. The events of 9/11 and subsequent increased worldwide travel security and delays have made "virtual meetings" and the use of teleconferencing much more attractive. The objective to have a meeting available in different areas through the use of telephone linkages with computer and AV equipment is now pursued quite extensively. For example, the AV equipment in this case could be a mini camera or a mini webcam placed on the computer PC with the picture or image projected to other meeting attendees simultaneously around the world.

Teleconferencing has evolved into videoconferencing as that technology has become more feasible. Academic users are now the emerging leader in some of these applications. College students now regularly complete *some* of their required courses online without ever seeing the teacher. Video lectures, discussions, and chats done in live time enhance the learning experience.

Here is a web page from a company that provides a wide variety of video and satellite conferencing services.

INSIDERS' TIP

Many colleges and universities worldwide book meeting groups during the summer break. Most have very reasonable meeting and meal packages with access to this technology in an educational retreat atmosphere. Better yet, a number of these school offer degrees in Hotel or Convention Management, so they know the importance of properly servicing meeting groups! Most schools with meeting facilities belong to a national organization. Check the following resources Web site for more information: www.acced-i.org (Association of Collegiate Conference and Events Directors International).

To use the present teleconferencing or videoconferencing technology in your upcoming meeting, ask the CSM or event manager. He or she most likely has handled your type of equipment needs before. The equipment description and pricing schedule, whether in-house or through an outside AV contractor, will be your best resource. Figure 9.4 shows a hotel AV equipment list. In this example, *Show Time Audio Visual Equipment* provides the actual equipment to meeting groups at the hotel.

Types of Audiovisual Equipment

Screens

Note: Check on the ceiling setup of the room to be used onsite. Review the banquet chart for sizing.

FIGURE 9.4

CAL-NEVA RESORT AV INFORMATION

SHOW TIME

AUDIO VISUAL EQUIPMENT

Show and tell. Snappy, upbeat, high tech. Make your point with a dramatic visual. Big impact. Crisp sound. Slides, videos, color. Whatever equipment you need to make your presentation a resounding success, we can supply it.

The show must go on and our Sales Executives will see to it that it goes on with style and ease and plaudits for you.

SOUND EQUIPMENT

6 Channel Microphone Mixer	$40
12 Channel Microphone Mixer	$50
8 Channel Mixer/Amp	$85
12 Channel Mixer/Amp	$175
Press Patch	$50

LECTERNS

Table Lectern	$30
Floor Podium	$30
Table Lectern w/Microphone	$65
Floor Podium w/Microphone	$65

MICROPHONES

Shure Podium, Table, Floor Microphone	$25
Shure Lavalier Microphone	$25
UHF Wireless Hand Held Microphone	$100
Shure SM99 Podium Microphone	$55

CD & TAPE PLAYERS

5 Disc CD Player	$60
Marantz 3 Head Cassette Recorder/Player	$30
Cassette/Sync Recorder	$50

DATA PROJECTORS

Color S-VGA LCD Projector	$450
Color S-VGA DLP Projector	$550
+Sony 1270Q Projector	$800
+Sony 127Q Projector	$1,000
Color LCD Overhead Panel (SVGA)	$550
Color LCD Overhead Panel (VGA)	$300

+ Requires Professional Operator

VIDEO EQUIPMENT

1/2" VHS Videocassette Recorder	$65
27" Monitor w/VHS VCR & Cart	$175
LCD Video Projector w/VCR, Cart, & 6' Screen	$350
1/2" VHS Videocassette Recorder	$65
3/4" Sony Videocassette Recorder	$75

EASELS

Tripod Easel	$10
Flipchart w/Easel	$25
White Bond Pad	$10

SPEAKERS

Anchor Liberty Self-Powered Speaker w/Stand	$50
Anchor Liberty Extension Speaker w/Stand	$30
Stereo Headphones	$20
2 Speaker Sound System	$80

PRESENTATION ACCESSORIES

Electric Pointer	$25
Laser Pointer	$50
3'x4' White Board w/Markers	$35
AC Power Strips	$10
AC Extension Cords	$5
Black 3" Duct Tape	$15
Masking Tape	$5

OVERHEAD PROJECTORS

Overhead Projector w/Stand	$40
4000 Lumen Overhead Projector w/Stand	$65
6000 Lumen Overhead Projector w/Stand	$125
Xenon Overhead Projector w/Stand	$165

SLIDE PROJECTORS

Slide Projector w/EXW Lamp & Stand	$45
Brite Lite Projector w/Stand	$70
Xenon Slide Projector w/Stand	$190
Wireless Remote Control	$25

PROJECTION SCREENS

6' Tripod Screen w/Skirt	$20
8'x8' Fast Fold Screen	$40
12'x12' Fast Fold Screen	$70
9'x12' Fast Fold Screen	$65
8'x8' Dress Kit	$40
12'x12' Dress Kit	$65
9'x9' Dress Kit	$60
10.5'x14' Dress Kit	$80

This is a partial equipment list only; please call for further details and pricing on specific equipment you may require.

Prices are subject to change.

CAL•NEVA
RESORT
L A K E   T A H O E

800-225-6382

Courtesy: Cal-Neva Resort.

Wall or ceiling screens: Designed to be hung from hooks or lines mounted on the wall or ceiling.

Tripod screens: Mounted permanently on a tripod stand so they are portable; ideal for smaller meeting rooms.

Screen Fabrics

- Silver metallic and lenticular surfaces offer maximum brilliance and wide-angle consistency but are more expensive than other types.
- Matte-surface screens offer consistent brilliance from a wider angle.
- Glass-beaded screens offer greater brilliance.

Setup Guidelines

- **Five-feet principle:** Bottom of the screen must be a minimum of five feet off the floor.
- **One-by-six principle:** No one should be seated closer than one times the screen's width and no farther than six times the screen's width.

Types of Projection

Rear screen projection: The projector is set behind a special translucent screen. All projection equipment is hidden from the audience, causing a more dramatic presentation. The speaker is able to be near the screen and cords are hidden and taped. This has become the standard. A technician should be available in case of malfunctions. Projectors must be positioned correctly.

Standard projection: The use of any standard screen placed in front of the projector (including the following projectors).

Projectors

Overhead projector: This industry workhorse is still requested but is being rapidly replaced by the LCD (liquid crystal display; considered an overhead projector). It can be mounted on the ceiling or on a projection table and used with a laptop or PC, primarily to project Power Point slides and Web presentations.

Opaque projector: This one reflects an image from paper material. It must be used from the rear of a dark room and must be cooled with a loud motor.

Slide projector: 35 mm carousel, mounted in standard frames that measure two inches square. The 35 mm slide is the industry standard. Wireless remote control devices or laser pointers are now commonly used.

Note: Keep spare lamps for all projectors, fuses, and extension cords on hand. Wireless remote control devices or laser pointer are also now commonly used.

Videotape VCR projectors: These projectors are used with a TV monitor to view VHS video. Most previous forms (Beta) are obsolete.

DVD players: Available at most hotels with meeting facilities. (VHS tapes are no longer being made.) Players will become standard when film production facilities convert all former VHS tapes to this medium. Recordable DVDs have a much sharper picture than a videotape, which also wears out as it passes over the metal play heads. DVDs are touched only by a beam of light and should remain in good condition even after you play them thousands of times.

Projector Stands

The safe lock and the rolling cart are the most common types of stands. They come in folding or rigid types, with or without wheels. Projector stands may need shelves to accommodate LCD projectors, VCR and monitors, and other AV equipment.

Note: Special lenses may have to be used for long projection distances.

Sound Systems

Most hotels own a supply of microphones, stands, amplifiers, and speakers. Speakers should be distributed so that there are no "dead spots." They should be placed near the screen for movies, slides, and videos.

Microphones

There are many types of microphones in use today. Most are standard and available from AV departments. Therefore, we will present them by name and definition. The following is a list of commonly used microphones and definitions, from the CIC glossary.

Microphone, portable: Operating on its own power source. Often used to pass through an audience for questions.

Microphone, cardioid: Pronounced "car-dee-oid." A microphone with a polar pattern that is heart-shaped. Cardioid microphones decrease gradually in sensitivity as they are rotated away from the source of sound they are aimed at.

Microphone, cordless: Portable microphone operating on its own power source. Often used to pass through an audience for questions.

Microphone, lavaliere: A wired or wireless microphone that hooks around the neck or is clipped to clothing. Sometimes called a *necklace*, *lapel*, or *pendant* microphone.

Microphone, omnidirectional: Microphone that picks up sound from all directions.

Microphone, roving: A small microphone, with or without a wire, that can be moved easily through an audience for questions or comments.

Microphone, stationary or standing: Microphone mounted on an adjustable floor stand and intended to remain in the same location throughout a presentation. Also called *floor* microphone.

Microphone, table: Microphone on a short stand placed on a table for seated speakers.

Lighting

The existing capabilities of the lighting system must be determined. Today, most hotel meeting rooms have individual light controls with dimmer switches. The master control box often is located in the first section of the ballroom. Additional lighting requirements should be handled by a specialist, if available. Rooms with permanent stages should be equipped with permanent lighting.

Note: Union regulations require the use of an operator for certain kinds of lighting.

Audiovisual Aids

Flipcharts and easels should be readily available, with pads of paper, chalkboards, or whiteboards.

Present and Future Needs

Demand among planners is increasing for simultaneous interpretation, multimedia presentations, dissolve units, and chalkboards. As previously mentioned, it is advisable to check with the CSM on-site to determine what is available.

MEETING ROOM DESIGN AND SPECIFICATIONS

All facilities with group meeting space have developed collateral materials that include diagrams of all available function and/or meeting exhibit space, including some guest rooms and suites that have been designated for this purpose. To secure groups that may need multiple breakout rooms at the same time, the property may have to commit every available space. The materials sent out by the group or convention sales department will include brochures and a sales kit or convention planning kit with the following:

- Master sheet listing room capacities for common types of function setup
- Diagrams of each room with dimensions
- Meeting room schematics
- CAD (computer-assisted design)

COMPUTER TECHNOLOGY IMPROVEMENTS

As more planners embraced the time-saving benefits of planning meetings, more Windows-based software programs became available. Most of these event-planning software packages include room floor plans with diagrams customized by the user. A wide variety of CAD driver features are included in the standard package as well. As technology has improved, the main objective,

FIGURE 9.5
CCC SPRING GALA FLOOR PLAN

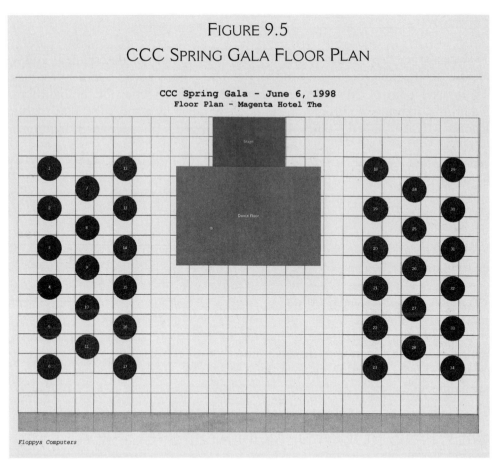

CCC Spring Gala - June 6, 1998
Floor Plan - Magenta Hotel The

Floppys Computers

Courtesy: Event Planner Plus.

making function room planning even easier, is continually evolving. Some now interface with the leading sales and catering software programs such as Delphi and Miracle. Figure 9.5 shows some examples of floor plans and directions for assigning seating from Event Planner Plus, a software program.

The use of event planning software for budgeting, program planning, registration, and other meeting planning applications is discussed in other chapters.

SUMMARY

Technological advancements impact the meeting industry on an almost daily basis. One of the latest trends (discussed in Chapter 12) is to "certify" meeting facilities. Industry facility leaders see this as an effective way to distinguish your meeting space.

The following enhancements are appearing in the newest renovated facilities and may become standard as production costs decrease due to wider availability:

- Open-structured ceilings
- Better soundproofing between ballroom airwalls and sections

FIGURE 9.5

CCC SPRING GALA FLOOR PLAN—*Continued*

On Your Own

The Floor Plan sub-tab allows you to create a diagram of the room and specify the location of tables, entertainers, and other elements for your event. You can then print the floor plan diagram using the Reports tab. A sample floor plan is provided with this event, but you may want to add and renumber the new tables.

Using Auto Seating

Event Planner Plus provides an Auto Seating feature that makes seating arrangements for you automatically based on information you have specified about the event facility and guests.

To run Auto-Seating:

1. **Click the Table Assignments sub-tab.**

   The Table Assignments sub-tab opens.

2. **Run Auto Seating to have Event Planner Plus automatically make seating assignments as shown below.**

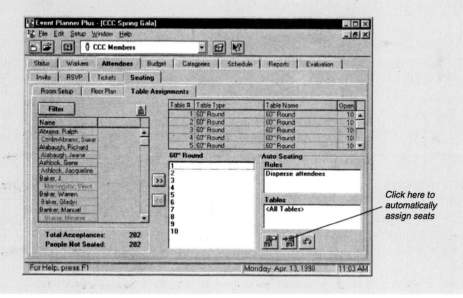

- Built-in plasma screens
- Concealed control panels for presentation equipment
- Increased computer banks in proximity to meeting facilities
- Virtual meeting or teleconferencing capability standardized

Function room charges vary by property and according to the amount of business the group brings, and can be used to compensate for discounted guestroom rates. They maintain a firm list of rates.

Many properties have sliding scales based on guest room pickup. There may be a charge for function rooms if guest room revenue does not cover setup, cleanup, and teardown costs. Also, release dates should be set in a letter of agreement or contract.

REVIEW QUESTIONS

1. List and describe the common types of meeting and function room setups.
2. List and describe at least two types of projectors used for meetings. What types of screens are used with each type listed?
3. List at least two ways computer technology has changed the projection systems.
4. What AV and meeting services are typically standard in conference centers but may not be available in hotels or resort meeting rooms?
5. List and describe the more common types of sound and lighting systems used in meeting rooms.
6. Discuss the key differences between manual and automated systems used in blocking function space.
7. List and describe the factors a convention service manager must consider in assigning function space.

ADDITIONAL RESOURCES AND WEB SITES

Note: Internet Web sites are current at publication, but are subject to change.

www.projection.com	Projection Presentation Technology
www.meetingmatrix.com	Meeting Planning Software
www.pcma.org	Professional Convention Management Association

Note: PCMA has formed a partnership with Meeting Matrix software.

www.presentations.com	Presentations Inc.
www.astd.org	American Society of Training and Development
www.avservices.com	Audio Visual Services
www.certainsoftware.com	Meeting Planning software
www.timesaversoftware.com	Event Sketch

REFERENCE

Jedrziewski, D. (1991) *The Complete Guide for the Meeting Planner*, Cincinnati: SouthWestern.

GLOSSARY

Auditorium Setup: Seating arrangement where chairs are arranged in rows facing head table, stage, or speaker. Variations are semicircular and V-shaped. Also called *theater* setup.

Classroom Setup: Seating arrangement in which rows of tables with chairs face the front of a room and each person has a space for writing. Also called *schoolroom* setup.

Classroom Table: Rectangular table, often narrower than regular tables and 30-inches high. Can be 6- or 8-feet long and 18- or 24-inches wide.

Schoolroom Perpendicular Setup: Variation of schoolroom setup in which tables are perpendicular to the head table, and chairs are placed on both sides of the tables.

Schoolroom V Setup: Seating arrangement where rows of tables and/or chairs are slanted in a V-shape facing a head table, stage, or speaker. Sometimes called *Chevron* setup.

Lectern: A stand on which a speaker may rest notes or books. May be "standing," which rests on the floor, or "table-top," which is placed on a table. Often confused with *podium*.

10

ON-SITE EVENT PLANNING: SERVICING THE EVENT

LEARNING OBJECTIVES

After studying this chapter, you will be able to discuss:

- The convention and event billing process standards
- The timelines involved in the planning through billing process
- The impact of computer technology on the billing process
- The forms, purpose, and agenda for the "pre-con"
- The "post-con" evaluation criteria and terms

INTRODUCTION

After reviewing the hotel's accounting department established policies, the scheduled group most likely has submitted the necessary documents for direct billing or credit approval months in advance. In this chapter, we discuss the use of the group master account, incidentals, extension of guest credit, suggested payment schedule, and gratuities. For a hotel facility to improve its marketing and servicing of conventions, it is important that each function is reviewed after it is held. This chapter discusses the importance of servicing the group during the events and the subsequent follow-up evaluation process.

Unlike the contractual rooms and function areas previously negotiated, the level of service provided during the event is intangible and subjective. However hard it is to measure, poor or inadequate service can be a determinant in how successful the sales department is in the rebooking process. Often, this becomes the pivotal point at which a rebooking for this particular group can occur.

Additionally, we will examine the forms and departmental procedures that correlate with each of these steps, from preconvention, to execution, to the postconvention evaluation. Before we begin, it is important to discuss computer technology and the tremendous improvements it has brought about in the billing process.

During the 1990s, many new Windows-based software programs were developed specifically for hospitality industry applications. Prior to that, DOS-based proprietary programs, developed by the hotel companies themselves, weren't considered user friendly. The new Windows-based applications were widely accepted throughout the hospitality industry relatively quickly by frontline employees who were mostly computer (Windows) literate. These programs allow charges from most hotel point-of-sale outlets to interface, and to be posted almost immediately to the guest folio at the front desk. This ensures accuracy of the total charges, and minimizes late posting charges, which streamlines the billing process for accounts receivable. This further allows accuracy of final charges during the postconvention evaluation.

As we learned in Chapter 7, contract negotiation has become an important skill for both buyer and seller to acquire. Now that the event has become *definite*—a term still used today—many details regarding billing arrangements need to be addressed by the convention services manager (CSM) or group sales coordinator.

Figure 10.1 is a checklist of areas for the planner to discuss with the facility service coordinator during the planning stage.

FIGURE 10.1
CHECKLIST

Topic:
√Discussed/Action:

Which events areas will the master account cover?	
How are individual charges to be handled? Will there be more than one master account?	
Name(s) of those authorized to sign?	
Department(s) Gratuities? Amount? Distribution method?	
Early arrivals/ late departures? Hotel Charge for these services	
Food &Beverage charges? Are there sponsored events?	
Audio Visual / related bills?	

ACCOUNTING AND BILLING PROCEDURES

The master account is established with the hotel accounting department to centralize billing for all related group and individual charges. The planner may also set up master accounts for other program segments. A list of persons authorized to sign on these accounts will also be set up at the front desk. This is called a *master account folio*. Posting will include all charges incurred by the delegates and paid by the named sponsoring organization. The charges to be posted by the account should be agreed upon in advance. Incidentals—individual expenses other than the guestroom charge and taxes—can also be billed to the master or to a guest and their individual folio. Some groups need to have split folios created. Essentially, the guest room charge for a double room is "split" in half when two guests wish to share the cost; this is popular with associations or SMERF groups.

Group Deposits

Group deposits may be required to secure some of the arrangements. Consideration commonly is given to factors such as creditworthiness or history of the group, which includes verification of payment of previous hotel charges. The preferred arrangement is for direct billing. If approved, the total typically is due in full approximately 30 days after the event. However, if credit cannot be extended, options are often available. Some hotels now offer a small discount to groups who pay 100 percent of their master account charges in less than 10 days after departure. The bill will list the discount as Net 10 percent, with the agreed upon discount amount or percentage.

Note: Hotels are now imposing interest charges on any unpaid balances if not paid within the agreed-upon net date.

GRATUITIES FOR HOTEL SERVICE EMPLOYEES STAFF

This topic has been the subject of many discussions and industry articles. Opinions and practices on tipping vary greatly by types of planners and world geography. In some regions of the world, this practice is largely ignored, partly due to the misconception that it is included automatically in the bill. Convention research shows that meetings are increasingly an international event. Therefore, the nationality, culture, and tradition of the meeting planner impact the amount of gratuity and the recipients who will receive it, or if it is even offered.

Experienced convention service managers are aware that some hourly service positions are still dependent on a gratuity, whereas others will have an automatic service charge (SC) added to the bill. The CSM should be knowledgeable of the hotel policies, while being prepared to provide the following guidelines or make recommendations on gratuity when requested to do so:

- Determine if an automatic service charge has already been added to the bill. (this is sometimes called a "blanket" charge). This is common for groups in the food/beverage, restaurant, and banquet areas. In cities where the restaurant and hotel workers are unionized, their contract stipulates the required service charge percentage. A portion of this SC usually is given to the banquet captains or similar supervisory staff in this department as well. Be aware that many experienced planners routinely ask for a written copy of the hotel's gratuity distribution policy.
- The group menus usually will list the SC/gratuity charges, currently between 17 and 21 percent. Determine which personnel will receive a gratuity from this, as well as any additional automatic charges as shown in the preceding example.
- Discretionary tipping: The postconvention meeting is the ideal opportunity for the CSM to discuss and identify exceptional staff whom the planner may not remember by name but would like to give an additional gratuity. The planner may then approve an amount to bill the master account for the CSM to distribute in envelopes.

Guidelines for tipping hourly staff, which varies by city or destination, are as follows:

Guest room cleaners (maids) two nights or less: $5 to $10 (typically left in your guestroom in an envelope)
Food servers: 15% of the check, or more for exceptional service
Bellperson: $1 per bag
Doorperson (hailing a cab, etc.): $1
Spa/recreational facilities service providers: 10 to 20 percent of fee for service provided.

Tips also may be given to food service personnel who do an extraordinary job; telephone operators, if there was heavy usage; front desk workers, if there was heavy check-in/out; chef, if the food is especially good; golf or tennis pros, if tournament or lessons are held.

Keep in mind that the meeting planner may elect to provide a gratuity to additional staff not mentioned here. Often they will attempt to distribute the cash themselves during the last day of the event.

BILLING AND GRATUITY GUIDELINES FOR CORPORATE AND NONASSOCIATION GROUPS

When it comes to the corporate meetings market and SMERFs (see Chapters 3 and 4), gratuities are handled quite differently from associations. The corporation or company holding the event most likely will pay for group functions and also the guest room charges of all attendees. Additionally, the corporation may pay incidental charges such as phone or room service.

The checklist at the beginning of this chapter is your best guideline. The final instructions from the meeting planner will be part of the group resume prepared by the CSM and discussed in great detail during the preconvention meeting shortly before the group's arrival. The front office manager should have a copy of the resume available at the front desk throughout the stay. This is designed to facilitate communication between the staff and planner and minimize confusion on master account charge postings.

POSTCONVENTION REVIEW

The purpose of a review is to evaluate performance and service during the event. Managers of all key departments responsible for a successful outcome should attend. It is held, ideally, at the conclusion of the event, after the main group departure (checkout). The primary meeting planner may have his or her on-site planner attend as well. The main objectives of the postconvention review are as follows.

Compare projected versus actual guestroom and function:
- Guest room pickup: number and type (Was the room block commitment met? Will there be meeting room charges due to attrition?)
- Guest room pickup at other hotels (whether a room block was contracted or not)
- No-shows and overbooking
- Early and late departures (many hotels now charge a penalty for this)
- Compare figures with those from past group history
- Function attendance (final food/beverage charges versus guaranteed amounts)

Review of general hotel service and specific departments utilized:
- Room service, restaurants, resort amenities, recreation (golf, recreational facilities), front desk clerks
- Responsiveness of CSM and support staff to changes throughout event
- Review of outside or ancillary vendors or off-site facilities; services utilized
- Reconcile charges, attendance, and level of service provided (DMC destination management company or audiovisual charges, etc.)

PRECONVENTION MEETING

Today most hotels hold a "pre-con" meeting at the property with all key department heads and the client or meeting planner in attendance. Typically held immediately prior to the beginning of the group's arrival, it is arguably the best way to ensure a successful event!

When possible, the general manager should attend preconvention meetings for groups that will significantly impact the properties' operation. The client will appreciate this type of "executive level" support. Even if the group is small in size, perhaps under 50 guest rooms per night or with little meeting space, they can still bring substantial revenue to the facility.

The CIC Apex glossary of definitions describes the pre-con agenda as "focusing on reviewing the purpose and details of the event and making final adjustments as needed." The CSM will present the final document.

The title of the document will vary, but the contents are standardized throughout the industry. Whether called a resume, a prospectus, or a specification guide, it provides a comprehensive overview of the entire program. Following the cover overview will be a function sheet for each event the group planner and CSM have finalized. With the meeting planner in attendance, questions from both sides—facility and client—can be addressed and acted upon as needed. Figure 10.2 shows sections of a planned program from a preconvention meeting group resume.

FIGURE 10.2
PROGRAM OF EVENTS FOR BOOKING NUMBER

PROGRAM OF EVENTS
For Booking Number: 1107895 s
CAP CURE
1250 4TH
SUITE 360
SANTA MONICA, CA 90401 US
(310) 458-2873 Fax: (310)458-8074

Meeting Name	Arrival Date	Departure Date	Contact Name	SLS Manager	CS Manager	CA Manager
ANNUAL SCIENTIFIC RETREAT	10/11/99	10/18/99	CYNDI MISKO	KRISTY OLK	UNKNOWN UNKNOWN	UNKNOWN UNKNOWN

Event Name	Event Type	Event Time	Attendance	Setup	Room
Event Date: Saturday, 10/16/99					
INFORMATION REGISTRATION DESX	OTHER	06:30 am-04:00 pm	2	OTHER	LAKESIDE LOBBY
CEO MEETING	MEETNG	08:00 am-06:00 pm	40	SCHOOL RM	ALDER AB
LUNCH	LUNCH	12:00 pm-02:00 pm	350	BANQUET	LAKESIDE COTTAGE GREEN
LUNCH DACKUP	LUNCH	12:00 pm-02:00 pm		BANQUET	BALLROOM
RECEPTION DINNER	DINNER	06:00 pm-12:00 pm	200	BANQUET	REGENCY CATERERS 1
DINNER BACK-UP	DINNER	06:00 am-12:00 pm		BANQUET	BALLROOM
Event Date: Sunday, 10/17/99					
BREANFAST	BREAKFAST	06:15 am-08:00 am	200	BANQUET	LONE EAGLE REST/PRIVATE ROOM
OFFICE	OFFICE	07:00 am-01:00 pm		OTHER	SPORTS SHOP

Number of Events: 44

FIGURE 10.2

PROGRAM OF EVENTS FOR BOOKING NUMBER—*Continued*

Event Name	Event Type	Event Time	Attendance	Setup	Room
Event Date: Thursday, 10/14/99					
INFORMATION REGISTRATION DESK	OTHER	06:00 am-11:59 pm	2	OTHER	LAKESIDE LOBBY
MEETING	MEETING	06:30 am-10:00 pm	350	SCHOOL RM	LAKESIDE BALlROOM
REGISTRATION	REGISTRATION	09:00 am-01:30 pm	2	OTHER	UPPER LOBBY 1
SURVIVOR WEETING	MEETING	10:00 am-12:00 pm	35	SCHOOL RM	DONNER
LUNCH	LUNCH	12:00 pm-01:00 pm	50	BANQUET	BEACH BARDEQUE
BACK UP LUNCH	LUNCH	12:00 pm-01:00 pm		BANQUET	CIAO NENCIAO MEIN LOUNGE
BACK UP DINNER	DINNER	06:00 pm-10:00 pm		BANQUET	BALLROOM
WELCOME DINNER	DINNER	06:00 pm-10:00 pm	350	BANQUET	LAKESIDE COTTAGE GREEN
ORACLE MEETING	MEETING	08:00 pm-10:00 pm	25	CONFERENCE	TAMARACK A
Event Date: Friday, 10/15/99					
OFFICE	OFFICE	06:00 am-12:00 am		OTHER	SPORTS SHOP
BREAKFAST	BREAKFAST	06:00 am-09:00 am		OTHER	LONE EAGLE GREAT ROOM
BREAKFAST	BREAKFAST	06:00 am-09:00 am	350	OTHER	LONE EAGLE REST/PRIVATE ROOM
MEETING	MEETING	08:30 am-10:00 pm	350	SCHOOL RM	LAKESIDE BALLROOM

BILLING INFORMATION

In order to set up a Master Account the Direct Billing Request Form must be received (4) weeks prior to the event.

CHARGES	MASTER ACCOUNT NUMBERS			
	22527			
All charges for guests	☐	☐	☐	☐
Room & Tax only, incidentals on own	X	☐	☐	☐
Incidentals guaranteed for these guests	☐	☐	☐	☐
See Accommodations & Special request list	X	☐	☐	☐
Food & Beverage functions as indicated	X	☐	☐	☐
Audio Visual Charges	X	☐	☐	☐
Meeting Room Rental	☐	☐	☐	☐
Transportation	X	☐	☐	☐
Telephone Charges	X	☐	☐	☐
Business Center	X	☐	☐	☐
Porterage		☐	☐	☐
Amenities	X	☐	☐	☐
Engineering / Electrical Charges	X	☐	☐	☐
Maid Gratuities	X	☐	☐	☐

Authorized Signatures:

FIGURE 10.2

PROGRAM OF EVENTS FOR BOOKING NUMBER—*Continued*

Tax-Exempt: **N/A**

COMMISSION INFORMATION

Terms: N/A
Payable: N/A

Special Billing Instructions/
Additional Information:

SEND BILL TO:

VIP's Compliuentary Accommodations & Staff Special Requests

Name/ Title	VIP Code	Accomo- dations	Check-in Date	Check-out Date	Billing	Rate	Amenities/ Comments
	III	1004	10.9.99	10.12.99	A	SHARE WITH	SWEATSHIRT (2) 6PKS BOTTLED WATERS (REFRESHED DAILY) (6) PK SIERRA NEVADA PALE ALE
	III	1004	10.9.99	10.19.99	A	SHARE WITH	SWEATSHIRT
	III	1001/1002	10.9.99	10.19.99	A	$395.00	SWEATSHIRT PICNIC BASKET
	III	266/267	10.13.99	10.17.99	A	$395.00	PICNIC BASKET BOTTLED WATERS REFRESHED DAILY

Courtesy: Hyatt Lake Tahoe.

THE BANQUET EVENT ORDER (BEO)

Also known as a function sheet, this becomes the document or guide from which all convention services employees will perform their tasks. Each function sheet has been previously approved and signed by the meeting planner. It is critical that every detail listed on the function sheet is correct and updated with final guarantees (number of people attending or amount ordered) discussed during the pre-con.

COMPUTERIZED GROUP SALES AND EVENT FORMS

Hotel sales and catering software programs such as Miracle and Adelphi are now widely adopted throughout the industry. These have the capability to copy or merge account information from those forms, which can then be "pasted" so that it doesn't need to be retyped for each function sheet. Many departmental form samples are provided in Chapter 8. Some larger hotel companies have developed their own software program for this application, known as "proprietary," which ideally should interface with front office systems. (Hotel computer systems are collectively known as Property Management systems.)

POSTEVENT FOLLOW-UP AND QUESTIONNAIRES

After the postconvention meeting, standard procedure is to mail a "thank you for your business" letter to the client and key meeting planners. It is worth the extra time it takes for the General Manager to write a personalized letter that should stress the importance of feedback and attach the questionnaire. Also included will be the final bill and support documentation, such as copies of banquet charges. Every effort should be made to encourage return of the completed questionnaires. Sometimes written recognition may be given to a well-deserving staff, who may not have received a gratuity. As stated in the beginning of this chapter, constructive and objective feedback facilitate the evaluation process. If the client's dissatisfaction is voiced in the questionnaire comments, further investigation of the disputed charges and the bill may be needed. Figure 10.3 is a sample questionnaire and postconvention evaluation form from the Reno, NV Hilton hotel.

GUEST GROUP ROOM BLOCK REPORTING

Hotels derive the majority of their revenue primarily from guest rooms. Additional large revenue sources includes food and beverage groups and all restaurant outlets. Recreational facilities and spa services also are good sources. So when the group room block doesn't fill, whether due to overbooking or booking outside the block, the hotel loses additional incremental revenue from these services that aren't utilized but must still have daily labor and operating costs.

FIGURE 10.3
SAMPLE QUESTIONNAIRE AND EVALUATION FORM

Sales Manager: _____
M&C Manager: _____
Catering Manager: _____

Group: _____
Dates: _____
Name: _____

	HIGH 1	2	3	4	LOW 5
CONVENTION SALES					
1) How satisfied were you with the overall performance of the hotel during your recent meeting or convention held at ?	○	○	○	○	○
2) How likely would you be to plan another meeting or convention at ?	○	○	○	○	○
3) How satisfied were you with the transition from the Sales Manager to the Meeting and Conventions Manager?	○	○	○	○	○
MEETINGS & CONVENTIONS					
1) Meeting & Convention Manager's overall knowledge of your meeting/convention requirements?	○	○	○	○	○
2) The review and confirmation of the arrangements?	○	○	○	○	○
3) The accuracy of the Convention resume?	○	○	○	○	○
4) With the amount of time you had to review the resume in advance of the event?	○	○	○	○	○
5) Your requests were responded to in a quick and efficient manner?	○	○	○	○	○
6) All correspondence was responded to promptly?	○	○	○	○	○
7) That all phone calls were returned promptly?	○	○	○	○	○
8) The Convention Service Manager's ability to resolve problems?	○	○	○	○	○
9) The level of communication between you and the Meeting & Convention Manager?	○	○	○	○	○
10) The Meeting & Convention Manager's visibility and accessibility during the meeting?	○	○	○	○	○
FACILITIES					
1) The condition and cleanliness of the overall meeting and banquet facilities?	○	○	○	○	○
2) The meeting/banquet rooms were set up according to your specifications?	○	○	○	○	○
3) The overall layout and functionality of the meeting/banquet rooms?	○	○	○	○	○
4) The meeting/banquet rooms were set-up on time?	○	○	○	○	○
CATERING & BANQUETS					
1) Catering Manager's overall knowledge of your food & beverage needs?	○	○	○	○	○
2) Timely review and confirmation of the BEOs?	○	○	○	○	○
3) The level of communication between you and the catering manager?	○	○	○	○	○
4) Requests were responded to in a quick and efficient manner?	○	○	○	○	○
5) That all correspondence was responded to promptly?	○	○	○	○	○
6) That all phone calls were returned promptly?	○	○	○	○	○
7) The Catering Manager's ability to resolve your problems?	○	○	○	○	○
8) The banquet rooms were set up according to your specifications?	○	○	○	○	○

Page 1

1/18/2005

Figure 10.3

Sample Questionnaire and Evaluation Form—*Continued*

Page -2-

	HIGH 1	2	3	4	LOW 5
9) The banquet rooms set-up on time?	◯	◯	◯	◯	◯
10) The quality of the banquet food & beverage selections?	◯	◯	◯	◯	◯
11) The banquet service level during meals?	◯	◯	◯	◯	◯

AUDIO VISUAL

	HIGH 1	2	3	4	LOW 5
1) A/V equipment was set-up according to your specifications?	◯	◯	◯	◯	◯
2) A/V equipment was working properly and according to your specifications?	◯	◯	◯	◯	◯
3) The request of your meetings attendees were responded to in a timely manner?	◯	◯	◯	◯	◯

OTHER HOTEL DEPARTMENTS

	HIGH 1	2	3	4	LOW 5
1) The type and condition of guest room accommodations?	◯	◯	◯	◯	◯
2) The cleanliness and servicing of guest rooms?	◯	◯	◯	◯	◯
3) The hotel's service and staff in general?	◯	◯	◯	◯	◯
4) The staff's responsiveness to your needs?	◯	◯	◯	◯	◯
5) Friendliness and helpfulness of our Front Service Staff such as Bellpersons, Guest Service Agents, etc.?	◯	◯	◯	◯	◯
6) The hotel's telephone and message service?	◯	◯	◯	◯	◯
7) Service in the food and beverage outlets was friendly and courteous?	◯	◯	◯	◯	◯
8) Quality and selection of Hotel restaurants?	◯	◯	◯	◯	◯
9) Quality of VIP Guest room accommodations?	◯	◯	◯	◯	◯
10) Quality of service & equipment provided by Priority Networks (if applicable)?	◯	◯	◯	◯	◯
11) How would you rate the Business Center services you received?	◯	◯	◯	◯	◯

12) *What Business Center services did you use? (check all that apply)*

☐ Copying ☐ Faxing ☐ Freight ☐ Internet Other _____

13) *What additional Business Center services would you use or recommend?*

_____

_____

14) *What did we do well, and where can we improve?*

_____

_____

15) *Were there any members of our staff that went above and beyond your expectations to meet your needs?*

_____

_____

Comments:

_____

_____

_____

_____

Page 2   1/18/2005

Courtesy: Reno Hilton.

The group room block reconciliation report, completed by the reservations manager, shows actual room occupancy and tracks all related areas. Early departures, also known as *understays*, are now routinely being charged a minimum of a one-night stay. As discussed in Chapter 7, association group room attrition has become a large problem. Planning professionals have developed a variety of strategies designed to combat this problem.

The room block/group room "pick-up" report is utilized primarily in the following ways:

- By the hotel to determine if meeting room charges must be applied (if the guest room block wasn't met)
- By the planner for the same reason, and to determine where attendees did stay (if multiple hotels were utilized), and future planning
- By the convention and visitors bureau if commission or a referral will be paid
- For filing group occupancy history and future business or rebooking

SUMMARY

By now it should be evident that the planning and servicing process is a complex one. This chapter examined the final chain of events and procedures that culminate in the postconvention evaluation.

The convention service manager assigned to a particular group is ultimately responsible for the success or failure of the event. In many hotel corporations today, the organization chart delineates that the CSM reports directly to the general manager. This usually helps to facilitate a quick response and resolution to challenges that must be immediately addressed. This demonstrates the importance of this position and the commitment to servicing and customer satisfaction. Ultimately, the future booking potential of a particular group or corporation is largely a result of the overall satisfaction level conveyed at the events' conclusion.

REVIEW QUESTIONS

1. List two types of folios that are used by hotels for group meetings.
2. Describe the key purposes of the preconvention meeting.
3. List the main topics at the postconvention meeting.
4. Define the term *attrition* and provide examples of its impact on the following: hotel, meeting group, and attendees.
5. List the suggested personnel and departments considered for a service gratuity. What criteria should be used in evaluating performance?
6. Describe the purpose and contents of the group room block report.

REFERENCES

Embassy Suites Hotel, Lake Tahoe.

Reno, Hilton. (2004) Annual planning state of the industry report, *Meetings West.*

ADDITIONAL RESOURCES AND WEB SITES

www.newsoft.com	Delphi-Newmarket Software
www.miracle.com	Miracle Software
www.eventweb.com	Event Web
www.astd.org	American Society of Training and Development
www.acom.org	Association for Convention Operations Management

GLOSSARY

Banquet Event Order (BEO): A form most often used by hotels to provide details to personnel concerned with a specific food and beverage function or event room set-up.

Function Book: Diary or log used to control and document the assignment of function space within a facility. May be computerized.

Function Sheet: See *Banquet Event Order (BEO).*

Gratuity: A voluntary payment added to a bill (e.g., a restaurant check), to signify good service. See *Service Charge.*

Guarantee: A promise of commitment to provide a minimum amount of sleeping rooms, F&B, or other revenues. Usually there is financial liability if the commitment is not met. The final number of persons to be served usually is required at least 48 hours in advance of a food and beverage event.

Guaranteed Late Arrival: Sleeping room that is guaranteed by credit card or advance payment in the event a guest's arrival is later than a hotel's predetermined arrival time.

Guaranteed Payment: A hotel reservation secured by the guests' agreement to pay for his room whether he uses it or not.

Guaranteed Reservation: Prepaid reservation held until agreed arrival time, or check-out time the next day, whichever occurs first. Guest is responsible for payment if reservation is not cancelled.

Incidentals: Expenses other than room and tax, billed to a guest's account (e.g., phone, room service, etc.)

Inclusive: Price charged, which includes all applicable gratuities and consumption taxes. Quoted cost; no extra costs to be added. Usually refers to tax and gratuity for food and beverage functions.

Inclusive Rate: 1) The amount charged for a room, usually including breakfast (or other meals), taxes, and service charge. 2) When applied to food or beverage, includes taxes, gratuities and/or service charges.

Pre-Con Meeting: A meeting at the primary facility at which an event will take place just prior to the event beginning. Attendees generally include the primary event organizer, representatives of the event organizer/host organization, department heads at the facility, other facility staff as appropriate, and contractors.

Specification Guide: Spec Guide. The industry-preferred term for a comprehensive document that outlines the complete requirements and instructions for an event. This document typically is authored by the event planner and is shared with all appropriate vendors as a vehicle to communicate the expectations of services for a project. The industry-accepted practice is to use the APEX Specifications Guide, which can be found at the Convention Industry Council (www.conventionindustry.org). Sometimes called Staging Guide, Resume, Bible.

APPENDIX

The following report is provided as a resource. Reprinted with permission.

The APEX Post-Event Report Template

Approved by the Convention Industry Council on October 30, 2003
Updated August 10, 2005

1. A report of the details and activities of an event is called a "Post-Event Report" or PER. A collection of PERs over time will provide the complete history for an event.
2. A face-to-face post-event meeting should be scheduled between the primary event organizer (the main planning contact person) and each venue and facility involved in an event. That meeting should occur immediately following the end of the event and should focus on an evaluation of the success of the event as well as the completion of the Post-Event Report.
3. The report shall be completed by the primary event organizer of an event and filed with each venue and facility that was used for the event. Detailed recommendations for this process are included in the "Suggested Uses" section of the APEX Post-Event Report template.
4. The most recent PER for an event should accompany any request for proposals (RFP) sent to solicit proposals for future occurrences of that event.
5. In regard to the actual APEX Post-Event Report:
   a. Some information in the APEX PER is required. Information must be included in these sections for the report to be considered complete. These items are designated within the template. While all items are not required, the more that are completed, the more valuable this report will be to the event organizer in the future.
   b. All sections and items will not apply to every event. If a section or item does not apply, it should be left blank.
   c. The APEX PER should be completed for events of all sizes, especially for those of 25 rooms on peak night and larger.
   d. It is recommended that the primary event organizer for an event, in partnership with the event's suppliers, complete all applicable sections of the report within 60 days of the end of that event.
   e. Once complete, the primary event organizer should file a copy of the report with each entity, venue or facility that was used for the event (i.e., Convention & Visitors Bureau, Hotel, Conference Center, etc.). The event organizer should also file the report internally for future reference.
   f. The "Comments" field in each section should be used for any information from the organizer, venue, facility, etc. that does not fit into one of the pre-established fields, but that provides insight or valuable information regarding the event.
6. There will be various stages in the evolution of the industry's Post-Event Report and the processes used to complete it. The Convention Industry Council will remain actively involved in this evolution and will provide resources as needed:
   a. Stage I – The form will be available as a word processing file that will be completed manually and will be filed by planners and suppliers in electronic and/or hard copy form.
   b. Stage II – As industry-related software is updated and new software is developed, programmers will ensure that the APEX data map is referenced so that all data fields are defined correctly and are able to efficiently capture, store, and share historical information. This will allow for more automated completion of the report.
   c. Stage III – When the industry determines that a central event history database is to be developed, this report and the resulting data map, will be the basis for the information collected by and stored in this database. At that time, the Convention Industry Council (CIC) will convene a special APEX panel to address the best practices and processes for the use of such a database.
7. The Convention Industry Council will hold the copyright to the APEX Post-Event Report template. However, members of the meetings, conventions and exhibitions industry are permitted to copy and/or reproduce the template, as permitted by applicable copyright law, provided such use of the APEX Post-Event Report template is for member services and educational purposes and not for commercial advantage or financial gain of any sort. All copies and/or reproductions of the APEX Post-Event Report template must include the following:

a. the copyright notice of "Copyright © 2003 by Convention Industry Council"

b. the date the information was copied or reproduced, and

c. a reference line that reads: "Refer to the on-line version of this report, located at www.conventionindustry.org for the most up-to-date content."

Any other reproduction, duplication, copying, sale, resale or exploitation of the APEX Post-Event Report template, or any portion thereof, for any other purpose, without the express written consent of the Convention Industry Council, is expressly prohibited.

8. The Convention Industry Council will annually convene a special committee of professionals from across the meetings, conventions, and exhibitions industry to review all recommendations to the contents of the APEX Post-Event Report that have been received in the preceding year. This special committee will consult and confirm that changes to the report are required. It will then make a formal recommendation to the Convention Industry Council for action.

9. The APEX Technology Advisory Council (TAC) will complete its work of defining the data specifications that correspond to the fields of data that the APEX Post-Event Report intends to capture and share. Those data specifications will be included in the APEX Data Map and will be released for industry use by December 31, 2003.

SECTION I: EVENT INFORMATION

*Event Name: _____

*Event Organizer/Host: _____

*Event Location City: _____   *Event Location State/Province: _____

*Event Location Country: _____

*Published Event Start Date: _____   *Published Event End Date: _____

Event Organizer/Host Overview (mission, philosophy, etc.): _____

Event Objectives: _____

Event Web Address: _____

Event Type:	Drop Down Options:
	❑ Board Meeting
	❑ City-Wide Convention
	❑ Committee Meeting
	❑ Customer Event
	❑ Educational Meeting
	❑ General Business Meeting
	❑ Incentive Travel
	❑ Local Employee Gathering
	❑ Product Launch
	❑ Public Show
	❑ Sales Meeting
	❑ Shareholders Meeting
	❑ Special Event
	❑ Team-Building Event
	❑ Trade Show
	❑ Training Meeting
	❑ Video Conference
	❑ Other: _____

Event Frequency:	Drop Down Options:
	❑ One Time Only
	❑ Bi-Annual
	❑ Annual
	❑ Semi-Annual
	❑ Quarterly
	❑ Monthly
	❑ Other: _____

*Primary Event Facility Name (the facility where most of the functions for the event were held): _____

*Primary Event Facility Type:	Drop Down Options:
	❑ Convention Center
	❑ Hotel
	❑ Conference Center
	❑ Other Venue

Was an off-site venue(s) used? Yes/No

Original Expected Attendance: _____

Total Pre-Registered Attendance: _____   Total On-Site Registrations: _____

No-Shows: _____

Number of Exhibitors Attending: _____

*Actual Attendance *(including exhibitors)*: _____

Number of Domestic Attendees *(Domestic Attendees live in the same country where the event is held)*: _____

Percentage of Domestic Attendees *(AUTO CALC: "Number of Domestic Attendees" DIVIDED BY "Actual Attendance" MULTIPLIED BY 100 = _____%)*: _____

Number of International Attendees: _____

Percentage of International Attendees *(AUTO CALC: "Number of International Attendees" DIVIDED BY "Actual Attendance" MULTIPLIED BY 100 = _____%)*: _____

Was shuttle service provided for attendees? Yes/No

Did the event make use of a Destination Management Company (DMC) or Professional Congress Organizer (PCO)? Yes/No

Did the event offer guest tours/guest programs? Yes/No

If a recurring event, complete the following for the last time the event occurred:
       Last Start Date: _____
       Last End Date: _____
       Last Primary Event Facility Name: _____
       Last Event Location City: _____
       Last Event Location State/Province: _____
       Last Event Location Country: _____

Event Information Comments *(Use this space to note important information not captured by the report such as unusual circumstances that positively or negatively affected attendance)*: _____

SECTION II: CONTACT INFORMATION

*Event Contact Type:	Drop Down Options: ❑ Employee of Event Organizer/Host ❑ Employee of Event Management Company ❑ Employee of Association Management Company ❑ Exhibit Manager ❑ Independent/Third Party ❑ Other: _____
*Event Contact Role *(check all that apply)*:	Drop Down Options: ❑ Volunteer ❑ Staff ❑ Event Organizer (Planner) ❑ Informational Contact ❑ Other: _____

Contact Person:

Prefix *(e.g., Mr., Dr.)*: _____   * Given Name: _____   *Middle Name: _____

*Surname Prefix *(e.g., Mac, Vander)*: _____   *Surname: _____

Suffix *(e.g., Jr., Sr.)*: _____   NameTitle *(e.g., CPA, Ph.D.)*: _____

*Preferred Name: _____

*Job Title: _____   *Employer: _____

*Mailing Address Line 1: _____   Mailing Address Line 2: _____

*City: _____   *State/Province: _____

*Postal/Zip Code: _____   *Country: _____

*Phone: _____   Mobile Phone: _____

Fax: _____   Email: _____   Web Address: _____

Repeat for additional contacts as necessary

SECTION III: HOTEL ROOM INFORMATION

*Did the event utilize sleeping rooms? Yes/No

If No, go to Section V. If Yes, complete the following:

ᵞNumber of Hotels Used: _____

ᵞTotal Number of Rooms Used on Peak Night: _____

ᵞBy whom were housing services performed?	Drop Down Options:
	❑ Event Organizer/Host ❑ Management Firm – Management Firm's Name: _____ ❑ Housing Bureau – Housing Bureau's Name: _____ ❑ Convention & Visitors Bureau ❑ Attendees Direct to Hotels ❑ Other: _____

Hotel Room Comments: _____

ᵞ *Denotes Required Information If Hotel Rooms Were Used*

SECTION IV: ROOM BLOCK INFORMATION

This information should be completed for each hotel used. List headquarters hotel first, then others alphabetically.

*Hotel Name: _____

*Headquarters Hotel? Yes/No

Hotel Type: _____

Drop Down Options:
☐ Airport
☐ Downtown
☐ Resort
☐ Suburban
☐ Other

No. of Single Occupied Rooms Used: _____

🛏 1 bed/1 person

No. of Double Occupied Rooms Used: _____

🛏 1 bed/ 2 people   OR   🛏 2 beds/ 2 people

No. of Suites Used: _____
No. of Complimentary Rooms Used: _____
No. of Staff Rooms Used: _____
No. of Sub-Blocks: _____

Room Block Contracted Date: _____
Final Room Block Date: _____
*Cut-off Date: _____
*Was the Cut-off Date Exercised? Yes/No
What was pick-up at the cut-off date? _____

^Day & Date (i.e. Monday, March 1, 2003) *Must Be Manually Entered*	Day 1	Day 2	Day 3	Day 4	Day 5	Day 6	Day 7	Day 8	Day 9	Day 10	Day 11	Day 12	Day 13	Day 14	Additional days as necessary
^Room Block when contracted															
Final RoomBlock															
90 day pick-up															
60 day pick-up															
30 day pick-up															
21 day pick-up															
14 day pick-up															
7 day pick-up															
^Actual pick-up															
Requested Oversell Percentage	From event contract														
Actual Oversell Percentage	Manual Calculation: [("Maximum Pick-up" MINUS "Actual Pick-up") DIVIDED BY "Maximum Pick-up"] MULTIPLIED BY 100 = ___%														
Slippage from 21 day pick-up	Auto calc: "21 day pick-up" MINUS "Actual pick-up" = ___														
% Sold (of contracted block)	Auto calc: "Actual pick-up" DIVIDED BY "Room Block when contracted" MULTIPLIED BY 100 = ___%														
% Sold (of final block)	Auto calc: "Actual pick-up" DIVIDED BY "Final Block" MULTIPLIED BY 100 = ___%														
^% to peak	Auto calc: "Actual pick-up" DIVIDED BY the peak night pick-up MULTIPLIED BY 100 = ___%"														

Room Block Comments: _____

Repeat for additional hotels as necessary

*Were food & beverage (F&B) functions included in the event? Yes/No   If No, go to Section VI.   If Yes, complete the following:

Attendance at Largest F&B Function: _____

What type of F&B function was the largest in attendance?

Drop Down Options:
☐ Break/Continental
☐ Breakfast
☐ Lunch
☐ Reception
☐ Dinner
☐ Other: _____

What type of F&B function was the largest revenue producer?

Drop Down Options:
☐ Break/Continental
☐ Breakfast
☐ Lunch
☐ Reception
☐ Dinner
☐ Other: _____

F&B Function Schedule (#guar=Total Covers Guaranteed; # fed=Actual Covers Per Function Period):

	Day 1	Day 2	Day 3	Day 4	Day 5	Day 6	Day 7	Day 8	Day 9	Day 10	Day 11	Day 12	Day 13	Day 14	Additional days as necessary
Break(s)/ Continental(s)	Date / # held / # guar / # fed	Date / # held / # guar / # fed	Date / # held / # guar / # fed	Date / # held / # guar / # fed	Date / # held / # guar / # fed	Date / # held / # guar / # fed	Date / # held / # guar / # fed	Date / # held / # guar / # fed	Date / # held / # guar / # fed	Date / # held / # guar / # fed	Date / # held / # guar / # fed	Date / # held / # guar / # fed	Date / # held / # guar / # fed	Date / # held / # guar / # fed	
Breakfast(s)	# held / # guar / # fed	# held / # guar / # fed	# held / # guar / # fed	# held / # guar / # fed	# held / # guar / # fed	# held / # guar / # fed	# held / # guar / # fed	# held / # guar / # fed	# held / # guar / # fed	# held / # guar / # fed	# held / # guar / # fed	# held / # guar / # fed	# held / # guar / # fed	# held / # guar / # fed	
Lunch(es)	# held / # guar / # fed	# held / # guar / # fed	# held / # guar / # fed	# held / # guar / # fed	# held / # guar / # fed	# held / # guar / # fed	# held / # guar / # fed	# held / # guar / # fed	# held / # guar / # fed	# held / # guar / # fed	# held / # guar / # fed	# held / # guar / # fed	# held / # guar / # fed	# held / # guar / # fed	
Reception(s)	# held / # guar / # fed	# held / # guar / # fed	# held / # guar / # fed	# held / # guar / # fed	# held / # guar / # fed	# held / # guar / # fed	# held / # guar / # fed	# held / # guar / # fed	# held / # guar / # fed	# held / # guar / # fed	# held / # guar / # fed	# held / # guar / # fed	# held / # guar / # fed	# held / # guar / # fed	
Dinner(s)	# held / # guar / # fed	# held / # guar / # fed	# held / # guar / # fed	# held / # guar / # fed	# held / # guar / # fed	# held / # guar / # fed	# held / # guar / # fed	# held / # guar / # fed	# held / # guar / # fed	# held / # guar / # fed	# held / # guar / # fed	# held / # guar / # fed	# held / # guar / # fed	# held / # guar / # fed	

Did the event have any in conjunction with (ICW) F&B functions? Yes/No   If No, go to Section VI.   If Yes, complete the following:

ICW F&B Function Schedule (#guar=Total Covers Guaranteed; # fed=Actual Covers Per Function Period):

	Day 1	Day 2	Day 3	Day 4	Day 5	Day 6	Day 7	Day 8	Day 9	Day 10	Day 11	Day 12	Day 13	Day 14	Additional days as necessary
ICW Breakfast(s)	Date / # held / # guar / # fed	Date / # held / # guar / # fed	Date / # held / # guar / # fed	Date / # held / # guar / # fed	Date / # held / # guar / # fed	Date / # held / # guar / # fed	Date / # held / # guar / # fed	Date / # held / # guar / # fed	Date / # held / # guar / # fed	Date / # held / # guar / # fed	Date / # held / # guar / # fed	Date / # held / # guar / # fed	Date / # held / # guar / # fed	Date / # held / # guar / # fed	
ICW Lunch(es)	# held / # guar / # fed	# held / # guar / # fed	# held / # guar / # fed	# held / # guar / # fed	# held / # guar / # fed	# held / # guar / # fed	# held / # guar / # fed	# held / # guar / # fed	# held / # guar / # fed	# held / # guar / # fed	# held / # guar / # fed	# held / # guar / # fed	# held / # guar / # fed	# held / # guar / # fed	
ICW Reception(s)	# held / # guar / # fed	# held / # guar / # fed	# held / # guar / # fed	# held / # guar / # fed	# held / # guar / # fed	# held / # guar / # fed	# held / # guar / # fed	# held / # guar / # fed	# held / # guar / # fed	# held / # guar / # fed	# held / # guar / # fed	# held / # guar / # fed	# held / # guar / # fed	# held / # guar / # fed	
ICW Dinner(s)	# held / # guar / # fed	# held / # guar / # fed	# held / # guar / # fed	# held / # guar / # fed	# held / # guar / # fed	# held / # guar / # fed	# held / # guar / # fed	# held / # guar / # fed	# held / # guar / # fed	# held / # guar / # fed	# held / # guar / # fed	# held / # guar / # fed	# held / # guar / # fed	# held / # guar / # fed	

Food & Beverage Comments (Use this space to note important information not captured by the report such as green meetings provisions, food bank donations, etc.): _____

APEX Post-Event Report Template
Copyright © 2003, 2005 by Convention Industry Council
Refer to the on-line version of this report, located at www.conventionindustry.org for the most up-to-date content.
Page 10 of 15

SECTION VI: FUNCTION SPACE INFORMATION

*Did the event require function space? Yes/No

    If No, go to Section VII. If Yes, complete the following:

+Attendance at Largest Function: _____

Was the space for the largest function on a 24-hour hold? Yes/No

+Room Setup for the Largest Function:	Drop Down Options: ❑ Theatre ❑ Conference Style Set-up ❑ U-Shaped Set-up ❑ Classroom Set-up ❑ Hollow Square/Rectangle ❑ Rounds for 8 ❑ Rounds for 10 ❑ Other _____
AV Setup for the Largest Function:	Drop Down Options: ❑ Front projection ❑ Rear projection ❑ None ❑ Other: _____
+Facility Type(s) Used for Functions *(check all that apply)*:	Options: ❑ Hotel ❑ Convention Center ❑ Conference Center ❑ Other: _____

Were there extensive AV or technology requirements for one or more functions? Yes/No

    If Yes, Number of Rooms with Extensive AV or Technology Requirements: _____

Total Number of Concurrent Breakout Sessions: _____

+Largest Daily Total of Concurrent Breakout Sessions: _____

Number of Seats Concurrent Breakout Sessions Typically Set For: _____

Typical Room Setup for Concurrent Breakout Sessions:	Drop Down Options: ❑ Theatre ❑ Conference Style Set-up ❑ U-Shaped Set-up ❑ Classroom Set-up ❑ Hollow Square/Rectangle ❑ Rounds for 8 ❑ Rounds for 10 ❑ Other _____

Was pre-function space required? Yes/No

Was a registration area(s) required? Yes/No   # of Registration Areas: _____

Was a lounge(s) area required? Yes/No   # of Lounges: _____

Was office space required? Yes/No   # of Offices: _____

Was table top exhibit space required? Yes/No   # of Table Top Exhibits: _____

Function Space Utilities Required:	Check from the following list:
	❑ Electricity
	❑ Water
	❑ Compressed Air
	❑ Natural Gas
	❑ Analog Phone Lines
	❑ ISDN Lines
	❑ Single Line Phone Set
	❑ Ethernet Internet Service
	❑ T-1 Lines
	❑ Other: _____

Was move-in and/or move-out time required? Yes/No

      If Yes, Number of Move-In Days Required: _____
      If Yes, Number of Move-Out Days Required: _____

Was tear-down time required? Yes/No

      If Yes, Number of Tear-Down Days Required: _____

Function Space Comments: _____

[+] *Denotes Required Information If Function Space Was Used*

SECTION VII: EXHIBIT SPACE INFORMATION

*Did the event require exhibit space? Yes/No

> If No, go to Section VIII. If Yes, complete the following:

^Facility Type Used for Exhibits (check all that apply):	Drop Down Options:
	❑ Convention Center
	❑ Hotel
	❑ Conference Center
	❑ Other Venue

Number of Exhibits: _____   Number of Exhibiting Companies: _____

^Type of Exhibits (check all that apply):	Drop Down Options:
	❑ 8'x10'
	❑ 10'x10'
	❑ Table Tops
	❑ Other: _____

^Gross Square Feet Used: _____   ^Gross Square Meters Used: _____

^Net Square Feet Used: _____   ^Net Square Meters Used: _____

^Number of Move-in Days: _____   ^Number of Move-out Days: _____

^Number of Show Days: _____   ^Show Days (i.e. M–W): _____

Show Hours: _____

Exhibit Utilities Required:	Check from the following list:
	❑ Electricity
	❑ Water
	❑ Compressed Air
	❑ Natural Gas
	❑ Analog Phone Lines
	❑ ISDN Lines
	❑ Single Line Phone Set
	❑ Ethernet Internet Service
	❑ T-1 Lines
	❑ Other: _____

Were there extensive AV or technology requirements for one or more exhibitors? Yes/No

> If Yes, Number of Exhibitors with Extensive AV or Technology Requirements: _____

Was a general service contractor (GSC) used? Yes/No

> If Yes, Number of Move-In Days Required for the GSC: _____

Was food & beverage required for any exhibitors (excluding concessions)? Yes/No

> If Yes, Number of Exhibitors that Required Food & Beverage: _____

Exhibit Space Comments: _____

^ Denotes Required Information If Exhibit Space Was Used

SECTION VIII: FUTURE EVENT DATES INFORMATION

*Have future dates been confirmed for this event? Yes/No

What is the next open date for this event? _____

Next Published Start Date: _____   Next Published End Date: _____

Next City: _____   Next State/Province: _____   Next Country: _____

Next Facility: _____

Future Dates Comments: _____

Additional future dates as necessary

SECTION IX: REPORT DISTRIBUTION TRACKING

*This report was completed on (DATE) _____ by (FULL NAME) ____, (TITLE) _____, (EMPLOYER) _____ . It was delivered
via (Checkbox: Postal Mail, Email, Fax, OTHER:_____) on (DATE) _____ to:
- (FULL NAME) ____, (TITLE) _____, (EMPLOYER) _____
- (FULL NAME) ____, (TITLE) _____, (EMPLOYER) _____
- (FULL NAME) ____, (TITLE) _____, (EMPLOYER) _____
- (FULL NAME) ____, (TITLE) _____, (EMPLOYER) _____
- *Additional lines as necessary*

This report was revised on (DATE) _____ by (FULL NAME) ____, (TITLE) _____, (EMPLOYER) _____ . A revised copy was
delivered via (Checkbox: Postal Mail, Email, Fax, OTHER:_____) on (DATE) _____ to:
- (FULL NAME) ____, (TITLE) _____, (EMPLOYER) _____
- (FULL NAME) ____, (TITLE) _____, (EMPLOYER) _____
- (FULL NAME) ____, (TITLE) _____, (EMPLOYER) _____
- (FULL NAME) ____, (TITLE) _____, (EMPLOYER) _____
- *Additional lines as necessary*

Additional revision notations as necessary

Post-Event Report (PER) FAQ
Information provided courtesy of Holly Hospel & AhhHah! Discovery Tools

What is a Post-Event Report?
   A Post-Event Report (PER) is a report of the details and activities of an event. A collection of PERs over time will provide the complete history of a recurring event. A PER is completed by the primary event organizer of an event, in conjunction with the suppliers for that event, and filed with each venue and facility that was utilized.

Why should I complete a report on an event that has already happened?
   Once complete, the information a Post-Event Report (PER) contains can do many valuable things – all of which can benefit the event organizer and host.

- **Convey the "Bottom Line":** The APEX PER can be used as a starting point to translate numbers to dollars and cents, which is the universal language of business. What decision makers (whether it is a boss or a supplier) really want to know is "How much did it cost? And how much was our net profit?"

- **Leverage Your Business:** Use it to analyze the numbers and conduct research. Numbers can act as a crystal ball while lending credibility and leverage. Numbers help an event organizer in two critical areas:
    1. Anticipation – Tracking numbers will reveal patterns that will help prepare for and predict the future of an event.
    2. Negotiation – Accurately demonstrating an event's value gives an event organizer the credibility and confidence needed to negotiate effectively. For example, good historical data on room pick-up is vital when leveraging business with a hotel. Without it an event organizer is losing amenities, losing complimentary rooms, and losing discounted exhibit space.
- **Decision Making Tool**: A PER can help answer questions like "How many registration counters and registration personnel will be enough?" or "What food and beverage guarantee should be made?" It can give you insight into the unique characteristics of an event's attendees. A PER can show if attendees bring their children to the event, if they make a vacation out of it, whether they drive or fly in, and whether they care about Saturday night airfare discounts. With this knowledge, an event organizer can make better decisions such as knowing that it is more important to negotiate for free parking instead of free health club passes.
- **Leverage Your Career:** Use it to demonstrate your professionalism and performance as a successful event organizer. If you have been tracking your numbers you can use this information during your annual performance review to demonstrate just how much you have contributed to the organization's bottom line. The value of your professionalism and skill will become indisputable.

11

EXHIBITION AND TRADE SHOW INDUSTRY OVERVIEW

LEARNING OBJECTIVES

After studying this chapter, you will be able to discuss:

- Exhibition and trade show planning and booth development
- The impact of the exhibition and trade show component, on the organization holding the event
- Effective marketing and sales techniques for trade shows
- The main services provided by exhibition and ancillary service contractors
- The key terms used in exhibition management and their use

INTRODUCTION

For both the event supplier and buyer, the exhibition trade show component segment has become a very significant part of the event. In this chapter, we present an overview of the key aspects of exhibition planning and execution for a convention.

As discussed in previous chapters, the convention sales and services manager (CSM) will be the key facility planning manager. All exhibition and ancillary service contractor arrangements will be coordinated through the facility CSM as well. In some destinations where the hotel structure is adjacent or connected to the convention center, exhibition attendees may travel between both facilities to attend events. Trade show organizers for citywide events, utilizing multiple exhibition facilities and venues, will likely use a document similar to the

CIC APEX Event Specifications Guide (see the Appendix) to plan and execute the event.

EXHIBITIONS

First let's define the term *exhibition*. The CIC glossary defines it as follows.

1. An event at which products and services are displayed. The primary activity of attendees is visiting exhibits on the show floor. These events focus primarily on business-to-business (B2B) relationships.
2. Display of products or promotional material for the purposes of public relations, sales, and/or marketing. The exhibition event can be held for and promoted to many different types of audiences.

We will also discuss *trade shows*. The CIC definition is:

An exhibition of products and/or services held for members of a common or related industry. Not open to the general public.

When open to the public, it is called a *consumer show*, with the CIC definition as follows:

Exhibition that is open to the public, usually requiring an entrance fee.

An exhibition or trade show is held in conjunction with a convention because it

- Provides a beneficial service to members or participants
- Provides a source of income for the organization from exhibitor space rental fees
- Promotes and showcases event sponsors

Also, the organization itself offers recruitment opportunities.

BOOTHS

There are four types of booths:

Tabletop: Used when space is limited. The actual exhibitor display board or case is small enough to fit on top of a 6- or 8-foot table. This size display commonly is identified as a "table top" by the trade show industry.

Standard: Dimensions are 10 feet wide by 10 feet long and 8 feet high. Also known as an *inline* booth. The booth can be up to 12 feet high, but is subject to restrictions. Standard inline booths, with foot traffic on both sides, are considered corner booths.

Island booth: A multiple booth space that is completely surrounded with aisles. Dimensions will vary but will be at least the equivalent of two standard booths. This is a popular choice for larger exhibitions. Island booth designs usually must be reviewed and approved to ensure they don't put neighboring booths at a visual disadvantage.

Peninsula booth: This is an exhibit with aisles on three sides. Two or more exhibit spaces, back to back, with an aisle on three sides is also known as an end cap. Peninsula booths also must not put neighboring booths at a visual disadvantage.

FLOOR PLANS AND DIAGRAMS

The design of the floor plan is often the most important part of the exhibition trade show planning. For large shows, floor plan layouts are done months in advance. Many large, well-designed shows have a waiting list for exhibitor space. Booth locations are preassigned within the booth type and size; placements are crucial factors in determining overall visibility.

The final floor plan should include:

- A description of each type of booth space
- The price for rental of each type of booth space
- Ceiling height, aisle width
- Restrooms
- Obstructions
- Utilities available through a GSC (general service contractor)
- Food and beverage/lounge/rest areas
- A security area
- Show management offices

Note: These items may also be listed separately with the appropriate form and/or also included in the exhibitor service kit.

WHO DOES WHAT IN PLANNING AN EXHIBITION TRADE SHOW?

In *Exhibitions* (2005), Ben McDonald describes the primary trade show industry providers and their respective roles or functions. "The *exhibition service contractor* (ESC) provides product and services to the *exhibition management company* and exhibitors. The trade show organizer will provide all exhibitors with a list of authorized service contractors to select from and enable the two parties to deal directly with each." Known as an *exhibitors service manual* or kit, the general or authorized service contractors will include, therein, all forms to order booth installation and dismantling; display and material shipping and storage; booth staffing; electrical, computer, AV, and utilities; furniture, carpet, and floral pieces; and the previously mentioned floor plan.

McDonald notes the following regarding the role of the *exhibition management company*. "Although it may be a trade organization, or a company subcontracted to a trade association, it may also be a separate company organizing the trade show as a profit-making venture. The organizing company is responsible for all aspects of the trade show. Think of it as the "systems integrator" responsible for implementing the show, marketing it to buyers and sellers, and gathering together all the resources needed for success.

Marketing

As the number of products and services available for all industries has grown, so have the marketing opportunities. Exhibiting at the right trade show(s) can be a very effective direct marketing tool in an overall marketing plan.

One example is the hotel and convention industry; both regularly use exhibitions to reach their target markets. At an industry trade *show*, the attendee would be a meeting planner, seeking a destination and accommodations. On the other hand, the attendee at a *consumer* or *public* show would be in search of the same, but for a vacation or travel getaway.

Today almost every industry has at least one or more trade shows with attendees waiting to buy.

Advantages of Trade Show Marketing

- Dealing directly with clients that buy—cuts out the middleman
- Show cost can be low when you consider number of attendees reached
- Networking opportunities
- Being able to see what the competition is doing—marketing sales strategies

How to Sell at a Trade Show

- Have a preshow action plan (identify prospects, consider purchasing the list of attendees from the previous year).
- Present a professional image while conducting business in your booth space.
- Don't leave the booth unattended for long periods of time.
- Consider giving away at least one prize, which will draw people into your booth and generate a database to develop qualified leads.
- To follow up quickly, develop a simple mail piece (prior to the show) for responses.

Planning Guideline

Many large convention hotels can accommodate guest room, meeting, and trade show exhibit space needs for groups of 500 to 1000 attendees, entirely within their own facility.

The checklist shown in Table 11.1 is useful for planners, to document discussions with the single hotel convention services manager. It will be used in tandem with the planning documents presented in previous chapters.

For complete exhibition planning, the Convention Industry Council (CIC) has created an accepted practices Event Specifications Guide (ESG). This APEX guide has been designed by the meetings, convention, and exhibitions indus-

TABLE 11.1
PLANNING CHECKLIST GUIDELINE

Subjects	Discuss	Outcome Action/Follow up	Notes
Show scheduling/dates other events at the same time?			
Convention space contracts deposits?			
Registration/Admission procedures, staffing			
Offsite planned activities Shuttle/ Transportation DMC/ suppliers			
Exhibit security			
Labor Regulations/contracts			
Additional as needed			

FIGURE 11.1
COMDEX COMPUTER SHOW HISTORY

COMDEX 2002

Each fall for more than two decades, the high-tech world has descended on Las Vegas to hype the industry's hottest wares at the Comdex trade show. Attendance had grown to over 125,000 people by the late 1990s. It became THE show for all computer companies to display their latest innovations. In some years, the floor of the Las Vegas Convention Center—the largest exhibition facility in the United States—got so packed that the show overflowed to the exhibit halls of nearby casinos. Potential customers and reporters got routed into private meeting rooms within the company exhibit spaces—or sent to meetings in hospitality suites at nearby casinos. Exhibiting and traveling to trade shows are among the first items to be axed as technology companies struggle to survive. The exhibit space this year is expected to shrink, after dropping from 1.2 million square feet in 2000 to 805,706 square feet sold in 2001. Only 1,000 or so exhibitors are expected this year, down from 1,685 in 2001 and 2,337 in 2000.

COMDEX 2005

For the third year in a row, Comdex has been cancelled. Former exhibitors IBM, Sony Electronics, and Gateway, are among the major corporations which abandoned Comdex for rival shows, which were better positioned, they believe, for their target industries. The Consumer Electronics Show (CES) is the leader in this arena. Comdex show management hope to return in 2006.

try to streamline business processes and create efficiencies. It is included in the appendix at the end of this chapter.

It is important to note that the decision to add an exhibit component to a convention is not an easy one. In recent years, some formerly successful, long-running annual trade shows have been canceled due to declining exhibitors, attendance, and competition from similar shows. Figure 11.1 is sections of a news story on the history and current status of the Comdex computer show. Many different industries worldwide are seeing formerly competing shows now consolidating, as attendees as well as exhibitors cut their own marketing budgets.

The CIC has established APEX (Accepted Practices Exchange), which has published an ESG, which includes a section on requirements for an exhibition or trade show. The comprehensive guide is a result of many leading practitioners cooperatively developing standards and procedures, recognized throughout the industry. The template is included in the appendix at the end of this chapter.

REVIEW QUESTIONS

1. What is an exhibition or trade show?
2. List and describe at least three different types of booths.
3. What is the difference between a consumer and trade show?
4. What does the Exhibitor Service manual (or kit) contain?
5. Discuss the role and responsibilities of the CSM and exhibition manager as described in this chapter.

REFERENCES

Convention Industry Council CIC. (2004, 2005).
Comdex 2002 /2005. *Meetings West*, Editorial comment (2005).
Fenich, G. G. (2005) *Meetings, Expositions, Events, and Conventions*. Boston: Pearson, Prentice Hall.
McDonald, B. (2005) Exhibitions. In G. Fenich, *Meetings, Expositions, Events, and Conventions*, Boston: Pearson, Prentice Hall.

ADDITIONAL RESOURCES, WEB SITES, AND PUBLICATIONS

American Trade Show Directory, CIC Web site.
Tradeshow Week Publication (www.tradeshowweek.com).
Lorimer, E.J. and Goldberg, M. Trade shows . . . Their hidden value during these uncertain times. White Paper: CIC Web site.

RELATED ORGANIZATIONS

| Exhibitor Magazine | www.exhibitornet.com |
| Exhibitors Service Contractors Association (ESCA) | www.esca.org |

GES Exposition Services   www.gesexpo.com
International Association of Exhibition Management www.iaem.org
  (IAEM)
Trade Show Exhibitors Association (TSEA)   www.tsea.org

GLOSSARY

Exhibit Booth/Stand: Individual display area constructed to exhibit products or convey a message.

Exhibit Designer/Producer: Person or company responsible for designing and constructing an exhibit booth/stand.

Exhibit Directory: Program or catalog for attendees listing exhibitors and exhibit booth/stand location.

Exhibit Manager: 1) Person in charge of individual exhibit booth/stand. 2) Event management staff member in charge of entire exhibit area.

Exhibit Producer: An individual or company that designs and/or builds exhibits. May also provide other services.

Exhibition: 1) An event at which products and services are displayed. The primary activity of attendees is visiting exhibits on the show floor. These events focus primarily on business-to-business (B2B) relationships. 2) Display of products or promotional material for the purposes of public relations, sales, and/or marketing.

Exhibition Area: Amount of floor space occupied by exhibitor.

Exhibition Contractor: The organizer or promoter of an exhibition; responsible for the letting of space, financial control, and management of the exhibition; sometimes an agent acting in this capacity.

Exhibition Manager: Preferred term for the specific person responsible for all aspects of planning, promoting, and producing an exhibition.

Exhibition Service Contractor: Supplier of booth/stand equipment, rental furnishings, floor coverings, labor, drayage and signs for exhibitions and trade shows.

Exhibitor: 1) Person or firm that displays its products or services at an event. 2) Event attendee whose primary purpose for attending the event is to staff a booth/stand.

Exhibitor Lounge: An area either on or adjacent to the exhibit floor where exhibitors may relax or meet with customers.

Exhibitor Manual: Also known as an *Exhibitor Kit*. Manual or kit, usually developed by the service contractor for an event, containing general event information, labor/service order forms, rules and regulations, and other information pertinent to an exhibitor's participation in an exhibition.

Exhibitor Move-In: The time period allowed for exhibitors to prepare their exhibit space for show opening. It generally begins after the exposition contractor to receive/unload show-site deliveries.

Exhibits-Only: The right to attend the exhibit-based portion of an event, not the paid conference or other fee events.

Peninsula: Two or more exhibit spaces back to back with an aisle on three sides. Also called *End Cap*.

Peninsula Booth/Stand: An exhibit with aisles on three sides.

Trade Day: Day of an exhibition restricted to attendance by professional or trade visitors.

Trade Fair: An international term for an exhibition.

Trade Missions: Group tour with a business rather than a vacation purpose. Usually planned for business or government representatives traveling overseas to secure new business in foreign markets for their product, city, or other entity.

Trade Publication: A magazine that targets a specific industry.

Trade Show: An exhibition of products and/or services held for members of a common or related industry. Not open to the general public.

Trade Show Facilitation Web Site: A Web site whose primary function is to provide attendees (buyers) and exhibitors (sellers) with online tools that help facilitate participation in an upcoming event.

APPENDIX

The following CIC guide is provided as a resource. *Source*: Convention Industry Council 2004, 2005. Reprinted with permission.

The APEX Event Specifications Guide Template
Approved by the Convention Industry Council on September 30, 2004

ACCEPTED PRACTICES

1. The term *Event Specifications Guide* or *ESG (acronym)* should be the industry's official term for the document used by an event organizer to convey information clearly and accurately to appropriate venue(s) and/or suppliers regarding all requirements for an event. This is a four-part document which includes:
    *   Part I: The Narrative – general overview of the event.
    *   Part II: Function Schedule – timetable outlining all functions that compose the overall event.
    *   Part IIIa: Function Set-up Order – specifications for each function that is part of the overall event (each function of the event will have its own Function Set-up Order).
    *   Part IIIb: Function Set-up Order (Exhibitor Version) – specifications for each booth/stand that is part of an exhibition.

    This is based on accepted terminology defined in the *APEX Industry Glossary*. The *Glossary* defines an event as "an organized occasion such as a meeting, convention, exhibition, special event, gala dinner, etc. An event is often composed of several different yet related functions." The *Glossary* also defines a function as "any of a group of related organized occasions that contribute to a larger event" (e.g. registration area, coat check, rehearsal, outside display, seating area, office, poster session, green room, emergency information area, breakout session, etc.).

2. The *APEX ESG* should be the industry's accepted format for the conveyance of information regarding the requirements of an event.

3. The following fields in the *Narrative* portion of the *ESG* require information input and are designated by *. An acceptable input is "Not Applicable" or "NA":
    Date Originated
    Date Revised
    Event Profile
    *   Event Name
    *   Event Organizer/Host Mailing Address Line 1
    *   Event Organizer/Host City
    *   Event Organizer/Host State/Province
    *   Event Organizer/Host Postal/Zip Code
    *   Event Organizer/Host Country
    *   Event Organizer/Host Phone
    *   Event Type
    Dates & Times
    *   Published Event Start Date
    *   Published Event Start Time
    *   Published Event End Date
    *   Published Event End Time
    *   Pre-Event Meeting
        -   Day & Date
        -   Time
        -   Location
        -   Attendees
    *   Post-Event Meeting
        -   Day & Date
        -   Time
        -   Location
        -   Attendees
    Key Event Contacts
    *   Complete information for a minimum of one (1) key event contact person
    Attendee Profile
    *   Accessibility/Special Needs
    Housing
    *   Room Block(s) - Complete information for a minimum of one (1) Hotel or Housing Facility
    *   Reservation method
    *   Accessibility/Special Needs Rooms
    Safety & Security
    *   Medical/Emergency Instructions

APEX Event Specifications Guide Template • Copyright © 2004 by Convention Industry Council
Refer to the on-line version of this report, located at www.conventionindustry.org for the most up-to-date content. • Page 2 of 27
*indicates required field

- Key Event Organizer/Host Contact in Case of Emergency/Crisis
- Crisis & Emergency Instructions
- On-site Communications
- Hours of surveillance
- Areas for surveillance
- Keys

Food & Beverage
- Special Requirements
- On-Site F&B Description
- Off-Site F&B Description
- Anticipated Outlet/Concession Usage
- Catered Food & Beverage Total Expected Attendance Chart
- "On Own" Food & Beverage Potential Attendance Chart

Transportation
- Attendee Shuttle Provided

Shipping/Receiving
- # Boxes Sent
- Address to Which Boxes Are Being Sent
- Expected Box Arrival Date
- Carrier By Which Boxes Were Sent
- Expected Outbound Shipping Requirements

Billing Instructions
- Group is tax-exempt
- Room & Tax to Master
- Incidentals to Master
- Guests Pay on Own
- Complimentary Items/Services
- Final Bill to Be Provided to (contact name)
- Final Bill to Be Sent to (mailing address)

Authorized Signatories
- Complete information for a minimum of one (1) authorized signatory

4. There should be various stages in the evolution of the *APEX ESG* and the processes used to complete it:

Stage I - The form will be a word processing file and be completed manually. It will be shared by event organizers and venues/suppliers in electronic and/or hard copy form.
- Every facility and vendor involved in an event should receive a complete copy of the final ESG.
- Each ESG will include dates for pre- and post-event meetings to review and revise information.
- The ESG should be shared in a way that, when changes are made, they can be properly tracked and identified. Specifically, when a change is made from the original published document, a revised date should be inserted, and any change should be highlighted and dated within the document.
- The Function Set-up Order (Exhibitor Version) should be used by exhibitors to communicate booth/stand needs to show management and other vendors. Additionally, show managers can use the form to guide exhibitors through the process of determining and relaying their set-up requirements.
- The suggested timetable for the completion and sharing of the information contained in this document is dependent upon the size and complexity of the meeting, convention, or exhibition.
  - *At a minimum,* an event organizer should send the ESG to all facilities and vendors four weeks prior to the start of the event.
  - *Also, at a minimum,* facilities and vendors should respond with completed orders [production schedules, Banquet Event Orders (BEOs), etc.] no later than two weeks prior to the event.

  While these are recommended guidelines, the needs of each facility and vendor will vary. Event organizers should confer with suppliers to determine the timeline and deadlines for this information. Also, all parties should consult the relevant contract because that could override any recommendation in this document.

Stage II - When industry-related software is updated and new software is developed, programmers will ensure that the APEX data map is referenced so that all data fields are defined correctly and are able to efficiently capture, store, and share information from the APEX ESG. This will allow for more automated sharing and updating of the report.

5. The Convention Industry Council will annually convene a special committee of professionals from across the meetings, conventions, and exhibitions industry to review all recommendations to the contents of the APEX Event Specifications Guide that have been received in the preceding year. This special committee will consult and confirm that changes to the report are required. It will then make a formal recommendation to the Convention Industry Council for action.

APEX EVENT SPECIFICATIONS GUIDE (ESG) TEMPLATE

Instructions for Use

The *ESG* is a written document that is all inclusive of event details. It includes three sections: 1) Narrative 2) Function Schedule and 3) Function Set-up Order. The following templates will assist event organizers in compiling complete information for a venue partner and contractor/supplier partners. Note the following:

1. Required Information: Several fields require information input. These items are designated by *.

2. Every function must have its own Function Set-up Order.

3. Every function must have a number. All diagrams, photos, sign copy, etc. refer to the function number at all times. When a new function is added, it is at the discretion of the planner whether to order in sequence, or to use "intermediate numbers." Anything other than whole numbers must be formatted as 1a, 1b, 1c, etc. When a function in sequence is cancelled, the function number should not be reassigned.

4. Every section may not apply for every event.

5. Changes & Revisions: ESGs should be shared in a way that, when changes are made, they can be properly tracked and identified. Specifically, when a change is made from the original published document, a revised date should be inserted, and any change should be highlighted and dated within the document.

6. The Function Set-up Order (Exhibitor Version) should be used by exhibitors to communicate booth/stand needs to show management and other vendors. Additionally, show managers can use the form to guide exhibitors through the process of determining and relaying their set-up requirements.

PART I – Narrative

Date Originated*: _____

Date Revised*: _____
Repeat for additional revisions as necessary.

A. EVENT PROFILE

Event Name*: _____

Event Organizer/Host: _____

Event Organizer/Host Mailing Address Line 1*: _____

Event Organizer/Host Mailing Address Line 2: _____

Event Organizer/Host City*: _____   Event Organizer/Host State/Province*: _____

Event Organizer/Host Postal/Zip Code*: _____   Event Organizer/Host Country*: _____

Event Organizer/Host Phone*: _____   Event Organizer/Host Web Address: _____

Event Web Address: _____

Event Organizer/Host Overview *(mission, philosophy, etc.)*: _____

Event Objectives: _____

Event
Scope:

Drop Down Options:
❏ Citywide
❏ Single Venue
❏ Multiple Venue
❏ Other: _____

Event Type*:

Drop Down Options:
❏ Board Meeting   ❏ Sales Meeting
❏ Committee Meeting   ❏ Shareholders Meeting
❏ Customer Event   ❏ Special Event
❏ Educational Meeting   ❏ Team-Building Event
❏ General Business Meeting   ❏ Training Meeting
❏ Incentive Travel   ❏ Trade Show
❏ Local Employee Gathering   ❏ Video Conference
❏ Product Launch   ❏ Other: _____
❏ Public/Consumer Show

Event
Frequency:

Drop Down Options:
❏ One Time Only
❏ Biennial
❏ Annual
❏ Semi-Annual
❏ Quarterly
❏ Monthly
❏ Other: _____

Event is mandatory for attendees: ❏ Yes   ❏ No

Spouses & Guests are invited to attend: ❏ Yes   ❏ No

Children are invited to attend: ❏ Yes   ❏ No

Event History
    Most Recent Past Date & Venue for this event (Enter NA if a first-time event): _____
    Most Recent Total Attendance for this event: _____
    Next Date & Venue for this event: _____

Other Event Profile Comments: _____

B. DATES & TIMES

Refer to the complete Schedule of Events (Part II of the ESG) for complete details on all functions and scheduled activities.

Published Event Start Date*: _____
    Published Event Start Time* (US & Military via auto calc): _____

    Published Event End Date*: _____
      Published Event End Time* (US & Military via auto calc): _____

Pre-Event Meeting
    Day & Date*: _____
    Time* (US & Military via auto calc): _____
    Location*: _____
    Attendees*: _____

Post-Event Meeting
    Day & Date*: _____
    Time* (US & Military via auto calc): _____
    Location*: _____
    Attendees*: _____

Targeted Move-in: ❏ Yes   ❏ No
    If Yes, Specific Schedule Will Be Provided By: _____ *(e.g. name of contractor)*

Other Dates & Times Comments: _____
    e.g. registration desk hours, daily review meetings

C. KEY EVENT CONTACTS

Use this section to list all key personnel for the event (e.g. staff, exhibits manager, general services contractor, A/V company, security company, preferred shipper).

Contact1 Name* Contact1 Title* Contact1 Company*	Contact1 Address* Contact1 Telephone* Contact1 Fax* Contact1 Email* Contact1 Mobile Phone*	Contact1 Responsibilities Description*	❏ On-Site* ❏ Off-site* *(during event)*
Repeat for additional Contacts as necessary.			

Other Event Contacts Comments: _____

D. ATTENDEE PROFILE

This section should not include information on Exhibitors. See Section E for the Exhibitor Profile.

Expected Attendance: _____

Pre-Registered Attendance: _____

Number of Domestic Attendees: _____
    Note: Domestic Attendees live in the same country where the event is held

Number of International Attendees: _____

Demographics Profile (Attendees Only): _____

Accessibility/Special Needs*: _____
  Note: Use this section to outline any special needs the group has.

VIPs – Very Important Persons

Name	Title	Employer	Arrival Date	Departure Date	Amenities	Upgrades	Relationship to the Event	Comments e.g. special billing, airport transfers
VIP1								
VIP2								
Repeat for additional VIPs as necessary.								

Other Attendee Profile Comments: _____

E. EXHIBITOR PROFILE

Number of Exhibitors Attending: _____

Number of Domestic Exhibitors: _____
  Note: Domestic Exhibitors live in the same country where the event is held

Number of International Exhibitors: _____

Demographics Profile (Exhibitors Only): _____

Number of Exhibiting Companies/Organizations Represented: _____

Accessibility/Special Needs*: _____
  Note: Use this section to outline any special needs the group has.

VIPs – Very Important Persons

Name	Title	Employer	Arrival Date	Departure Date	Amenities	Upgrades	Relationship to the Event	Comments e.g. special billing, airport transfers
VIP1								
VIP2								
Repeat for additional VIPs as necessary.								

Other Exhibitor Profile Comments: _____

F. ARRIVAL/DEPARTURE INFORMATION

Major Arrivals: _____

Major Departures: _____

Group Arrivals/Departures: _____

Luggage Storage Requirements: _____

Porterage/Luggage Delivery Requirements: _____

Drive-in Instructions: _____

Parking Instructions: _____

Fly-in Instructions: _____

Other Arrival/Departure Comments: _____

G. HOUSING

Amenities: _____

In-room deliveries: _____

Room Drops (outside doors): _____

Room Block(s)*:
For a multi-hotel/housing facility event, name all housing facilities and specify the headquarters

Facility Name	HQ Hotel?	Day 1	Day 2	Day 3	Additional days as necessary
Facility Name1	❑ Yes ❑ No	Final Room Block #	Final Room Block #	Final Room Block #	
Additional facilities as necessary					

Reservation method*:_____

Suites: _____

Accessibility/Special Needs Rooms*: _____

Double/Single Occupancy: _____

Third-Party Housing Provider Used: ❑ Yes ❑ No
If Yes, Housing Provider Company Name: _____

Other Housing Comments: _____
Note: *See Section D for VIP information*

H. FUNCTION SPACE
Use this section to address any special issues or situations that apply to the event.

Off-site Venue(s): _____

Function Rooms: _____

Message Center: _____

Office(s): _____

Registration Area(s): _____

Lounge(s): _____

Speaker Ready Room(s): _____

Press Room: _____

Storage: _____

General Reader Board Information: _____

Other Function Space Comments: _____

I. EXHIBITS

Location(s) of Exhibits: _____

Exhibitor Registration Location(s) : _____

Number of Exhibits: _____

Gross Square Feet Used: _____   Gross Square Meters Used: _____

Net Square Feet Used: _____   Net Square Meters Used: _____

Rules & Regulations Attached: ❑ Yes   ❑ No

Show Days & Dates: _____

Show Hours: _____

Storage Needs: _____

Anticipated POV (Privately Owned Vehicle) Arrivals: _____

Exhibitor Schedule

Move-in Begin Date: _____   Move-in End Date: _____
Move-in Begin Time: _____

Move-out Begin Date: _____   Move-out End Date: _____
Move-out End Time: _____

Service Contractor Schedule

Move-in Begin Date: _____   Move-in End Date: _____
Move-in Begin Time: _____

Move-out Begin Date: _____   Move-out End Date: _____
Move-out End Time: _____

See Section B: Dates & Times for Targeted Move-in Information

Other Exhibits Comments: _____

J. UTILITIES
Use this section to describe any special situations in regard to Engineering, Rigging, Electrical, Water, Telecommunications, etc.

K. SAFETY, SECURITY & FIRST-AID

Medical/Emergency Instructions*: _____

Key Event Organizer/Host Contact in Case of Emergency/Crisis*: _____

Crisis & Emergency Instructions*: _____

On-site Communications*: _____

General Security/Surveillance: ❑ Not Required   ❑ Group To Provide   ❑ Venue To Provide
                                   ❑ Outside Vendor To Provide: _____ (company name)

Hours of Security/Surveillance*: _____

Areas for Security/Surveillance*: _____

First-Aid Services: ❑ Not Required   ❑ Group To Provide   ❑ Venue To Provide
     ❑ Outside Vendor To Provide: _____ (company name)

Hours of First-Aid Services: _____

Location of First-Aid Services: _____

Keys*: _____

Pedestrian Traffic & Vehicular Traffic Patterns *(include specific group movements)*: _____

VIP and/or Police Escorted Movements: _____

Other Security Comments: _____

L. FOOD & BEVERAGE

Special Requirements*: _____

On-Site F&B Description*: _____

Off-Site F&B Description*: _____

Anticipated Outlet/Concession Usage*: _____

Catered Food & Beverage Total Expected Attendance*

	Day 1	Day 2	Day 3	Day 4	Repeat for additional days as necessary.
Breakfast(s)	#	#	#	#	
AM Break(s)	#	#	#	#	
Lunch(s)	#	#	#	#	
PM Break(s)	#	#	#	#	
Reception(s)	#	#	#	#	
Dinner(s)	#	#	#	#	

"On Own" Food & Beverage Potential Attendance*

	Day 1	Day 2	Day 3	Day 4	Repeat for additional days as necessary.
Breakfast(s)	#	#	#	#	
AM Break(s)	#	#	#	#	
Lunch(s)	#	#	#	#	
PM Break(s)	#	#	#	#	
Reception(s)	#	#	#	#	
Dinner(s)	#	#	#	#	

Other Food & Beverage Comments: _____

M. SPECIAL ACTIVITIES

Recreational Activities: _____

Guest Programs: _____

Tours: _____

Pre- & Post-Event Programs: _____

Entertainment: _____

Children's Programs: _____

Other Special Activities Comments: _____

N. AUDIO/VISUAL REQUIREMENTS
Use this section to address any special issues or situations that apply to the event.

O. TRANSPORTATION

Attendee Shuttle Provided*: ❏ Yes   ❏ No
If Yes, complete the following:

Day & Date (i.e., Monday, mm/dd/yyyy)	Official Stop #1	Official Stop #2	Additional Stops as Necessary
Day 1	Departure times	Departure times	
Day 2	Departure times	Departure times	
Day 3	Departure times	Departure times	
Day 4	Departure times	Departure times	
Day 5	Departure times	Departure times	
Day 6	Departure times	Departure times	
Day 7	Departure times	Departure times	
Repeat for additional days as necessary.			

Transportation Provider: _____

Shuttle(s) Provided for Off-Site Events: ❏ Yes   ❏ No
If Yes, complete the following:

Departure location: _____

Drop-off location: _____

Transportation Provider: _____

Other Transportation Comments: _____

P. IN CONJUNCTION WITH (ICW) GROUPS
Use this section to list and describe any In Conjunction With (ICW) groups of which suppliers for this event should be aware. Full contact information for the main point of contact should also be included. Additionally, note any important rules and regulations regarding these groups.

Q. MEDIA/PRESS
Use this section to address any special issues or situations that apply to the event (e.g. contact information for the person to whom all media inquiries should be sent).

R. SHIPPING/RECEIVING

Boxes Sent*: _____

Address to Which Boxes Are Being Sent*: _____

Expected Box Arrival Date*: _____

Carrier By Which Boxes Were Sent*: _____

Expected Outbound Shipping Requirements*: _____

Dock Usage: _____

Freight Elevator Usage: _____

Drayage To Be Handled By: _____

Other Shipping/Receiving Comments: _____

S. HOUSEKEEPING INSTRUCTIONS
Use this section to address any special issues or situations that apply to the event.

T. FRONT DESK INSTRUCTIONS
Use this section to address any special issues or situations that apply to the event.

U. OTHER REQUIREMENTS

V. BILLING INSTRUCTIONS

Group is tax-exempt*: ❑ Yes ❑ No

Room & Tax to Master*: ❑ Yes ❑ No

Incidentals to Master*: ❑ Yes ❑ No

Guests Pay on Own*: ❑ Yes ❑ No

Special Concessions and Complimentary Items/Services*

Description	Responsible Party
Item/Service1	
Item/Service2	
Repeat for additional items/services as necessary.	

On-Site Bill Review Instructions: _____

Third-Party Billing Instructions: _____
Use this section to give specific instructions for goods & services that the event organizer is not responsible for (e.g. contractors expenses, etc.)

Final Bill to Be Provided to*: _____ (contact name)

Final Bill to Be Sent to*: _____ (mailing address)

W. AUTHORIZED SIGNATORIES

Full Name	Title	Maximum Approval Authority
Signatory1 Full Name*	Signatory1 Title*	Signatory1 Maximum Approval Amount*
Repeat for additional Signatories as necessary.		

PART II – Function Schedule

Date Originated: _____

Date Revised*: _____
Repeat for additional revisions as necessary.

Event Name: _____

Event Organizer/Host Organization: _____

Contact Name: _____

Contact Phone: _____

Day & Date	Function Start Time (US & Military via auto calc)	Function End Time (US & Military via auto calc)	Function Name	Facility	Room Name	Set-up	Set For	Function #	Posting Instructions	24-Hour Hold?
						^			☐ Post ☐ Do Not Post	☐ Yes ☐ No

Function Schedule Comments: _____

^enter primary set-up designated on the function's function order.

PART IIIa – Function Set-up Order

Date Originated: _____

Date Revised*: _____
Repeat for additional revisions as necessary.

A. EVENT DETAILS

Event Name: _____

Event Organizer/Host Organization: _____

Contact Name: _____

Contact Phone: _____

B. FUNCTION DETAILS

Function #: _____

Function Name: _____

Function Type:
    Drop Down Options:
    ❑ Break Out
    ❑ Coat Check
    ❑ Dressing/Green Room
    ❑ Exhibit
    ❑ General Session
    ❑ Meeting
    ❑ Office
    ❑ Photo Room
    ❑ Poster Session
    ❑ Registration
    ❑ Speaker Room
    ❑ Storage
    ❑ Workshop
    ❑ Other

Post to Reader Board? ❑ Post ❑ Do Not Post
    If Post, Post As: _____

Function Location: _____

Key Event Personnel for this Function: _____

Attendance: _____

Function Start Day/Date: _____
Function Start Time (US & Military via auto calc): _____

Function End Day/Date: _____
Function End Time (US & Military via auto calc): _____

Set Up By (US & Military via auto calc): _____

Dismantle No Later than (US & Military via auto calc): _____

Catered Function: ❑ Yes ❑ No

C. ROOM SET-UP

Room Set-up Diagram Attached: ❑ Yes ❑ No
   Note: The set-up diagram should indicate A/V placement and electrical needs.

Room Set Room For: _____ (qty.)

Primary Room Set-up: *Drop Down Options:*
                             ❑ 10x10 exhibits
                             ❑ 8x10 exhibits
                             ❑ Island Exhibit
                             ❑ Peninsula Exhibit
                             ❑ Perimeter Exhibit
                             ❑ Tabletop exhibits
                             ❑ Banquet Rounds for 10
                             ❑ Banquet Rounds for 12
                             ❑ Banquet Rounds for 8
                             ❑ Board Room (Conference)
                             ❑ Classroom - 2 per 6 ft. tables
                             ❑ Classroom - 3 per 6 ft. tables
                             ❑ Classroom - 3 per 8 ft. tables
                             ❑ Classroom - 4 per 8 ft. tables
                             ❑ Classroom (Chevron) - 2 per 6 ft. tables
                             ❑ Classroom (Chevron) - 3 per 6 ft. tables
                             ❑ Classroom (Chevron) - 3 per 8 ft. tables
                             ❑ Classroom (Chevron) - 4 per 8 ft. tables
                             ❑ Cocktail Rounds
                             ❑ Crescent Rounds of 5
                             ❑ Crescent Rounds of 6
                             ❑ Crescent Rounds
                             ❑ E-shaped
                             ❑ Existing
                             ❑ Flow (no tables or chairs)
                             ❑ Hollow square
                             ❑ Perimeter Seating
                             ❑ Registration
                             ❑ Royal conference
                             ❑ Talk Show
                             ❑ Theater
                             ❑ Theater - Semi-circle
                             ❑ Theater - Chevron
                             ❑ T-shaped
                             ❑ U-shaped
                             ❑ Other: _____

Secondary Room Set-up: *Choose all that apply:*
                             ❑ Perimeter Seating set for _____ (qty.)
                             ❑ Talk Show Set-up set for _____ (qty.)
                             ❑ Head Table for _____ (qty.)
                             ❑ Lectern *[see Section D (A/V) for style & quantity]*
                             ❑ Rear Screen Projection *[see Section D (A/V) for details]*
                             ❑ Riser
                                If yes,
                                     Riser Height: _____ in. (_____ cm)
                                     Riser Width: _____ in. (_____ cm)
                                     Riser Depth: _____ in. (_____ cm)
                             ❑ Dance Floor
                                If yes,
                                     Dance Floor Length: _____ in. (_____ cm)
                                     Dance Floor Width: _____ in. (_____ cm)
                             ❑ Other: _____

Other Set-up Requirements *(choose all that apply)*:

    ❑ Water Service for Speaker(s)/Moderator(s)
    ❑ Water Service for table(s)
    ❑ Water Service for back of room
    ❑ Pads/Pens for tables
    ❑ Candy for tables
    ❑ VIP Set-up   *If yes*, Describe: _____
    ❑ Table(s) in back of room (for literature, etc.)   *If yes*, Quantity: _____
    ❑ Other: _____

Special Requirements: _____

Room Set-up Comments: _____

D. AUDIO/VISUAL (A/V)

❑ Not Required   ❑ Group To Provide
❑ Venue To Provide ❑ Outside Vendor To Provide
    If Not Required, go to Section E. Otherwise, complete the following:

A/V Company Name: _____

A/V Equipment/Services Needed *(choose all that apply)*:

Item	Quantity	Item Price	Item Detail/Comments
❑ 35mm Projector w/ Remote			
❑ Audio Recording			
❑ Background Music			
❑ Blackboard w/ Eraser & Chalk			
❑ Closed Circuit Video			
❑ Data Projector			
❑ Dry Erase Board w/ Eraser & Markers			
❑ DVD Player			
❑ Easel			
❑ Electric Pointer			
❑ Flipchart & Markers			
❑ Lectern (standing)			
❑ Lectern (table)			
❑ Microphone – Wired Lavaliere			
❑ Microphone – Wired Lectern			
❑ Microphone – Wired Standing			
❑ Microphone – Wired Table			
❑ Microphone – Wireless Lavaliere			
❑ Microphone – Wireless Lectern			
❑ Microphone – Wireless Standing			
❑ Microphone – Wireless Table			
❑ Monitor Cart			
❑ Overhead Projector			
❑ Personal Computer – Desktop			
❑ Personal Computer - Laptop			
❑ Personal Computer - Mac			
❑ Powered Speaker			
❑ Projection Stand			
❑ Screen (indicate size in comments)			
❑ Television			
❑ VHS Player			
❑ Video Camera			
❑ Video Monitor			
❑ Video Recording			
❑ Other: _____			

A/V Comments: _____

Include special information such as lighting needs or labor needs (e.g. AV technician).

E. FOOD & BEVERAGE (F&B)

❑ Not Required   ❑ Group To Provide
❑ Venue To Provide ❑ Outside Vendor To Provide
   If Not Required, go to Section F. Otherwise, complete the following:

F&B Service Time (US & Military via auto calc): _____

Anticipated Attendance: _____

F&B Guarantee: _____

Set for: _____

Meal Type: *Drop Down Options:*
                              ❑ Continental Breakfast
                              ❑ Breakfast
                              ❑ Brunch
                              ❑ Lunch
                              ❑ Dinner
                              ❑ Break
                              ❑ Reception
                              ❑ Hospitality
                              ❑ Other: _____

Service Type: *Drop Down Options:*
                              ❑ Boxed
                              ❑ Buffet
                              ❑ Plated
                              ❑ Other: _____

F&B Menu

Description	Quantity	Price	Per
			Person, gallon, tray, etc.

F&B Comments: _____

Note: This can address dietary requirements, alcohol policies, and other special issues.

F. DÉCOR

❑ Not Required   ❑ Group To Provide
❑ Venue To Provide ❑ Outside Vendor To Provide
   If Not Required, go to Section G. Otherwise, complete the following:

Decorator Company Name: _____

Décor Instructions/Requests: _____

G. SECURITY

of Keys Required: _____

Key(s) should be: ❑ House/Standard Key   ❑ Re-keyed

Security Required: ❑ Not Required   ❑ Group To Provide
                    ❑ Venue To Provide   ❑ Outside Vendor To Provide

If Not Required, go to Section H. Otherwise, complete the following:

Security Company Name: _____

Security Start Time (US & Military via auto calc): _____

Security End Time (US & Military via auto calc): _____

Security Instructions/Requests: _____

H. ACCESSIBILITY

Accessibility/Special Needs Instructions:

I. ENTERTAINMENT/SPEAKER

Entertainment/Speaker: ❑ Yes ❑ No
If No, go to Section J. If Yes, complete the following:

Speaker Name(s) : _____

Entertainment/Speaker Company: _____

Entertainment/Speaker Instructions/Requests: _____

J. SIGNAGE

❑ Not Required   ❑ Group To Provide
❑ Venue To Provide ❑ Outside Vendor To Provide
If Not Required, go to Section K. Otherwise, complete the following:

Signage Company: _____

Easel Required: ❑ Yes   ❑ No

Signage Instructions/Requests: _____

K. TRANSPORTATION

Transportation Required: ❑ Yes   ❑ No
If No, go to Section L. If Yes, complete the following:

Transportation Company: _____

Transportation Instructions/Requests: _____

L. SHIPPING/RECEIVING

Shipping/Receiving Required: ❑ Yes   ❑ No
If No, go to Section M. If Yes, complete the following:

Shipping/Receiving/Mail Instructions/Requests: _____

M. UTILITIES

Electrical Connections: ❑ Not Required   ❑ Group To Provide
❑ Venue To Provide ❑ Outside Vendor To Provide

Optional:

Connection Type	Quantity	Price

Connection types can include specific service type such as 120 volt (10 amp) service or power strip quad box etc.

Electrical Notes:

> *Include Electrical needs, description of use and quantity.*

Telecommunications Connections: ❑ Not Required ❑ Group To Provide
❑ Venue To Provide ❑ Outside Vendor To Provide

Voice Services

Item	Quantity	Price	Comments
❑ Analog Phone Line	_____	_____	❑ Long distance
			❑ Restricted
			❑ Other_____
❑ Multi-Line Phone Set	_____	_____	_____
❑ Single Line Phone Set	_____	_____	_____
❑ Speaker Phone	_____	_____	_____
❑ Voice Mail Box	_____	_____	_____
❑ Other: _____	_____	_____	_____

Data Services

Item	Quantity	Price
❑ Internet Connection – Ethernet	_____	_____
❑ Internet Connection – Wireless	_____	_____
❑ ISDN Line	_____	_____
❑ T-1 Line	_____	_____
❑ Other: _____	_____	_____

Telecommunications Notes:

> *Include placement information and other requirements here.*

Cleaning Services: ❑ Not Required ❑ Group To Provide
❑ Venue To Provide ❑ Outside Vendor To Provide

Cleaning Contractor: _____

Cleaning Refresh Times and Instructions:

> *Specify multiple cleaning and refresh times as needed. Also indicated trash removal times if different from refresh times*

Other Utilities: ❑ Not Required ❑ Group To Provide
❑ Venue To Provide ❑ Outside Vendor To Provide

Item	Quantity	Price
❑ Air (indicate PSI/Pascal: _____)		
❑ Drain	_____	_____
❑ Natural Gas/Propane	_____	_____
❑ Water (indicate minimum pressure: _____)	_____	_____
❑ Fill & Drain (indicate gallons: _____)	_____	_____
❑ Steam	_____	_____

☐ Other: _____   _____

Other Utilities Notes:

N. BILLING INSTRUCTIONS

Billing Instructions: _____
Note any instructions that are unique to this function and not covered by information in the narrative.

Organizer Cost Center: _____

PART IIIb – Function Set-up Order (Exhibitor Version)

Date Originated: _____

Date Revised*: _____
Repeat for additional revisions as necessary.

A. EVENT DETAILS

Event Name: _____

Event Organizer/Host Organization: _____

Contact Name: _____

Contact Phone: _____

B. BOOTH DETAILS

Booth #: _____

Booth Location: _____

Booth Type:
❏ 8'x10'
❏ 10'x10'
❏ Island
❏ Peninsula
❏ Perimeter
❏ Table Top
❏ Other: _____

Booth Name: _____

Company Name: _____

Key Contact Person for Booth: _____

Booth Start Day/Date: _____
Booth Start Time (US & Military via auto calc): _____

Booth End Day/Date: _____
Booth End Time (US & Military via auto calc): _____

Set Up By (US & Military via auto calc): _____

Tear Down No Later than (US & Military via auto calc): _____

C. BOOTH SET-UP

Booth Set-up Diagram Attached: ❏ Yes   ❏ No
Note: The set-up diagram should indicate A/V placement and electrical needs.

Inventory Needed *(list all that apply)*:

Description	Quantity	Price/Per	Comments

Special Requirements: _____
e.g. double-decker, floor load

Booth Set-up Comments: _____

D. AUDIO/VISUAL (A/V)

❑ Not Required   ❑ Booth To Provide
❑ Venue To Provide   ❑ Outside Vendor To Provide
    If Not Required, go to Section E. Otherwise, complete the following:

A/V Equipment/Services Needed *(choose all that apply):*

Item	Quantity	Item Price	Item Detail/Comments
❑ 35mm Projector w/ Remote			
❑ Audio Recording			
❑ Background Music			
❑ Blackboard w/ Eraser & Chalk			
❑ Closed Circuit Video			
❑ Data Projector			
❑ Dry Erase Board w/ Eraser & Markers			
❑ DVD Player			
❑ Easel			
❑ Electric Pointer			
❑ Flipchart & Markers			
❑ Lectern (standing)			
❑ Lectern (table)			
❑ Microphone – Wired Lavaliere			
❑ Microphone – Wired Lectern			
❑ Microphone – Wired Standing			
❑ Microphone – Wired Table			
❑ Microphone – Wireless Lavaliere			
❑ Microphone – Wireless Lectern			
❑ Microphone – Wireless Standing			
❑ Microphone – Wireless Table			
❑ Monitor Cart			
❑ Overhead Projector			
❑ Personal Computer – Desktop			
❑ Personal Computer - Laptop			
❑ Personal Computer - Mac			
❑ Powered Speaker			
❑ Projection Stand			
❑ Screen (indicate size in comments)			
❑ Television			
❑ VHS Player			
❑ Video Camera			
❑ Video Monitor			
❑ Video Recording			
❑ Other: _____			

A/V Comments: _____

E. FOOD & BEVERAGE (F&B)

❑ Not Required   ❑ Booth To Provide
❑ Venue To Provide   ❑ Outside Vendor To Provide
    If Not Required, go to Section F. Otherwise, complete the following:

F&B Service Time (US & Military via auto calc): _____

Anticipated Attendance: _____

F&B Guarantee: _____

Set for: _____

Meal Type:	Drop Down Options:
	❑ Continental Breakfast
	❑ Breakfast
	❑ Brunch
	❑ Lunch
	❑ Dinner
	❑ Break
	❑ Reception
	❑ Hospitality
	❑ Other: _____

Service Type: *Drop Down Options:*
                     ❑ Boxed
                     ❑ Buffet
                     ❑ Plated
                     ❑ Other: _____

F&B Menu

Description	Quantity	Price	Per
			Person, gallon, tray, etc.

F&B Comments: _____
   Note: This can address dietary requirements, alcohol policies, and other special issues.

F. DÉCOR

❑ Not Required   ❑ Booth To Provide
❑ Venue To Provide ❑ Outside Vendor To Provide
   If Not Required, go to Section G. Otherwise, complete the following:

Exhibitor Appointed Contractor: _____ (include company name and contact information)

Décor Instructions/Requests: _____

G. SECURITY

of Keys Required: _____

Key(s) should be: ❑ House/Standard Key   ❑ Re-keyed

Security Required: ❑ Not Required   ❑ Booth To Provide
                      ❑ Venue To Provide   ❑ Outside Vendor To Provide
   If Not Required, go to Section H. Otherwise, complete the following:

Security Company Name: _____

Security Start Time (US & Military via auto calc): _____

Security End Time (US & Military via auto calc): _____

Security Instructions/Requests: _____

H. ACCESSIBILITY

Accessibility/Special Needs Instructions:

I. ENTERTAINMENT/SPEAKER

Entertainment/Speaker: ❑ Yes   ❑ No
  If No, go to Section J. If Yes, complete the following:

Speaker Name(s) : _____

Entertainment/Speaker Company: _____

Entertainment/Speaker Instructions/Requests: _____

J. SIGNAGE

Signage Instructions/Requests: _____

K. MATERIAL HANDLING

Shipping/Receiving Required: ❑ Yes   ❑ No

Customs/Brokerage: ❑ Yes   ❑ No

Shipping Information:

To	From	Sender	Venue

Shipping to Show Carrier: _____
(Include Company name, address, contact, phone, fax and e-mail.)

Shipping from Show Carrier: _____
(Include Company name, address, contact, phone, fax and e-mail.)

Material Handling Instructions: _____
(Specify fragile, oversized etc.)

L. UTILITIES

Electrical Connections: ❑ Not Required   ❑ Group To Provide
                              ❑ Venue To Provide   ❑ Outside Vendor To Provide

Optional:

Connection Type	Quantity	Price

Connection types can include specific service type such as 120 volt (10 amp) service or power strip quad box etc.

Electrical Notes:

Include Electrical needs, description of use and quantity.

Telecommunications Connections: ❑ Not Required   ❑ Group To Provide
                                      ❑ Venue To Provide   ❑ Outside Vendor To Provide

Voice Services

Item	Quantity	Price	Comments
❑ Analog Phone Line	_____	_____	❑ Long distance
			❑ Restricted
			❑ Other_____
❑ Multi-Line Phone Set	_____	_____	_____
❑ Single Line Phone Set	_____	_____	_____

❑ Speaker Phone
❑ Voice Mail Box
❑ Other: _____

Data Services

Item	Quantity	Price
❑ Internet Connection – Ethernet		
❑ Internet Connection – Wireless		
❑ ISDN Line		
❑ T-1 Line		
❑ Other: _____		

Telecommunications Notes:

Include placement information and other requirements here.

Cleaning Services: ❑ Not Required   ❑ Group To Provide
       ❑ Venue To Provide   ❑ Outside Vendor To Provide

Cleaning Contractor: _____

Cleaning Refresh Times and Instructions:

Specify multiple cleaning and refresh times as needed. Also indicate trash removal times if different from refresh times

Other Utilities: ❑ Not Required   ❑ Group To Provide
       ❑ Venue To Provide   ❑ Outside Vendor To Provide

Item	Quantity	Price
❑ Air (indicate PSI/Pascal: _____)		
❑ Drain		
❑ Natural Gas/Propane		
❑ Water (indicate minimum pressure: _____)		
❑ Fill & Drain (indicate gallons: _____)		
❑ Steam		
❑ Other: _____		

Other Utilities Notes:

N. BILLING INSTRUCTIONS

Booth is tax-exempt: ❑ Yes   ❑ No

Tax-Exempt ID#: _____

Authorized Signatories: _____

Booth Cost Center: _____

Send Final Bill To:

Company Name: _____
Address: _____
City, State, Postal Code, Country: _____
Contact Person: _____

Title: _____
Phone: _____
Fax: _____
Email: _____

Method of Payment:

Purchase Order, Credit Card Type, Master Account, etc.

Method of Payment #:

PO #, Credit Card # with expiration date, Master Account #

Billing Instructions: _____
Note if any aspect of the function is complimentary and the responsible party.

12

INDUSTRY TRENDS AND RESOURCES

The following complete articles are provided at the conclusion of this book as a resource. Each article presents a concept that has been recognized by both the author and leading convention industry publications as an emerging trend during the first six years of the twenty-first century.

Additional articles and viewpoints on these trends can be located at the Web sites listed throughout this text. As a reminder, the CIC Web site, www.conventionindustry.org, provides a very comprehensive list of links to their 30-member related trade organizations and the corresponding publications.

NEW AND EMERGING TRENDS

The following sections describe new and emerging trends recognized by meeting and convention industry leaders, in no particular order.

Meeting Facilities Designed and Approved by IACC (International Association of Conference Centers)

Leading hotel companies—in this example, Hilton Hotels—now design and build meeting facilities "which meet the rigorous standards of the IACC for optimized productivity," according to advertisements placed by the Hilton Corporation. For years, convention center facilities and hotels with meeting facilities have actively sought design input from meeting planners. This came about originally due to the fact that for years, surveyed meeting planners complained that poor facility design—meeting rooms built for banquets (not soundproofed or comfortable for 8-hour meetings)—could not make up for great service.

As we've seen in Chapter 6, endorsements, testimonials, and awards by satisfied groups have been a popular advertising method for decades. Therefore this newest trend in advertisements is a natural progression. Whether this will help achieve one objective of advertising—impressing the planners with the endorsement—will be determined by market tracking of the business sources.

Figures 12.1 and 12.2 show the hotel advertisements that were both placed in meeting planner trade publications. Both hotels include the IACC certification in their ad copy.

Greening of Hotels and Meetings

"What can my hotel do to help the environment?" is a question being asked increasingly by hoteliers. It is no longer acceptable for hotels, and all businesses, to *not* have an environmental impact program. Throughout the United States, city agencies and utility companies have partnered to increase employer awareness, provide program supplies, and create incentives for reduction in energy costs.

Since 1990, Fairmont Hotels & Resorts has been actively involved in this issue through their Green Partnership program. National Geographic Traveler magazine has called the program "the most comprehensive among North American hoteliers and has raised the bar for other industry leaders." Hoteliers are now making environmentally correct building and conferences a priority, after many years of leaving this issue on the back burner.

In 2004, the second annual U.S. Greenbuild International Conference and Expo was held, with over 5000 hotel executives in attendance. The event was held at Oregon Convention Center, in Portland, Oregon. According to the article "Centered on Sustainability" by Ralph DiNola and Elaine Aye, the OCC (Oregon Convention Center) became, in 2004, (only) the second building to become certified by the U.S. Green Building Council (USGBC).

Figure 12.3 is an excerpt from the article that lists guidelines for building owners to calculate the USGBC energy requirements.

The USGBC has created the following "test" for hotels to distribute internally.

IS YOUR HOTEL GREEN?

Experts say there's much more to the hotel environmental responsibility equation than reusing linen. Is solar power or natural energy sources incorporated into the building design? Meeting planners may take up the gauntlet by inserting some or all of the following questions in their RFPs to determine whether a hotel is really committed:

- Is the hotel certified by Green Seal?
- Does the hotel use shampoo and soap dispensers instead of replacing amenities?
- Does the housekeeping staff shut blinds and turn down the HVAC in guest rooms when they are vacant?

FIGURE 12.1

ESTANCIA LA JOLLA, IACC CERTIFIED HOTEL

Courtesy: Estancia La Jolla.

FIGURE 12.2
HILTON LONG BEACH, IACC CERTIFIED HOTEL

Courtesy: Hilton Long Beach.

FIGURE 12.3
LEED-EB AND ENERGY STAR

LEED-EB and ENERGY STAR

For some building owners, calculating energy requirements seems to be the most daunting part of the U.S. Green Building Council's LEED®-certification process. LEED for Existing Buildings (LEED-EB), however, uses the Environmental Protection Agency's (EPA) straightforward ENERGY STAR® program as its reference standard.

ENERGY STAR draws on its database of thousands of buildings across the nation. Once a building owner enters his building's information into the program, it compares the data with other buildings of the same type in the region. The program even corrects slightly for specific climate conditions. Then ENERGY STAR generates a number from 1 to 100 that ranks the building's percentage among those in its region.

SOME GENERAL INFORMATION IS NEEDED TO DETERMINE A BUILDING'S RATING:

- Total floor area
- Rough percentage of the floor area allocated for different uses, such as office space, classrooms and meeting areas
- Weekly operating hours
- Number of building occupants
- Number of personal computers
- Building ZIP code
- At least 12 months of gas and electric meter data

An ENERGY STAR rating of 60 is the prerequisite for LEED-EB certification. Beyond this baseline, LEED-EB awards up to 10 points as ENERGY STAR ratings climb higher. A medium or low rating reveals opportunity for improvement, and that's a good indication that the owner can realize cost savings, as well.

The Portland-based Oregon Convention Center's ENERGY STAR rating of 70 encouraged the staff to consider actions that will increase the building's performance, such as installing variable frequency drives on the chillers and performing a lighting retrofit. They also are looking into other energy-efficient measures appropriate for the facility.

ENERGY STAR is an excellent tool for benchmarking building performance. The program not only is a prerequisite for achieving LEED-EB, an ENERGY STAR rating is valuable for any owner interested in quality control and performance enhancement.

Source: R. DiNola and E. Dye, LEED-EB/Energy Star.

- Does the F&B department use locally grown products (to reduce energy in transport) and glass or china (nondisposable) plates, cups, and glasses?
- Does the hotel use any Styrofoam products?
- Is useable leftover food donated to charity?
- Is food waste picked up by composting vendors or donated to local farms?
- Will there be electronic checkout?
- What types of paint and cleansers are used on a regular basis?
- Do they recycle paper, cardboard, cans, and bottles?

The CIC Green Report

In 2003, the Convention Industry Council's Green Meetings Task Force was charged with creating minimum best practices for event organizers and suppliers to use as guidelines for implementing policies of sustainability. The task force was composed of individuals from the EPA, the Ocean's Blue Foundation, the Society of Incentive Travel Executive's Green Meeting Group, the World Travel Organization, hotels, convention and visitor's bureaus, convention centers, and meeting-planning organizations.

The results of the task force's work are a series of guidelines for event organizers and event suppliers on running environmentally friendly events. Those guidelines are available in this report, as described next.

What Is a Green Meeting or Event?

A green meeting or event incorporates environmental considerations to minimize its negative impact on the environment.

What Are the Benefits of Green Meetings and Events?

The Economic Bottom Line—Green Meetings and Events Can Save Money
Planning and executing a green meeting isn't just about being environmentally responsible. They can have economic benefits for the event organizer. In fact, many of the minimum recommended guidelines in the Green Meetings Report can actually save money. For example, collecting name badge holders for reuse at an event of 1300 attendees can save approximately $975 for the event organizer.

The Environmental Bottom Line—Green Meetings and Events are Good for the Environment
Using recycled materials, recycling materials used, reusing items, and reducing materials used can significantly lessen the environmental impact an event has. For example, if a five-day event serves 2200 people breaks, breakfasts, lunches, and receptions using china instead of plastic disposables, it prevents 1,890 lbs. of plastic from going into a landfill. That's nearly one ton! Another example is by not prefilling water glasses at banquet tables during three days of served lunches for 2200 attendees; 520 gallons of water can be saved.

Best Practices for Event Suppliers

Additionally, the task force created "Best Practices for Event Suppliers" (see Table 12.1). The entire report can be accessed at the Web site www.conventionindustry.org.

Radio Frequency Identification Badges (RFID)

RFID chips are small (approximately one quarter of an inch across) chips that are able to broadcast information over a limited range. Though the technology has been around for a while, it has just been introduced to the convention industry mainstream.

At the 2005 PCMA (Professional Convention Management Association) annual convention, so-called SMART Badges were used to track CEUs (continuing education credits—attendees held their name tag in front of a reader station and then collected a printed receipt to prove their attendance. In the meeting industry this is the most prevalent application for RFID; however, the IATA (International Air Transport Association) is calling for all luggage to be tagged by 2007.

Some of the possible uses of this technology being researched and tested include:

- Collecting data for attendee research on trade show exhibits, traffic flow
- Event registration check-in
- Tracking attendance at general meeting sessions

TABLE 12.1
CONTENTS

Introduction	**Page 3**
Section 1: Best Practices for Event Suppliers	**Page 5**
— Convention & Visitors Bureaus/Destination Management Companies	
— Accommodations (Lodging/Cruise Lines)	
— Event Venues	
— Transportation Providers	
— Food & Beverage Providers	
— Exhibition Service Providers	
— General Office Procedures & Communications	
Section 2: Best Practices for Event Organizers	**Page 10**
— Destination Selection	
— Accommodations Selection	
— Event Venue Selection	
— Transportation Selection	
— Food & Beverage	
— Exhibition Production	
— Communications & Marketing	
— General Office Procedures	

- Keeping track of length of time people attend a session (to evaluate effectiveness)

Of course, there are (some) concerns about the loss of privacy and possible misuse of the personal data gathered through this method. Table 12.2 shows the results from a survey question posed to meeting planners by *Meeting West*, in their April 2005 issue.

Figure 12.4 is the art titled "Spy Responsibly," by Josh Krist, which accompanied the results of the questions shown in Table 12.2. Useful information is provided to meeting planners considering utilizing this technology.

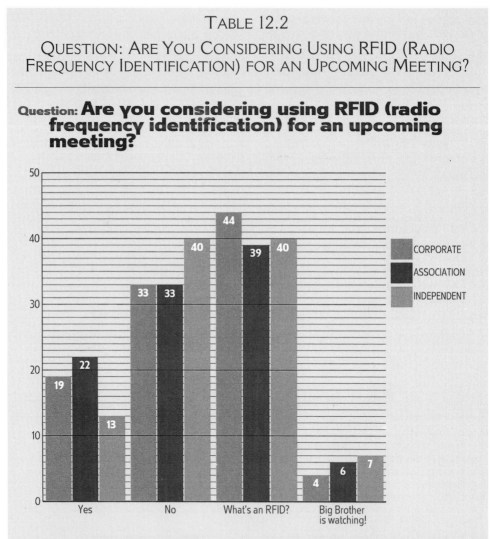

TABLE 12.2

QUESTION: ARE YOU CONSIDERING USING RFID (RADIO FREQUENCY IDENTIFICATION) FOR AN UPCOMING MEETING?

Question: Are you considering using RFID (radio frequency identification) for an upcoming meeting?

The Skinny: C'mon, where's the paranoia? Less than 10 percent of all planners surveyed think radio frequency identification (RFID) is an evil government plot to control our lives. Go figure! A sizeable number of planners don't know what RFID is. Well, we've got something just for them this month—a cover story detailing the wonders of this new technology. Read the story. Spread the word.

Source: Krist (2005).

FIGURE 12.4
SPY RESPONSIBLY

A position paper issued by a number of respected privacy advocates, including the American Civil Liberties Union and the Electronic Frontier Foundation, provides valuable guidelines for meeting planners who might be thinking of incorporating RFID technology into meetings.

Following are some guidelines for using RFID technology responsibly:

➤ **Openness, or transparency:** RFID users must make public their policies and practices involving the use and maintenance of RFID systems, and there should be no secret databases. Individuals have a right to know when products or items in the retail environment contain RFID tags or readers. They also have the right to know the technical specifications of those devices. Labeling must be clearly displayed and easily understood. Any tag reading that occurs in the retail environment must be transparent to all parties. There should be no tag reading conducted secretly.

➤ **Purpose specification:** RFID users must give notice of the purposes for which tags and readers are used.

➤ **Collection limitation:** The collection of information should be limited to that which is necessary for the purpose at hand.

➤ **Accountability:** RFID users are responsible for implementation of this technology and the associated data. RFID users should be legally responsible for complying with the principles. An accountability mechanism must be established. There must be entities in both industry and government to whom individuals can complain when these provisions have been violated.

➤ **Security Safeguards:** There must be security and integrity in transmission databases are system access. These should be verified by outside third-party, publicly disclosed assessment.

There are some uses, however, that privacy advocates say should be flatly prohibited:

➤ Merchants must be prohibited from forcing or coercing customers into accepting live or dormant RFID tags in the products they buy.

➤ There should be no prohibition on individuals to detect RFID tags and readers and disable tags on items in their possession.

➤ RFID must not be used to track individuals absent informed and written consent of the data subject. Human tracking is inappropriate, either directly or indirectly, through clothing, consumer goods or other items.

➤ RFID should never be employed in a fashion to eliminate or reduce anonymity. For instance, RFID should not be incorporated into currency.

The paper asks that companies not use RFID to track individual products "until a formal technology assessment process involving all stakeholders, including consumers, can take place."

"Radio Frequency Identification (RFID) is an item-tagging technology with profound societal implications. Used improperly, RFID has the potential to jeopardize consumer privacy, reduce or eliminate purchasing anonymity, and threaten civil liberties, " reads the report.

The paper notes that privacy advocates have deep concerns about government use and abuse of RFID. The position statement notes that the Department of Defense has issued a mandate to its suppliers to start using RFID on the crate and pallet level, libraries have begun using RFID, and that Japan and the European Union are investigating using RFID chips in currency.

"Some uses of RFID technology are inappropriate in a free society, and should be flatly prohibited. Society should not wait for a crisis involving RFID before exerting oversight: the writers declare.

Other highlights of the "Position Statement on the Use of RFID on Consumer Products" include a section on threats to privacy:

➤ Hidden placement of tags
➤ Unique identifiers for all objects worldwide
➤ Massive data aggregation
➤ Hidden readers
➤ Individual tracking and profiling

Source: Krist (2005).

Marriott Changing Bed Linens / Donating Old Bed Linens

The following two press releases demonstrate a dual benefit, which reinforces the trend and need that many corporations have to "give back," or volunteer and assist those less fortunate. Many hotel companies, such as Marriott, have programs that honor their own employees who benefit the communities they serve. The company Web site should provide press releases on all community service programs. Figure 12.5 is a press release from the Marriott Web site on one such program that will benefit guests as well as the communities they serve.

FIGURE 12.5
MARRIOTT CHANGES TO BE MORE GREEN

Marriott News

MARRIOTT TO CHANGE 628,000 BEDS WORLDWIDE IN 2005

Marriott is Creating More Luxurious Bedding With Plusher Mattresses, Softer Sheets, More Pillows, and a New, Fresh, White Look

CONTACT:
John Wolf/Stephanie Hampton
(301) 380-5718/1217
john.wolf@marriott.com/stephanie.hampton@marriott.com

WASHINGTON , DC - 25 January 2005 -

Photography of our new bedding is available for download >>

Marriott International, Inc. (NYSE:MAR) today announced that by year-end, 628,000 beds at approximately 2,400 hotels worldwide, across eight brands, will have a new, more luxurious look and feel. The global bedding makeover will utilize over 30 million yards of fabric – enough to stretch more than two-thirds of the way around the world – creating softer sheets, plusher mattresses, stylish duvets, more pillows – and a new fresh, white look.

J.W. Marriott, Jr., chairman and chief executive officer of Marriott International, said, "Together with our hotel owners and franchisees, we are launching an unprecedented bedding makeover, continuing our invitation to guests to experience the new look and feel of Marriott. This initiative draws on the finest designs and service traditions at our best hotels worldwide to position each of our brands as the most luxurious in their segment. And our new bedding is already getting rave reviews."

The company said its owners and franchisees are investing nearly $190 million in the new bedding. And, to speed the makeover, Marriott is offering owners and franchisees a one-time incentive, to ensure that guests can enjoy the comfort and luxury of the new bedding by year-end.

The company conducted extensive consumer research on the new bedding for all its brands. More than four out of five of the 1,000 guests surveyed preferred the new bedding and said they liked the stylish design and appearance, calling it fresh, inviting and comfortable. They also said the new bedding would increase their preference for a Marriott brand.

The more luxurious bedding is the new brand standard for the JW Marriott Hotels & Resorts, Marriott Hotels & Resorts, Renaissance Hotels & Resorts, Courtyard, Residence Inn, Fairfield Inn, TownePlace Suites and SpringHill Suites brands. As part of the makeover, the company is replacing traditional bedspreads with freshly laundered linens, making Marriott's new bedding the cleanest and freshest of any major hotel chain.

JW Marriott Hotels & Resorts, Marriott Hotels & Resorts and Renaissance Hotels & Resorts --
Full-service JW Marriott, Marriott and Renaissance hotels and resorts will replace the traditional bedspread with down comforters nestled inside sheeted duvets. The duvet covers will be freshly laundered for each new guest. The bedding will feature 300-thread-count, cotton-rich, white top and fitted bottom sheets, making them among the finest and softest sheets of any global hotel chain. The new JW Marriott, Marriott and Renaissance bedding will also offer thicker, more comfortable mattresses with the addition of a two- to four-inch mattress topper and more pillows. The stylized bedding will be accented with euroshams, a decorative bed scarf and an optional bolster. This spring, the new Marriott Hotels & Resorts bedding will be available for purchase.

Courtyard, Residence Inn, SpringHill Suites, Fairfield Inn and TownePlace Suites --
The company's select-service and extended-stay brands will feature comforters snuggly fit between triple sheeting, including 200-thread-count, cotton-rich top and fitted bottom sheets that will be "mercerized," a process that elevates the softness of the linens. The bedspread will be replaced by triple sheeting, which is commonly found at luxury hotels and resorts, including a decorative top sheet with colorful trim. All linens will be laundered daily at Courtyard, SpringHill Suites and Fairfield Inn. Linens will be freshly laundered for new guests at Residence Inn, and TownePlace Suites. Comforters will fit neatly between the new triple sheeting. The new bedding also features more pillows, enhancing its home-like appeal. Thicker mattresses will become standardized across these brands. Courtyard hotels outside North America will also feature elements of the upgraded full-service bedding in some markets.

Marriott ExecuStay --
Marriott ExecuStay, the company's corporate and temporary housing brand, will offer the Elite Dreamer™ bedding package, offering featherbed comfort with a mattress topper wrapped in luxurious Tru Val™ sheets and a climate-customized blanket. On top is a deluxe goose down comforter with a cover and skirt designed exclusively for ExecuStay. Five pillows of two varieties, both Down Surround and fiber-filled, will also be offered. Marriott ExecuStay is the first corporate housing provider to offer deluxe bedding nationwide.

Under Marriott's "Spirit To Serve Our Communities" program, participating hotels will have the opportunity to make charitable contributions of the replaced bed linens, including sheets, bedspreads, blankets and pillows. Marriott, on behalf of its owners and franchisees, is working through United Way of America and Gifts in Kind International to identify nonprofits serving local communities, as well as the tsunami-affected region of Southeast Asia. Beginning in February, nonprofit organizations interested in receiving a Marriott bedding donation can link to www.volunteersolutions.org/marriottdonations, courtesy of United Way of America's online tool called United eWay, to access linens from participating Marriott hotels as they become available throughout the year. Agencies may also register online with Gifts in Kind at www.giftsinkind.org.

Source: Marriott Corporation.

Source: Chapman, B. *Successful Meetings*, (2003).

In many programs that "give back," a local food bank will be the recipient of the donation. Figure 12.6 is an article from *Successful Meetings* magazine on donations made to food banks in San Diego after the Super Bowl. As the article mentions, "the San Diego-based nonprofit, event philanthropy specialists, CharityDirect, facilitated the donation."

Many would say that the convention industry helped to create what has now become a trend—donating leftover food from events to local shelters. Organizations like PCMA and MPI have worked with hotel and convention centers for over 10 years to ensure donations occur when the convention ends.

Note: For further information and examples of these trends, read the appendix at the end of this chapter.

REFERENCES

Chapman, B. (2003) The short report, *Successful Meetings*.

DiNola, R. and Aye, E. (2004) Centered on sustainability, *eco-structure magazine* (www .eco-structure.com). Reprinted from www.greenbuildingservices.com Web site).

Estancia Hotel La Jolla, California.

Hilton Hotel Long Beach, California.

Krist, J. (2005) Spy responsibly, *Meetings West.*

Krist, J. (2005) What's the frequency? RFID badges have attendees positively beaming, *Meetings West.*

APPENDIXES

The following articles and materials are provided as a resource. Reprinted with permission.

Appendix A: Centered on Sustainability: The Oregon Convention Center Gets Certified

Oregon Convention Center was the second convention center in the nation to be LEED rated and the first to be LEED-EB certified.

Interior photos provided by Randy Craig.
Exterior photos courtesy of Richard H. Strode.
Rain garden photos by Bruce Forster.

eco-structure | 44 | may/june 2005

FASCINATING THINGS HAPPEN WHEN PEOPLE COME TOGETHER AROUND A SINGLE PURPOSE. They spark new ideas, forge partnerships and create synergy. As the largest convention center in the Pacific Northwest, the Oregon Convention Center (OCC), Portland, often has witnessed this dynamic. But last fall, the center was part of the excitement during the U.S. Green Building Council's 2004 Greenbuild International Conference and Expo.

The conference launched LEED® for Existing Buildings (LEED-EB) and OCC officials recognized the best way to showcase this new program was through OCC itself. They started making preparations not simply to host the conference but also to become one of the first 12 projects certified under the LEED-EB pilot program. By the time more than 7,800 Greenbuild attendees from across the globe poured through the facility's doors, OCC was the second convention center in the nation to be LEED rated and the first to be LEED-EB certified.

A COMMITMENT TO SUSTAINABILITY

Situated across the Willamette River from downtown Portland, OCC lies in the middle of a bustling

area that is served by the city's light-rail line and multiple bus routes. The 1 million-square-foot (92900-m²) center was built in two phases on an 18-acre (7-hectare) campus. Portland-based Zimmer Gunsul Frasca (ZGF) Partnership designed the original portion of the building, which was constructed in 1990, and the 2002 expansion that nearly doubled the center's size. During the expansion, OCC and ZGF initially pursued LEED for New Construction (LEED-NC) certification, but the requirement to retrofit the existing chillers to a non-CFC (chlorofluorocarbons) refrigerant became an obstacle to achieving this goal.

Despite the setback, officials were dedicated to sustainability and incorporated as many green measures as possible into the expansion. When LEED-EB was launched, a window for certification reopened. New funding was available to retrofit the chillers, and it was determined the expansion portion of the building would pursue LEED-EB for initial certification only. Jeff Blosser, OCC's executive director, was a strong advocate for obtaining certification from the start.

"Being certified helps you tell your story," Blosser says. "It validates our internal processes and says there's value here that's recognized on a national level."

OCC assembled a team led by the facility's staff, ZGF and Portland-based Green Building Services, a green-building and facilities-management consulting practice, to pursue certification and refine building operations.

A PROCESS FOR IMPROVEMENT

LEED-EB certification is a journey, not a point in time. The program was designed as a long-term, ongoing certification process. After initial certification, a building owner has one to five years to recertify the facility. This peaked the interest of OCC officials; it meant they could obtain certification at the level of their current capability and then raise the bar as future funds became available for additional improvements.

LEED-EB provides a holistic approach to building operations and maintenance. The rating system addresses criteria in the following categories: sustainable sites; water efficiency; energy and atmosphere, materials and resources, including on organization's environmental purchasing policies; indoor environmental quality, such as cleaning and pest-management practices; and innovation and design process, including a point for having a LEED-accredited professional working on the project.

Unlike LEED-NC, where building performance is estimated, LEED-EB evaluates the actual performance of energy, water and other systems in the building. Because the team is working with actual measurements, it's easier to evaluate opportunities for increased efficiencies and accurately gauge progress.

An ideal approach to implementing LEED-EB has three fundamental components: a building audit, adoption of selected practices, and performance tracking and documentation. During the initial assessment, the team examines how the systems are working and identifies areas for improvement. In addition, it determines what practices and policies need to be instituted to meet the team's goals. The next step is to implement the new practices and policies and make them a part of the daily operation. Then the team tracks and documents the performance for up to one year. The entire process can take six to 18 months from the project's inception.

MAKING THE GRADE

Blosser was surprised when the initial assessment revealed many of OCC's current characteristics and practices already met LEED-EB requirements.

The expansion's design included abundant glass with low-E glazing to provide generous amounts of daylight in the space and generate energy savings. An engery-efficient lighting system and advanced control systems also helped the building achieve an ENERGY STAR® score of 70. (For more information about ENERGY STAR's role in LEED-EB, see "LEED-EB and ENERGY STAR," left.)

An existing on-site oil- and water-separation system prevents contaminants from entering the storm-water system, and a rain garden designed by the landscape architecture firm of Mayer/Reed, Portland, captures and filters storm-water runoff through specially selected plantings.

The expansion's design also reduced the heat-island effect with an ENERGY STAR-compliant roof that has high reflectance and high emissivity. Recycled-content building materials were used in the center's construction, such as steel, concrete and gypsum board. Inside, recycling containers, kiosks and a wall display that explains the facility's sustainable measure make OCC a green-building demonstration project, which earned the facility an innovation credit for helping educate visitors about green features.

In addition to the building's existing characteristics and practices, the LEED-EB team found other ways to meet LEED-EB requirements.

OCC has worked closely with its electricity provider, PacifiCorp, to purchase 12 percent of its energy from wind power, becoming one of the utility's largest green-power buyers in the area. While it does not meet the LEED-credit requirement (25 percent off-site renewable power for one point), the OCC team continues to explore opportunities to reduce energy use and purchase enough green power to earn the LEED credit.

OCC earned two points for water efficiency. The OCC expansion utilizes low-flow restroom fixtures that meet or exceed the U.S. Environmental Protection Agency's Energy Policy Act of 1992, the LEED reference standard.

The center also uses low-environmental-impact materials in its daily operations, such as concentrated cleaning products with low toxicity and paper products with at least 30 percent past-consumer recycled content. IAQ also is enhanced through minimizing sources of pollution, such as gases, particles and bio-contaminants, as well as controlling moisture in occupied spaces.

Waste management is an important business consideration at OCC. Materials that are routinely recycled include paper, glass, plastic, metals, cardboard, mercury-containing lamps, magazines, newspaper, wood and yard debris. To achieve LEED-EB, the center added a clause into all its contracts that encourages exhibitors and decorators to recycle.

As a government-run entity, OCC's purchasing policies typically were low bid and needed some adjustment. According to Bob Spier, OCC's director of operations, officials are changing their policies to no longer solely look at the lowest price.

"We want to make sure paper and office products are ecologically sound," Spier explains. "We're also purchasing only certain kinds of lighting fixtures with energy-efficient ballasts; their longer life means we spend less man hours changing bulbs."

The OCC LEED-EB team already has its sights set on recertification as it incorporates additional improvements. In addition to eliminating CFCs, the team plans to install variable frequency drives in the chillers, which will save the facility money in the long run. The staff also is considering occupancy sensors and other energy-efficient measures. In fact, OCC officials are so pleased with the results of upgrading the building's expansion, they now are working to get the entire facility certified. The team hopes to achieve at least a Silver rating when the building is recertified.

ENHANCED VALUE FOR ANY BUILDING OWNER

Like OCC, other building owners already may be close to qualifying for LEED-EB certification but simply haven't tracked their buildings' performance. One of the most beneficial outcomes of going through the LEED-EB process is the discovery of what's actually happening in the building.

INSIDE, RECYCLING CONTAINERS, KIOSKS
AND A WALL DISPLAY THAT EXPLAINS THE
FACILITY'S SUSTAINABLE MEASURES MAKE
OCC A GREEN-BUILDING DEMONSTRATION
PROJECT

"I have a better handle on how well each piece of equipment is performing," Spier explains. "With the recertification process we're keeping better records and performing mechanical tune-ups more frequently. This gives us better operations now and should lengthen the facility's life span and further reduce costs."

In addition, LEED-EB certification reaps benefits on social, economic and environmental levels. As building owners conserve resources, they reduce a building's environmental footprint by minimizing resource depletion and extraction, lessening fossil fuel use, generating less solid waste and minimizing the use of toxic materials.

By providing an improved workplace, building owners can reduce employee absenteeism and increase productivity. With optimized systems' operation, owners reduce building operating and maintenance costs and save money on their energy, water, sewer, waste and materials' expenses. Financial incentives for building upgrades and retrofits also frequently are available.

Certification also demonstrates environmental leadership to the community and building occupants. Blosser said it helped OCC staff to think holistically about building operations, and the reporting process helps them demonstrate the positive effects of their efforts. In addition, Blosser found LEED-EB certification to be a very viable marketing tool when speaking with clients across the nation; green practices are a growing request among organizations seeking conference facilities. OCC now proudly displays its certification plaque in the building and on its Web site, www.oregoncc.org.

As building owners, tenants, employees and facilities' staff come together to achieve LEED-EB, they discover how their facility truly performs, realize the importance of their day-to-day choices and make a difference in the quality of their workplace as they protect the environment.

Ralph DiNola, associate AIA, is a senior design consultant for Green Building Services, a Portland, Ore.-based professional consulting firm that helps clients successfully adopt green-building and -facility-management practices. He also is a LEED New Construction advanced faculty member. Elaine Aye, IIDA, is a senior design consultant for Green Building Services and LEED Commercial Interiors faculty member. DiNola and Aye can be reached at (866) 743-4277 or through www.greenbuildingservices.com.

MATERIALS & SOURCES

GLAZING—VIRACON, Owatonna, Minn., www.viracon.com
LIGHTING CONTROL SYSTEM—LEVITON MANUFACTURING CO. INC., Little Neck, N.Y., www.leviton.com
LOW-MERCURY LAMPS—PHILIPS LIGHTING CO., Somerset, N.J., www.lighting.philips.com
GREEN CLEANING PRODUCTS—COASTWIDE LABORATORIES, Wilsonville, Ore., www.coastwidelabs.com
FLY-ASH IN CONCRETE MIXES—GLACIER NORTHWEST, Seattle, www.glaciernw.com
STEEL FRAMING, 90 PERCENT RECYCLED CONTENT—VULCRAFT, Charlotte, N.C., www.vulcraft.com
FIBER-GLASS INSULATION, AT LEAST 25 PERCENT RECYCLED CONTENT—JOHNS MANVILLE, Denver, www.jm.com
CEILING TILES, 37 PERCENT RECYCLED CONTENT—ARMSTRONG, Lancaster, Pa., www.armstrong.com
VINYL COMPOSITION TILE, 10 PERCENT RECYCLED VINYL—MANNINGTON, Salem, N.J., www.mannington.com
METAL TOILET PARTITIONS, MORE THAN 35 PERCENT RECYCLED CONTENT—ACCURATE PARTITIONS, Lyons, Ill., www.accuratepartitions.com
ROOF DECKING, 14 PERCENT GYPSUM—GEORGIA PACIFIC, Atlanta, www.gp.com

The Oregon Convention Center
LEED-EB TEAM

OREGON CONVENTION CENTER
Portland, www.oregoncc.org
- JEFF BLOSSER, executive director
- BOB SPIER, director of operations

FACILITY OPERATIONS—METROPOLITAN EXPOSITION RECREATIO COMMISSION, Portland, www.merc-facilities.org
ARCHITECTS—ZIMMER GUNSUL FRASCA PARTNERSHIP, Portland, www.zgf.com
LEED-EB PROJECT MANAGEMENT—GREEN BUILDING SERVICES Portland, www.greenbuildingservices.com
MECHANICAL AND ELECTRICAL ENGINEERING—CBG CONSU ENGINEERS, Portland, www.cbg-engrs.com

Appendix B: What's the Frequeny? RFID Badges Have Attendees Positively Beaming

Like lasers, the Internet, global positioning systems, or any other technology that's had a profound influence on our society, radio frequency identification (RFID) tags are starting to transmit their way into our daily lives, much to the delight of big business and the government.

An RFID chip is basically a very small chip (one-quarter of an inch across, if that) that is able to broadcast information over a limited range. Because of security concerns, newer chips don't broadcast unless they are "woken up" by a compatible reader nearby.

The information each chip broadcasts is usually nothing more than the electronic equivalent of "I am chip #337." This doesn't mean much, but when linked with an RFID reader, "I am chip #337" can translate into "Name: John Doe. Company: XYZ Productions. Shopping for: Lighting production, live entertainment, set decor."

Basically, any information that attendees put on a registration form can be programmed into an RFID chip. If all of this sounds a little cloak and dagger, it is—the KGB supposedly developed RFID chips to help it track surveillance subjects, and before that, large RFID transmitters were used by the British during World War II to help them distinguish which planes heading toward London at night were theirs.

In the meetings industry, the most prevalent application for RFID is for "smart" name badges. With a smart name badge, tracking attendees for educational credits, on the trade show floor, or anywhere else, is much easier. The International Air Transport Association is calling for all luggage to be RFID-tagged by 2007, and declared, "The future is always knowing exactly where your bag is."

For meeting planners, this could be amended as, "The future is always knowing where—and who—your attendee is."

WELCOME TO THE MACHINE

Although RFID chips and smart badges have been around for a few years, the 49th annual PCMA Annual Meeting at the Hawaii Convention Center last January probably marked their official debut into the convention industry mainstream.

At that convention, RFID "SmartBadges" were used to track continuing education unit (CEU) credits—attendees held their name tag in front of reader stations and then collected a printed receipt to prove their attendance. The badges were also used to track overall attendance at general sessions; verify a delegate's identity at the cyber cafe; and help people find their friends and colleagues during banquet seating.

As convenient as all of this is, says Corbin Ball, CMP, an attendee at PCMA and president of Bellingham, Wash.-based Corbin Ball Associates, as well as a partner in meetings industry technology consultancy Tech3 Partners, the dawn of the RFID age is just now upon us.

"We're very much in the early adoption phase," says Ball, who recently published an article about RFID technology on his website (www.corbinball.com). "We're going to see lots of stuff come out of this. It's kind of like when the laser was invented—they had no idea how many applications would come out of it. In the same way, I think RFID has a lot of potential for things—like exhibit marketing, lead retrieval, and all sorts of things in addition to what they demonstrated at the PCMA conference.

"The things I didn't see there, but I think it really has huge potential for, is the marketing aspect for exhibits, and knowing how you can build a better exhibit hall for the traffic patterns through it, and those kinds of things," Ball adds.

Tony Melis, vice president of business development at Washington, D.C.-based Laser Registration, the company that supplied the RFID SmartBadges to PCMA, says that the technology opens the door to a completely new way of collecting and using information.

"We're helping meeting planners can exhibitors arm themselves with better data," he says. "We can report on traffic patterns, we can report on the people who come in and come out over time. We can tell, in real time, that we have x number of first-timers or second-timers out on the trade show floor. We can also tell exhibitors how many people are on the floor at different times of the day, so they can make sure people are at the booths or out walking the floor accordingly."

Organizations can take this information one step further and include even more demographic information, so exhibitors, for instance, can spend their time on the trade show where attendees will most likely have a genuine interest in their product. Financial breaks on registration for attendees willing to be "pre-qualified" will likely be a thing of the very near future.

"I know that there are organizations that spend thousands of dollars trying to find out and analyze what kind of attendees are at a certain trade show, or prove to exhibitors what kind of traffic a show can draw," Melis says. "Then, for access control and security, I know there are times when it would be nice to make sure in an unobtrusive way that the people who are in a certain room really do belong there."

Melis says that RFID attendee-tracking also has applications for rating the popularity of speakers or new programs—putting a whole new spin on the phrase "vote with your feet."

"Let's say that a planner has a gut feeling about a certain new program or speaker," Melis offers. "If we can read everyone going in and out of that presentation, we can see the average length of stay and traffic patterns in and out of the room—if it's empty or halfway empty, we can see that maybe the subject wasn't appropriate, or maybe the delivery wasn't appropriate."

PRIVACY ON PARADE

All of this is great for planners and exhibitors, but attendees might not be so thrilled. After all, any technology developed to basically spy on people understandably causes some privacy concerns.

"It's scary to people, and if you don't understand it, the normal tendency is to fear it," Ball says. "I think there's going to be a hue and cry—I mean, there are much bigger issues that we're facing in terms of privacy, and I think that people should be rightfully concerned about government and corporate intervention into their own privacy. This is going to play into those fears. I think it all comes back to, 'What is the trade-off?'"

There are already organizations aligned against the widespread use of RFID, which some privacy advocates maintain will be so tempting for the government and big business to abuse that it's a matter of when they cross the line, not if.

Or, as California state Sen. Debra Bowen famously asked: "How would you like it if, for instance, one day you realized your underwear was reporting on your whereabouts?"

"Not very much, senator," is probably how most people would respond to her hypothetical question. Just knowing that an RFID tag is in use to track your movements in a given environments is the first step to deciding whether you want to be tracked, experts note. After all, the chips are small, but not microscopic, and can be removed from whatever they are attached to.

"You could have ripped off the RF tag on the [PCMA] name tags," Ball contends. "People have speed passes in their cars. Those are RF tags, essentially. Someone could conceivably set up some sensors and track cars as they go all around to different areas—that could be a [privacy] problem. But, people are willing, happy in fact, to have those things in their car for the convenience of being able to sail through the fast lane on toll roads. In the same way, if there's a good justification for use—a perceived benefit for the attendee—I don't think there will be significant push-back."

Ray Verhelst, vice president of Las Vegas-based Expo2.net, a trade show and event marketing technology company, has worked with RFID and some of the registration/lead-management companies. His company has studied the privacy issues as well as the potential of hacking into RFID systems.

"The data which is stored on the device is completely under the control of the operator," he says. "Therefore, if certain elements of data could be considered as being questionable in a privacy issue, don't publish it.

"The concept of an RFID tag is to be able to deliver information to a receiver freely within a predetermined proximity of the sending unti," he continues. "This eliminates physical counting, swiping or individual scans. Furthermore, this memory-based technology can store and transport a much greater volume of information than any static—barcode, and certainly more data than a magnetic stripe. This alone should make [operators of] traditional lead-retrieval systems nervous."

The issue, however, isn't the medium but the message—the data itself—he contends. Things get interesting when one considers that RFID chips can transmit much more information that is commonly shared on the trade show floor.

"Think about the last time you registered for a trade show and the volumes of information you had to enter to complete the registration process," Verhelst says. "Typically, there are tremendous demographic profiles you are required to complete before your confirmation arrives. Now look at the lead device the next time you have your badge swiped. You will see only basic information about yourself—none of the detailed information about your decision-making responsibilities, interests or objectives for attending this show. Certainly, this information could be very important to an exhibitor trying to fulfill your request for product-specific information, right?"

Of course, he notes, this is the eternal tug-of-war in all marketing endeavors—companies who are paying money to get their message out want to know who they're reaching. Trade show organizers need to prove that they have a qualified audience. The consumer is left feeling like a roasted chicken in a room full of starving people.

Consumers often do benefit from companies having knowledge of their needs and preferences, but increasingly it seems that even our personal health issues are no longer private. Anyone who has researched a health issue online may have noticed a sudden spike in online advertising and e-mails that offer to fix their problem. Imagine similar scenarios when walking into a drug store . . .

CONVENTION WISDOM

Laser Registration's Melis notes that for convention uses, his company has adopted the following criteria: 1.) The RFID has to be explained to attendees and the process has to be transparent; 2.) No special behavior of the attendee is required; and 3.) It has to be a disposable technology so that it's affordable to planners and attendees can throw it away or let it expire.

"We're very aware of any privacy issues that people might have." he says. "We like to explain that RFID is only valid if you are in a certain range of an antenna. It's more about getting an understanding of an aggregate flow, rather than getting a report on one particular person. We encrypt this data, and we don't store any personal information. Before you could penetrate through that layer of encryption security, you'd have to be pretty sophisticated. And, once you are outside the range of an antenna, it's impossible," he says.

At PCMA, Ball asked the people giving out badges if they had heard any complaints. Two people were slightly concerned and asked about the RFID capabilities, but they seemed assuaged by the answers given to them.

"A few inquiries out of 2,600 people—I think it was perceived as value. [But] I think that in general, in society at large, it will be a really big issue," Ball says. "I think being concerned about privacy is legitimate. It's the same thing when e-commerce started happening on the Web—that's a perfect analogy. You heard then, many times, people saying that they would never put their credit card on the Web. Then, that same person happily hands their credit card to the waiter who takes it into the back room where it's much more likely to get scanned than from a secure website. So, it's just getting used to the idea."

THE FUTURE

A growing number of major retailers, including Wal-Mart, are requiring that their suppliers use RFID chips, and as of this writing there is a controversy raging over a California school that wants all of its students to wear RFID tags for their own safety. Libraries across the country are hoping to balance convenience of book check-in and checkout with privacy concerns. Hospitals are discussing incorporating RFID for a number of uses, and the Department of Homeland Security is considering RFID for passports and border control.

If there's a good reason to track something, or someone, RFID is becoming the device of choice.

"In meetings, the commodity that you're tracking is people," Ball says. "That can be used in dozens of different ways—but it really focuses around lead retrieval, exhibit marketing, access control, all those things that I've really seen focused around the attendee."

He says that a badge with an RFID tag in it currently costs anywhere from 50 cents to $2. As the costs go down, as they almost always do, the adoption rate will go up.

"It's a refinement of how the processes are already done," Ball says. "It's not a total revolution. But, when the lasers were first developed, they had no idea it would be used for CDs and CD players and medical imaging and Lasik eye surgery—there are so many applications, and in the same way, the jury is still out on RFID. I think it has great potential."

And that potential is poised to impact the meetings industry in myriad ways.

"Through our research and in my opinion, this type of technology has tremendous benefits for the conference and trade show industry," Expo2. net's Verhelst says. "Realize that for an organizer to become directly involved with the lead-capture process would ultimately require them to become accountable for the quality and quality of leads generated. In a word of unaudited shows, that could be a deathblow to many."

So, the brave new RFID world may have attendees beaming—their personal information and buying power, at least—but this doesn't mean they'll be happy about it.

The three keys to smooth adoption—or points on the pitchfork, depending on your perspective—are education, respecting privacy and making sure the use of RFID on the trade show floor is a benefit both to exhibitors and organizers as well as attendees.

Source: Krist, J. *Meetings West*, April 2005.

Source: *Meetings Guide to the West*, 2006/2007 Edition.

INDEX